WILDFLOWERS

A BLACK WOMAN'S JOURNEY TAKES ROOT

MARGARET EDWARDS

Wildflowers

Cover design by Eliza Osborn
Interior formatting by Eliza Osborn for Hallard Press.

Published by Hallard Press LLC.

This book is a work of nonfiction. However, some names, places, and dates have been modified for confidentiality and storytelling purposes.

Library of Congress Control Number: 2023909506

Publisher's Cataloging-in-Publication data

Names: Edwards, Margaret, 1945-, author.
Title: Wildflowers: A Black Woman's Journey Takes Root / Margaret Edwards.
Description: The Villages, FL: Hallard Press LLC, 2023.
Identifiers: LCCN: 2023909506 | ISBN: 978-1-962326-06-3 (hardcover) | ISBN: 978-1-951188-87-0 (print) | 978-1-951188-88-7 (ebook)
Subjects: LCSH Edwards, Margaret, 1945-. | African American women--Illinois--Biography. | African American women--Middle West--Biography. | United States--Race relations--History--20th century. | BISAC BIOGRAPHY & AUTOBIOGRAPHY / Cultural, Ethnic & Regional / African American & Black | BIOGRAPHY & AUTOBIOGRAPHY / Personal Memoir
Classification: LCC E185.915 .E39 2021 | DDC 977/.0496073/092--dc23

ISBN: 978-1-962326-06-3 (hardcover)
ISBN: 978-1-951188-87-0 (print)
ISBN: 978-1-951188-88-7 (ebook)

CONTENTS

Dedication

For those who helped me become who I am.

Book I

"Do you suppose
she's a wildflower?"

Daisy, *Alice in Wonderland*

1

HOME AWAY FROM HOME

"There's one!...

Over there...Look!...There!"

I'm pointing into stragglers and groups of White jubilant faces blocking my view of that Black girl I know I saw. Jean is trying to get her eyes to follow my pointing finger. We're at Southern Illinois University, standing in our church clothes on the two bottom steps of Old Main a tall building with a clock tower on the top. The brochure said Old Main is one of the oldest buildings on SIU's campus with three floors of offices, classrooms and even a museum.

Every morning, Jean and I stand on the steps of Old Main looking toward the campus entrance gate. We're on the lookout for Black faces.

The brochure said, "There are over 13,000 students at Southern Illinois University." So we figured at least half must be Black. From the steps of Old Main, we can see every Black student coming and going. So far, I have only twelve pencil marks on my chart. That brochure must be wrong.

"I don't see nobody." Jean is ducking her head up and around and squinting her eyes.

"I know I saw her. Look! There's another one...He's coming this way. He's in the green shirt. Don't look! Let's just look at our schedules and pretend to talk."

"Ooh wee, I see him." Jean is not looking at our schedules.

I make another pencil mark on my chart. That makes thirteen Black faces so far this week, eight girls and five boys.

I raise my head and see Jean smiling at this guy in the green shirt. He's smiling back at her as he passes by. I smile too because they're smiling.

Jean said, "He wanted to say something to me. I can tell. He was so good looking!"

Ever since Daddy left us in the pink and green room at Mrs. Hathaway's boarding house, we have been trying to figure things out. At home in Mt. Vernon, we didn't have to figure things out. Everybody knew the Edwards Sisters. We knew the "decent" people and we knew to "keep our dress tails down." We had rules.

Here at SIU, we don't have rules to tell us what to do. We have to make our own rules. So far, college has just set us free to feel lost.

After a few weeks of counting Black faces from the bottom steps of Old Main, our numbers hadn't grown past fifteen. So we stopped counting. We started meeting in front of the library so we could walk home together.

At first, we left campus at around three-thirty in the afternoon and arrived at Mrs. Hathaway's house at around four o'clock. When we walk in the door, Ms. Hathaway is always sitting in her orange couch chair with a brown throw pillow on her lap. Her gray, stringy hair is pulled back in a ponytail with a few strands hanging alongside her ears. Her flowered house dress dips between her stocking covered knees. She engages us as we walk in the door.

"Y'all home early today so you got time to set for a while 'fore you start sturding."

We sat on the brown couch holding our books and notebooks on our laps, smiling and nodding.

"The Lord sho don blessed me. Nobody woulda did what I did, marry a man with eight chirdrens! Eight! And I raised them all! The Lord is watching what we do…He wont us to do good. We gotta put our troubles in the hands of the Lord...'cause He comin' back."

We started getting home later. By the time we got home and closed the door to our little pink and green room with the twin cots, Mrs. Hathaway was in her room with her door closed.

We could avoid sitting with Mrs. Hathaway on weekdays, but there were no classes on weekends. We couldn't be with her alone all weekend! We asked Daddy to pick us up on Friday evenings and bring us home to Mt. Vernon. On Sunday after supper, he drove us back to Mrs. Hathaway's. After about a month, Daddy said, "I can't keep doing this ripping and runnin' evry weekend. It's too merch driving. Y'all gon havtah stay at dat skool on weekends."

2

THE CROSSOVER

I was standing in front of the library, looking in the direction Jean was supposed to come from. I see Black faces. There seems to be more on campus these days. Maybe I'm seeing the same one over and over again. No…that's a new face. That guy...I've seen him somewhere before. I know that guy! *Oh, my goodness...That's Roland! I knew we would meet again!*

"Roland...Roland!"

I run to him, over sidewalks, grassy lawns and around curious White faces. My black church shoes with the gold buckle click on sidewalks and sink into manicured grass. Roland is not looking in my direction. He's turning around, looking off into the distance. He's looking for somebody.

I shift my French book and my shorthand book to my left hand so I can wave my right hand to get his attention. I can't wave with my right hand. I have to use that hand to pull down my yellow dress with the tiny flowers to keep the skirt from sticking to my pantyhose.

I know that's him. That neat crew cut, those tight leg muscles, that strong, football body...*he's looking my way.*

"Roland!...Roland!"

I smile big now, the same big wide smile that intoxicated him when we first met back at the church conference five years ago. He squints at me as I get closer...I slow down, smooth my hair on the right side of my face to ensure acne coverage. I take three deep breaths to slow down my beating heart. I don't want to seem too anxious. He walks across the grass toward me, still squinting his brow.

"Hi, Roland." I'm trying to control my breathing. He is smiling now.

"Hi," he said, just standing and looking at me with that "who are you?" look on his face.

I refresh his memory. "Roland, it's me, Margaret. Remember? We met at the church conference...you and your cousin Sonny and my friend, Lindy..."

His eyes light up. He throws up his arms, which are draped with football stuff, a helmet, and shoes.

I like his delighted, wide-eyed smile. He's coming towards me. He's going to wrap me in his arms, football stuff and all and tell me how much he missed me and how he thought of me...

"Oh, yeah...Margaret! How are you? It's been so long! My goodness...how long have you been here?"

We are standing in the middle of a sidewalk. He doesn't drop his helmet and shoes and rush to me and wrap me in his arms and tell me...

"This is my first year...my sister Jean is here too, she's a junior...I'm a sophomore...I went to junior college first." *Shut up...I'm talking too much!*

"How about you...I mean, how long have you been here?"

"Wow, I can't believe we ran into each other...at the same college! Yeah, I'm a sophomore, too. I got a football scholarship, so I've been playing football. So, how you been...that church conference seems like so long ago..."

I caught him. He is still looking around. *Who is he looking for?*

He's not happy to see me...he's changed from the guy who couldn't stay away from me to a guy who has nothing to say to me.

"I have been doing well...just trying to get used to being away from home...but doing good."

I switch my two books from the arm holding my French and shorthand book to the other arm. I just want to end this conversation. He seems to want to do the same.

"Well, it is nice seeing you," he said, smiling with all thirty-two teeth showing. "I gotta get to practice...and don't you worry about this place, you'll get used to it in no time."

"Oh, I'm sure I will," I said.

He was shifting his helmet and shoes from hand to hand, still looking around for somebody. I didn't want to be left standing so I walked away smiling and giving a weak wave as I turned.

"You take care, Roland...and maybe I'll see you around."

He returned my wave and added as his eyes were still searching in the distance.

"Oh, yeah," he yells toward me. "I have a game on Friday...why don't you come and cheer us on?"

He is showing all his teeth again. I see them glistening in the sunlight. I am all smiles as I turn to acknowledge his invitation.

"Great. I'd love to see you play. I'm definitely gonna try to be there." I gave another wave. He didn't see it. His back was to me.

I pull my French book and my history book up to my chest, push my hair away from acne coverage and head back to my waiting post in front of the library. Halfway there I looked over my shoulder to see if he had found who he was looking for.

He had. His strong Black football arms were wrapped around a tall blonde girl. His football helmet and shoes are sprawled on the grass.

I won't be going to his football game to cheer him on.

3

CHASING "CITY"

The Black girls Jean and I met and became friends with were just like us. We came from small towns like Herrin, Harrisburg, Du Quoin, Marion, and Mounds. Our friends lived at home with their parents. Jean and I were living in a boarding house.

We all lived on the Black side of town. When we spotted a Black face, we flashed a big smile and called out too loud, "Hi." When not pointing out Black guys among the White masses who acted like they owned the shaded walkways, we gathered at a table in the back of the cafeteria.

A skinny girl with thinning hair and buck teeth named Lola did most of the talking. She must know what she's talking about since she's the only one of us with a boyfriend.

"A piece of fresh meat...that's all you are to these boys. Yeah, when you go out with them, they start out just kissing and stuff. But before you know it, they done tricked you. And you know what that means? That means there ain't no turning back. Girl...I'm telling you...y'all better watch yourself or you gon be kicked outta school and be on your way home!"

Small town Black boys were just like small town Black girls. Their lips were always whispering in the ear of another small-town boy. They just stood there grinning and playing with their hands. It was easy to tell they had never been away from home before.

My inspiration was those Black girls from the city. They came from places like Chicago, St. Louis, and Memphis. They were grouped together in rented houses and trailers. Some even lived in on-campus houses for Greeks. They mingled with the city boys who also lived in rented houses, trailers, and houses for Greeks. Their eyes focused on nobody, except other city folks. Their clothes were big shirts and jeans, and their hair was straightened by a chemical instead of with a hot comb. And they used a lot of bad words!

"That fool did that...shit...you did?"

"I said 'the hell with you'...I'm not letting no damn man get away..."

"Yeah, that son-of a-bitch had the nerve to call me again...I said get away from me you jive turkey."

I sat in the cafeteria with the small-town girls sipping hot chocolate. Those city girls sat with their hands circling cups of black coffee. They talked about "standing up" to guys. We small town girls sat with our hands encircling cups of hot chocolate, listening to Lola warn us against becoming "fresh meat."

"Shit! Shiiit...Damn you!...don't be such a fool. You bastard."

Jean and I are walking home from the library. Jean is listening to me practice my 'city girl' talk.

"You're crazy!" She is staring with disgust in her eyes. "You don't need to be like those old stuck-up girls."

"I don't think they're stuck up...they are just so confident and...listen to this...Ok, here goes, 'Shit, you bastard. You are not going to send me home! You 'F'ing turkey!' How was that?"

"That's ridiculous...you sound phony...you can't even say all the bad words! You should just stop trying to be 'city'."

"How about this, 'Damn you...you son-of-a-bitch. You are a no-good rascal'."

"No...No...No...I don't know why you're trying to talk like that. You're never gonna be 'city.' You may as well stop trying. And what if you slip up and say that stuff in front of Daddy!"

I stopped practicing bad words...out loud. But my mind was a cesspool of 'city girl' filth.

Sometimes, I had to walk past the game room in the Student Union. Most of the Black guys hung out there playing cards or just hanging outside the door. When small town girls like me walk by, the guys yell and make comments like, "Girl, Girl you got some legs on you!"

The other guys around laugh, jostle each other and make some other inaudible comments. They all laugh and laugh some more.

Sometimes a blind guy in a wheelchair named Will sits among the guys. He is always laughing and asking questions about the girls he can't see.

"Man, what her butt look like?"

"Whoo-whee!...she got a handful...but them legs, you'd be going crazy, Will! Them some good-looking legs on you girl...whoo-whee."

Will bangs on the arm of his wheelchair and grins big, turning his head from side to side.

"You gon talk to her, man...you should. With a butt and legs like that...what else you want?"

His friends try to slow him down.

"Not yet, man...here come another piece...oh my goodness..."

I used to be like the other small-town girls around guys like that. I used to just throw a hand over my giggling mouth, look to see who made the comments, smile big like a Cheshire cat, and hurry on by. No more. Now I focus. I am learning how to be like those city girls.

All the Black guys didn't hang out and jeer at every small-town girl. The coat check guy, Lawrence never did. He was mature and manly. He always gave me eye contact and a no-teeth side grin every time I handed him my coat. I knew his work schedule. I went to the Student Union sometimes just so he could check my coat.

I always wanted to meet a quiet, mature, city guy like him. His body is slim, his brown face is slim, and his long fingers are slim. He wears church pants every day with a pink or blue collared button-down shirt with the sleeves rolled up to his elbows. I watch him watching me as he grabs that hanger, inserts it into the shoulders of my brown trench coat and hangs it face forward on the hanging rod. He's really good with his hands. That's because he's from Chicago and very experienced.

When he's working behind the coat check counter, he's not allowed to talk to students except to say, "How you doing this afternoon." His name plate on the counter says "No Loitering."

One Wednesday when I was placing my trench coat on the check coat counter, he looked straight into my eyes and slowly placed my coat check ticket in my hand. I looked at my ticket. The words, "Meet me at 7" were scribbled on the back of the ticket. I nodded, grinned, and rushed to our meeting place in front of the library to tell Jean to go home without me.

"Where are you going?" she asked.

"I'm going out with Lawrence. He wrote on my coat ticket..."

"Are you talking about that skinny butt coat check guy?" Jean was looking at me with a grimacing face.

"Why are you fooling around with that guy...he's just after one thing!"

"I gotta go...he's not what you think...see you later."

I went to the bathroom to prepare for my date with Lawrence.

I wiped under my arms with a soapy paper towel and parted my hair on the left side to ensure maximum right-side acne coverage.

Lawrence was not the first guy at SIU to show an interest in me. During my first week, a guy named Barry approached me while I was sipping my morning cup of hot chocolate in the cafeteria. He said, "You look too innocent and good-looking to be left alone. Some of these guys around here are animals. You need a mentor." I put on my small-town girl grin and said, "Ok." After that, I listened to Barry's guidance over hot chocolate almost every morning.

I met Ed, a small-town boy from Quincy, Illinois in my Culture, Society and Behavior class. After two days of talking after class, he asked me to go home with him to meet his Mama. He said, "You're gonna love her down-home cooking."

I hadn't had any "down home" cooking for a while, so I went home with him to Quincy, Illinois for the weekend. I met his Mama, his cousins, his aunts, and the neighbors.

When we got back to school, he asked me to marry him! He even gave me a picture of himself with the words 'If you don't say yes, I will turn to stone' written on the back.

I thanked him for the picture. He was clueless about girls. Ed was a small-town boy without the sophistication of a city guy like Lawrence.

Felton said he was a Greek. I said to my mentor, Barry, "There's this guy named Felton...he said he's Greek...I have never heard of a Black person being Greek!"

Barry took my right hand in his. He spoke to me with awe in his eyes. "The Greeks on campus are not people from Greece. That's the name for girls and guys who join together...they become friends, but mostly they party together. The guys join fraternities and the girls join sororities. You've been to parties at the Alpha house. I'm not saying you shouldn't be friends with those 'frat' boys...I'm saying they are 'party hogs,' and hanging out with those guys will get you sent home real fast. You just gotta watch yourself."

I tried to shake Felton loose, but he was persistent. My small-town friend Joyce was persistent too. She said, "He's an Alpha… they're the best. You can't give up a Alpha man...you so lucky. I'm working to get me one."

Felton asked me to come to parties at his Greek House. I went, but I was out of place. I said to Felton, "I can't dance."

He said, "Everybody can dance."

He pulled me onto the floor. I tried to remember some of the dance steps from American Bandstand. I couldn't remember. But I could do "The Walk." So Felton would just stand with me on the sidelines and wait for "The Walk" music to come on.

I came out of the bathroom and walked over to the coat check room. Lawrence was locking up as I approached. The sight of his full body with those slim hips in gray church pants with a pink button-down shirt with the sleeves rolled up to his elbows made me count my lucky stars. *This son-of-a bitch is fine!*

"Hi," he said, flashing that same no-teeth side grin. That's the way those city guys grin.

We started walking toward the Black side of town. He was walking briskly like he was in a hurry. I didn't ask him where we were going. City guys know where they are going.

He took my cold right hand. His hand was slim and warm. My heart was beating fast. He started asking me questions.

"What's your name?

"Where are you from?"

"How long have you been here?"

"What's your major?"

He was interested in me. He wanted to get to know me. I talked about myself all the way to the trailers.

"Where do you live?"

We stopped walking. We were standing at a crossroad. He was looking one way and then the other.

"I live right down that street." He let go of my right hand so I could point toward my residence.

"You live in a trailer?" he asked.

"No," I said, with incredulity in my voice. "I live in a house…a boarding house."

"A boarding house? Who are you boarding with?"

His voice rose an octave. He folded his arms across his chest and into his pressed pink shirt.

I spoke slowly.

"I live in a boarding house with Mrs. Hathaway, and in a room with my sister, Jean."

Lawrence went silent.

"Well," he said finally. "I've got to get back...you know, papers to write. It was nice talking to you...you think you can make your way to your boarding house from here?"

"Sure," I said, waiting for him to make his move…to begin with a hug and then...

He turned and left me standing there, waiting.

I didn't even get a chance to ask him where he lived.

4
RULES OF THE GAME

After about two months, I refused to look in the direction of those guys standing in and around the Student Union watching, commenting, and laughing.

I focused my eyes straight ahead. I held my head high and I rushed out into the open air.

One time, I had made it outside unscathed when I felt a hand on my arm. A voice said, "Hey, Little Mama. Where you going so fast?"

I kept walking, shrugging that hand off me. *Who's this bastard putting his hands on me? He doesn't know me...and...I don't know where I am going so fast...just getting away from you, you rude jive talking...!*

"Hey, wait a minute. Where you going?" I stopped and turned around ready to

Oh my...he is so good looking...

"Nowhere, I was just..."

Stop stammering! City girls don't stammer. They know where they are going.

"...thinking about going to the library."

I looked at his face, expecting him to smirk and call me "legs."

He just smiled down at me.

"What a coincidence!" He threw up his arms.

"I'm on my way to the library too. Mind if I walk with you?"

"Uh, no, no, uh…" *Shucks!*

"Ok, let me get my bike."

I moved to the side of the wide, paved concrete walkway near the bike rack. I looked around expecting the Student Union guys to yell out something about my legs. They were smiling onlookers. *What's going on?*

I returned my attention to this guy as he retrieved his bike from the rack. He was light-skinned, tall with a football player body, a shaved head, and a goatee.

Ooh...this guy's got a body...better than Roland's...and he's a city guy!

He's wearing khaki, knee-length shorts, a no collar gray tee shirt and brown flip-flops in sixty-degree weather!

Why is he talking about walking me to the library? Why is he even talking to me? I'm in my striped knee-length raincoat and my black patent leather low black heels. *Shit...I'm dressed like a church lady.*

I'm looking up at his face...his cropped black mustache above his smiling lips and those bright expressive eyes.

He probably has a girlfriend and is just looking for 'fresh meat' on the side. Well, not me.

We are walking and he's guiding his bike along his right side. He's asking me questions...*another Lawrence!* I answer like a city girl.

"You been here long?"

I knew it...he's after fresh meat! Lola is right! You bastard!

"No, my first year here."

"Where you from?"

"St. Louis...well, uh...just outside St. Louis."

I couldn't tell him Mt. Vernon…too small...too country.

"Where are you staying here?"

"In a house not too far from here."

I will never tell you that I am boarding with a scripture quoting grandma. Small town girls live in places like that. And anyway, it's none of your damn business!

"With a roommate?"

"Well, sort of…with my sister."

He leaves me alone.

What, you don't want a girl with a roommate?

He starts talking about himself.

"This is my second year. I live nearby in a trailer...with my roommate."

You're not gonna get me to your trailer, big guy…

"By the way, my name is Sid. What's yours?"

"Marg." 'Margaret' was too long and plain. 'Marg' was fresh and suggested city casual.

"Marg, huh...how about I just call you 'Little Mama'?"

We both had smiles on our faces when he continued on his way, and I headed to the third floor of the library.

When he appeared again the next day outside the Student Union ready to go to the library with me, I was suspicious. Jean was suspicious, "He's so good-looking, why couldn't he talk to me!"

Lola was suspicious.

"That guy has been around, girl. Every year girls like you come here and before you know it, you gone...honey, gone home! You better watch yourself."

I was conflicted about Sid. I trusted Lola. She and her boyfriend have been together since high school. So when we were sitting at a table in the cafeteria sipping hot chocolate from white mugs, I asked her advice.

"Lola, what am I supposed to do if Sid asks me to do something…"

"Marg. Marg...have you had a boyfriend before?"

"Well, sort of...when…" Lola cut me off, her head shaking and her pointer finger jabbing into the plastic table.

"There is no such thing as 'sort of.' You do know how to play baseball, right?"

"Of course, everybody knows how..." Lola interrupts me again.

"And you know the point of the game is to make home runs...right?"

"Yes, of course I know that!"

"So let me try to make this simple." Lola opens her SIU burgundy notebook with a Saluki on the cover. She turns to a clean sheet of paper and begins to draw lines as she speaks.

"In baseball, you have two teams. Let's say Team A is Sid, and Team B is you. See?"

She heads two columns as she speaks.

"Sid team is trying to make it around ***your*** bases. You have three bases…you understand?"

"Yeah…we used to play..."

She draws a female stick figure and draws lines as she speaks,

"Your first base is from your neck to the top of your head. See...that's easy and harmless...that's like kissing and stuff. Your second base is from your waist up. Now, second base can be dangerous because it can lead to third base, which is everything below your waist."

She stops drawing lines and looks me in the eyes.

"Now third base is a red-light zone...a stop sign. If you like this guy and you have been with him for a while, like me and Freddie, it's up to you how many bases you gonna let him take. If you're gonna play ball you gotta know that getting a 'home run' is what the game is all about. And these guys at this school, honey, they all about getting home runs!"

I shake my head.

"No...Sid's not like that...we've been going out for...almost a month!

He has never tried anything. This second and third base stuff...not Sid."

Lola started laughing and shaking her head.

"You just wait...I've heard that line before. Give him another month...no...another week!"

She closed her notebook, picked it up with her right hand and stood up.

"I gotta go to class. Good luck...and don't say I didn't warn you."

Those small-town boys were always talking with us small town girls. When a boy named Arthur heard about me and Sid, he told me right to my face, "Yeah, your body looks good and everything, but you got that shit all over your face!"

That shit on my face was acne. It was still with me even into my second year of college. I would get a bump on my forehead and another on my cheek or my chin. Most of the time, my hair saved me. I gave myself a part and let it hang long on the side of my face that had the greatest need for coverage. Sometimes the coverage hid the entire side of my face. I had to learn how to navigate stairs and walkways with just one eye.

I expected this "studying in the library" with Sid to end real fast. I was twenty years old with "pretty hair, a great body and the best legs on campus," but I also had "shit" all over my face. Plus, my goal in life was to be an executive secretary like the ones I saw on TV. Sid, on the other hand, was twenty-six years old, and returning to school after having done "stuff." He was taking pre-law classes.

Somehow, that "shit" all over my face didn't stop us ending up every day in that third-floor glassed study room in the library. We took breaks to talk about my classes, my major and his roommate, Chris. We started spending less time in the library and more time around the campus walking, talking, and laughing. Soon, we were walking with his bicycle to his trailer. He never came to my boarding house except to drop me off at the gate.

Sid still sometimes stood outside the game room with his

friends. But things had changed. None of the guys tried to get my attention, and nobody yelled at me about my "beautiful legs" or my "round butt." Instead, they stood around smiling, and looking at Sid like there was some secret among them. I asked Sid one time, "What are you guys smiling and talking about?"

"Nothing," he answered. "They're just jealous."

5

MRS. HATHAWAY

Jean and I got home on school nights and on weekends no later than nine o'clock. We got home by nine o'clock even though according to the University rules curfew was eleven on weeknights and one o'clock on weekends. When we walked in the front door, Mrs. Hathaway came out of her room and locked the front door.

After a month of coming home before her bedtime, Jean said, "I want a house key so I can stay out as long as I want to."

"I don't think she's gonna give us a key. And she is not going to like getting out of bed to let us in if we stay out past nine." I said.

"I don't care," Jean said. "I'm not going to be treated like I'm a kid still at home in Mt. Vernon..."

"And she's not going to like it if we go into the kitchen late and start banging around pots and pans. She'll be yelling, 'Do y'all have to make all dat noise?'"

One time we were in the kitchen at around eight-thirty in the evening. We had just finished eating a plate of mayonnaise smeared baloney sandwiches cut in half. I ran a little water from the sink over our used plates. I was about to put them in the drying rack when I saw Ms. Hathaway standing in the doorway glaring at me through her rimless bifocals.

"You puttin' dem plates in the drying rack without washing 'em with soap and water?"

Her hands were on her hips. A long pink flannel housecoat was hanging from her shoulders. It was open in front, like she didn't have time to tie the belt. Her blue night gown was showing. A matching blue night cap covered her hair, except for a few strands of gray that had escaped and were hanging down the right side of her face. She hobbled toward me. I was standing there holding a dripping plate in midair.

"If y'all ain't gon wash them dishes right, just leave 'em in the sink. I'll wash 'em myself!"

She grabbed the dripping plate out of my hand, pushed me aside, squirted lots of soap on a dishrag and started rubbing the plate like it was covered with burned on barbecue sauce.

From that day forward, we packed extra baloney sandwiches in the morning before we left for class so that our evening routine did not include going into Ms. Hathaway's kitchen.

From her orange couch chair where she sat reading *The Bible* and fanning herself with her church fan with a picture of Jesus on one side, Mrs. Hathaway was always urging us to go to church even though she never went herself. She reminded us to "Remember the Sabbath to keep it holy."

"I raised dem eight chillin...and all of dem never been in no trouble. Nobody else would marry a man wit eight kids. I'm a Christian woman. I made shor to bring them chillin up in church. Hit's all right to go out sometime wit yo friends, but y'all outta be goin to church."

Jean and I tried church. We went with a girl named Essie. It was a Baptist church like the one Big Mama went to. At this Baptist Church they were singing songs we didn't know. We only knew songs from the Methodist church hymnal, like "Jesus Keep Me Near the Cross" and "Yield Not to Temptation."

At this Baptist church, the preacher didn't ask us to stand up and say a few words like in Mt. Vernon when a new face appeared in the pews. Nobody asked Jean to play the piano and nobody asked us to sing "Did you Stop to Pray This Morning." Nobody knew that we were two sisters from the well-known gospel group, The Edwards Sisters. Nobody knew that we had sung in churches in small towns like Murphysboro and Centralia and that we had won a sing-off contest in Mt. Vernon. We were nobody at this church. So, we stopped going.

One time Sid walked me from his house on a Friday night. We ended up sitting on the porch swing and doing first base stuff. It was almost eleven o'clock, way past Mrs. Hathaway's bedtime. On this night, I didn't feel like being constrained by her bedtime clock.

We were just talking and staying on first base. I don't know how it happened, but soon, I was sitting on Sid's lap. His hands started to roam like he was trying to steal second base.

What did Lola say?

The top buttons of my blouse somehow got opened and I could feel Sid's hands, then his lips, on my neck. His hands were reaching and I was helpless to keep them from meandering. My eyes were closed. I was warm and amenable. Sid took off his glasses. Was he heading for second base…on a screeching swing on Mrs. Hathaway's porch? *Red light...red light...flashing red light! "Stop...stop!"*

The screeching sounds from the chains on the swing were soothing. I leaned back. My head was reeling, waiting for ecstasy to overcome me. I was not listening to Lola's voice warning me. I was...*What? What's he doing? What's happening?*

Sid's hands were fumbling. His breathing slowed and quietened.

I pushed myself upright and opened my eyes. Sid was staring straight ahead. I followed his gaze, squinting and trying to bring my surroundings into focus.

There in front of me was a light. A tall figure was outlined and surrounded by light. It had stringy white hair hanging on each side of its face and was wearing something long, white and flimsy. *Oh, my God...it's an angel from Heaven or is it Jesus Christ himself!*

I couldn't take my eyes off that figure.

I slid off Sid's lap onto the wooden seat of the swing. My hands grasped at the buttons of my open blouse as I erected my body to face that tall figure surrounded by shining lights.

Sid's left hand was patting the seat of the swing to his right hoping his fingers would hit upon his glasses.

A voice cut through the warm air, "Don't you know what time it is?"

My heart was fluttering. Is that the voice of an angel...I have never heard Jesus speak.

No..no...that's not Jesus...that's Mrs. Hathaway!

I sat there staring straight ahead and breathing anger through my nostrils. Sid's hands stumbled upon his glasses. Both his hands were fiddling to get them placed on his face. His breathing was staccato.

"You gon be out here all night? Hit's almost midnight...I cain't keep waiting on you to come in here. I need to go to bed!...Dis staying out half the night..."

She stepped out of the light, opened her screen door, and left the porch.

We both sat there staring into the space where the light had been. Sid finally took a deep breath and let the air out slowly from his lips. He looked at me and shook his head.

"That was close...too close."

I put my lips close to his ear and whispered, snickering,

"Don't worry. She saw nothing. She's as blind as a bat without her bifocals."

6
HOMEFRONT TURMOIL

Jean didn't like her life at SIU.

"I want to leave this place, it's too much like Mt. Vernon. The girls are stuck up and the good-looking boys are just looking for 'pretty' girls…I wanna go and stay with Mae and Leeah. All my friends went up there."

I said, "Daddy's not gonna let you leave school now and go work at some hospital! You only got one more year down here."

Jean said, "I'm going. I can finish my last year up there...somewhere. I'm twenty-one years old, I can go where I want to go!"

She was right. She could say, "I'm leaving this school" and do it. Daddy was too busy trying to figure out how to keep his job at Wagner Electric.

During my first year at Mt. Vernon Junior College, Wagner announced that the company was moving to St. Louis. Because Daddy had worked there for over ten years, he was given a month to decide if he was moving with the company to St. Louis or giving up his job. With twelve mouths to feed and paying college fees for four kids, Daddy had to keep his job.

Those of us who knew what the choices were just stood around in the dining room watching and listening to Mama and Daddy talk. Mama always ended up crying and wiping her nose on an old white dishrag.

"You mean dat after living in dis house...fer almost twenty yeahs, we just gon pick up an move? What about Pavey Chapel and...dis house?"

We all looked at Daddy.

"You thank I wanna leave heah?"

Mama was crying and wiping and throwing her arms around.

"Eveythang we own is heah in Mt. Vernon. We gon havta fin new skools fer the kids. We can't take the kids outta school in the middle of de yeah...we don't know nothin 'bout them St. Louis skools. And dis house...what we gon do wit dis house? We can't just leave this house...and go to Missuri! Everybody is heah...Sista and Mama and..."

"What you wont me to do, Cora Mae?" That's all Daddy said.

What he did was become a boarder, like Jean and me. He rented a room from an old woman recommended to him by our St. Louis cousins. He slept in his rented room from Sunday night through Thursday night. Every day after work, he spent his time looking for "a decent house to live in." Fridays after work until Sunday evening, he was home in Mt. Vernon.

When Daddy was in St. Louis, Mama was in charge of everything. She didn't have Daddy around to enforce the rules. She was cleaning, cooking, and trying to get my younger siblings to "turn dat TV off and go do yo skool werk."

She constantly threatened my brothers Dale and Ray for being "hard-headed," and my younger sisters Helena and Leena for "letting dem dirty clothes pile up in the corner." Her mantra was, "Y'all just wait til yo daddy git home!"

Jean and I became the enforcers. Friday afternoons before Daddy got home, we made sure that when he opened the front door, he saw what he expected to see. He expected the floors to be mopped and waxed. He expected Helena and Leena to be folding the wash. He expected Ray and Dale to be sitting at the dining room table doing homework. I was to be ironing and Jean was "not to be making noise on dat piana."

Daddy had a nose for shoddiness. He uncovered dirt in the bathroom and bad grades on report cards. From Friday night to Saturday night, he had Helena, Leena, Ray and Dale, racking, sweeping, painting, and re-cleaning.

On Sunday, we went to church. After church, we had our family dinner of greens, beans, potatoes, cornbread, and chicken. While Mama packed up some leftovers in little tins so Daddy could have decent food to eat during the week, we all gathered around to listen to Daddy lay out what "Y'all better do while I'se in St. Louis."

When we heard the car back out of the driveway, a big sigh of relief could be heard as we watched that green Buick speed away down Twenty-Eighth Street. I settled on the couch in the living room, switched on the TV and dared anyone to switch channels. *The Ed Sullivan Show* was on.

7
UPROOTED

In the Spring of 1965, when I was near the end of my sophomore year at SIU, Daddy bought a house. It was in a suburb of St. Louis called University City.

One Saturday, he brought us all to St. Louis to see the house. First, he wanted us to see the neighborhood before he showed us our house.

"One of dem Cardnal ball players live in dat house."

"Dats the elementary skool ret dere."

"Dere's a Target store ret down dat street."

Tree-lined wide streets, brick ranch houses with garages, big picture windows, chimneys and patches of green covering the front lawns were everywhere. I didn't see any people walking on the sidewalks and no cars parked on the street.

I asked Daddy, "Do Black people live in this neighborhood?"

He kept driving.

"I wusn't lookin fer no Black peeples...I wuz looking fer a house. I don't care nothin 'bout no Black peeples."

The house Daddy bought was on Fern Street. It had five bedrooms, three upstairs and two more in the basement. It had a long family room that looked out into a small grassy backyard. It had two fireplaces, a small one in the family room and a larger one surrounded by glass in the living room.

When we finally got inside the house, everybody was running around touching walls and counting bedrooms and bathrooms.

"This house so big. This is my room."

"Uh..Un..you gon be in the basement."

"It got a basement, too? Oh, my goodness, this is a really big house."

Mama didn't have any say in the kind of house Daddy bought. He just bought what he liked. Mama didn't seem to care. She was just walking around saying,

"This shor is nice...it's got two bathrooms...dat's good.

I wandered through the long family room and out to the small back yard. I could see through the fences into the backyards of the houses on either side of ours. I guess you have to also be real quiet in this neighborhood.

The next time I came to our new house, it was moving-in time. School was out, furniture was delivered, and beds were assigned. I was no longer a country girl from Mt. Vernon. Home was now a ranch house in the suburbs on Fern Street in University City, Missouri. I never again slept in our house on 28th Street. It became the residence of my sister Ruth, her husband and their two kids.

Having a Black family like ours move into this quiet predominantly White community was hard on our neighbors, Black and White.

I was there one time to witness Daddy being summoned by the president of the neighborhood association to appear before the board to answer some questions. The President was a Black man and was one of two Black families in the neighborhood. The notice said, "The Association is concerned that you are violating the single-family household rule. This neighborhood does not allow multiple families to occupy single family homes."

Daddy was ready for 'dem peckerwoods and 'dat der ole Unca Tom.'

When he got home from the meeting, he told us what happened.

"I asted dat 'Uncle Tom,' 'Why you astinging me 'bout sangle-family houses. Do you know who you talkin' to? I know dese is sangle family homes. You thank I got all kinda peeples living in my house?'...Dat old 'Unca Tom' says, we is jest tryin to make shor dat the rules of the Association'...I cut him off.

"I didn't wont to heah nothin he wuz sayin. He wuz a fool, while dem White folks jest setting dere listening to Black men pit on a show...I said,' eveybody in my house is my family...ain't nobody else in my house. I got my nine chilren and my wife livin in my house. I got kids in high skool, junior high skool and elementary skool...I got kids in college and my son...he gon be a lawyer. All my chilren come heah to my house....I gotta right to hav my family living heah, no matter how many they is."

Daddy said, "I knowed what wus goin on. Dem crooked real astate folks gon start telling dese heah White folks dey better sell they house befor the naborhood is full of poor Black folks...and soon they house will be worth nothin. I seed stuff lak dis befor. You jes wait!"

It took a few months after that meeting for the Black president of the association to sell his house and for another Black family to buy it. Some White families noticed and followed his lead. By the time I graduated from college, the neighbors on both sides of our house were Black.

8
GREEKS AND 'ALL THAT JAZZ'

I was very happy with my social life at SIU. I had no thoughts of leaving. But when Jean left, I could no longer stay in Mrs. Hathaway's house.

It was my small-town friend, Joyce, who said we should move on campus.

"All we have to do is become a Greek! All the really popular guys live on Greek Row...and we will be able to go to all the Greek parties. . .and the Alphas..."

The Black Greeks with houses on Greek Row were the Alpha Kappa Alpha sorority for Black women, and the Alpha Phi Alpha fraternity for Black men. At the beginning of my second year at SIU and my junior year in college, I pledged AKA and moved into the AKA Sorority house.

On campus housing was expensive. My tuition scholarship had run out. To pay the bills, I got a National Defense Student Loan, and the Work/Study Program found me a part-time job as a secretary for the upcoming Winter Term.

I worked three days a week for a retired Lieutenant Colonel who headed the one- man Campus Security office. His name was

Mr. Alderman. He was a big, tall White man with a ring of white hair around a balding top. He spent most of his office time leaning back in his large brown leather chair, twiddling a blue Bic pen, and looking at the phone waiting for it to ring. His office was on the edge of the campus where the faculty and the student body would have little reason to traverse. So with no visitors and rarely a phone call, I spent most of my time reading and doing class assignments. Mr. Alderman spent most of his office time sitting in his brown swivel chair with an eye on the phone.

My secretarial skills had not improved since high school. I was still typing twenty words a minute. I used a lot of typing paper and eraser strips. When it took me an hour to type a memo, Mr. Alderson just smiled patiently, and waited.

He tolerated my lack of secretarial skills because he wasn't very good at his job either. He was rarely in the office. He was at the construction site of his new "dream house" located about an hour from the campus. If a call came in, I knew to say, "He just stepped out. Can I take a message?"

At the end of the Winter Term, I no longer wanted to be an Executive Secretary.

The AKA Sorority house was home to about thirty Black girls, some pledging, some AKA Big Sisters, and some others who the University placed to fill empty rooms. Some of those non-pledging girls were "fast." Everybody acted "fast" and "city" to me. There was a lot of chatter about going out and lots of running in and out of each other's rooms without knocking. Those good at hair grooming were busy giving perms and 'touch ups' amidst screams of pain and anxious yells to "get the phone!" Those with dates took extra-long showers.

There were some girls who went out with too many boys and spent too many nights breaking curfew. Night after night, these girls would sneak back into the house through a prearranged open back door. By the end of the semester, these "fast girls" were gone. That's how I got my own room on the second floor.

The House had a housemother named Ms. Johnson. Her job was to walk through the halls at curfew, count heads and check to see that doors to the outside were properly closed.

Every evening at about six o'clock, she emerged from her first-floor apartment. She strolled the lobby between the couches, couch chairs and coffee tables. She always dressed in a suit with matching church shoes. She finished her look with pressed beauty parlor hair, powdered cheekbones and too much mascara. The word around the House was, "Ms. Johnson loves her vodka."

She also had a sharp tongue. One time she said to me with a smirk on her face," I haven't seen your boyfriend around lately...did he dump you?"

I didn't have time to engage with Ms. Johnson, I was too busy becoming a city girl.

I had a lot of demands on my time when I was pledging Alpha Kappa Alpha. I had to go to meetings, learn and follow rules. I was expected to get involved in school activities, so I became a Model UN delegate representing the African country of Gabon where I did research and sat in meetings. One of the most important rules emphasized studying hard and maintaining good academic standing.

There was one Big Sister in the House who was always touted as the example we pledges should follow. She was studying law. She was admired by the other girls for "pulling all-nighters." We Pledges were paraded by her room. There she was, sitting blurry-eyed on the floor in her short pajamas surrounded by books, papers, and packages of No-Dose sipping black coffee from a stained paper cup. We were in awe of her.

In addition to pledging, Joyce and I had a boyfriend. I wanted to see Sid, and Joyce wanted to see Jason, and her other suitors. But being with our boyfriends while pledging was forbidden. We were under constant observation by day and allowed out of the House evenings only "if you are going to the library to study'.

So, most evenings, Joyce would say to a Big Sister, "Marge and I need to go to the library to meet our study group. Is that all right? We will be studying on the third floor."

Permission was always granted. We went to the library, walked around a few minutes to ensure that we were 'seen,' then we went our separate ways.

I spent these 'library forays' at Sid's trailer. We spent the evenings mostly talking, eating, and getting to first base. But center stage at all these rendezvous was the sounds of jazz blaring from his record player.

Sid asked me one time when he was putting a record on the record player. "Do you like Lou Rawls?"

"Who? Who's Lou Rawls?" I was sitting on his sofa bed munching on carrot sticks.

"You don't know Lou Rawls, the greatest jazz singer ever? Who do you think we have been listening to every night?" He stopped and stared at me.

"How about Gloria Lynne?" He was still staring at me with his eyes still bulging and his mouth ajar.

I threw up my arms.

"Sid, I don't know these people! I like how they sing, but in Mt. Vernon, we…I never listened to these kinds of songs."

"So, what kind of songs did you listen to...Hillbilly and Honky-Tonk?" He laughed and shook his head.

I never told Sid that I was a famous Edwards Sister. I never told him that in our house was music played by gospel singers like Mahalia Jackson, Rosetta Tharpe, and the Blind Boys. I never told him that drinking 7 Ups and dancing were forbidden in my house. I didn't want him to think I was out of his league.

Night after night in his trailer, we listened to, sang along with, and swayed to the voices of Gloria Lynne, Lou Rawls, and Nina Simone. Sometimes we switched to Etta James, Barbara Streisand, and Billie Holiday. His kind of music became my kind of music.

In the Winter Term of my junior year, I became an Alpha Kappa Alpha.

Sid and I were free to roam. We went to loud dance parties at the Kappa house on the Black side of town. We went to fancy events at the Alpha fraternity house. I liked dressing up in my loosely fitted black sleeveless dress and being escorted by Sid in his matching black suit.

My jazz repertoire was expanding. Sometimes Sid didn't put a record on the record player. Instead, he said to me, "I want to hear you sing."

"Ok," I said.

I stood before him as Gloria Lynne and belted out "Impossible" or as Billie Holiday and emoted through "God Bless the Child." With exaggerated expressions and total body involvement, I did my best to bring each song to life. Sid just sat on the sofa bed looking at me with that city boy side grin on his face. After my big finale, he said, "You're good...you're very good."

I guess not good enough for you to throw me on the couch and finish what you started on Mrs. Hathaway's swing!

9

THE CHOICE

Academically, I was in trouble. By the time I became an AKA, I had a D in French and a D in Climate 331. I dropped French. That ended my backup plan to become a French-speaking Black woman working for the United Nations. I had already abandoned my dream of becoming an executive secretary after practicing on Mr. Alderman, and after being shamed by Sid.

"You don't go to a four-year college to become a secretary! How are you going to make a decent living typing letters?"

I switched my major from Secretarial Sciences to History.

I couldn't drop Climate 331. It was a required class. I blamed Sid and the sounds of jazz singers in my head for some of my lack of focus in the Climate class. I also had a hard time understanding the slides and charts of pictures, graphs, lines and scribbles the little balding Professor Cramer was pointing to from the front of the lecture hall. I couldn't share notes or confer with any of the other two hundred students in the hall since I didn't know any of them. I needed the Professor's help. If I passed the final, I could pass the class.

I made an appointment to meet with Professor Cramer one

afternoon at four o'clock. I was nervous because I had not had a conversation with a White person or a White professor since I got to SIU. I did not relish asking this White professor for help.

Professor Cramer's office door was closed when I arrived. I knocked. I heard a "Come in." I opened the brown door, closed it behind me and stood near the door. I stood there in my church clothes looking around waiting for further instructions.

The Professor's back was to me. He was sitting at his desk in a large brown swivel chair surrounded by scattered piles of papers. All I saw was a bald head encircled by a fringe of choppy white hair.

He finished doing what he was doing. The brown chair slowly swirled around. There sat a small man wearing gray tweed pants, a brown belt with a gold buckle and a tucked in, wrinkled white shirt. With a blue Bic pen in hand, he motioned me to a brown wooden chair at the round black table facing him. I sat down, placed my clutch black purse on the scarred black table and crossed my legs.

He started the conversation.

"So, what can I do for you?" He was twiddling his pen and looking at me.

I answered like a White person would with a little small talk first.

"Thank you for seeing me, Professor Cramer. I am in your Climate Class 331 and uh, I am not doing very well. I was just wondering if there are any study groups that I can join to prepare for the final."

He was quick to answer.

"There are no more study groups this late in the term."

He sat there looking at me like he had answered my question and it was time for me to leave. I didn't leave. So, he said, "What's your name?"

"Margaret Edwards."

He swiveled his large brown chair around to face the piles on his desk. He rummaged through papers and came up with what looked like a grade book. He swiveled back to face me. He flipped through a few pages and ran a finger from left to right on a page. His nodding confirmed my assessment of my academic status.

"Yes, you are not doing well."

He looked up from the grade book to face me, still fingering that blue Bic pen.

He rubbed in another point.

"And the final is the only test left and that will be in two weeks."

I persisted, leaning forward, and splaying my hands.

"Yes, I know. But I was wondering if it is possible for the teaching assistants to offer one last study group before the exam, since there are so many other students having trouble in this class."

He stopped twiddling that blue Bic and started tapping it on his desk.

"I don't know about that. A lot of students are having no problem and are doing very well. Why don't you start your own study group?"

"I don't know any other students in the class." I said with a helpless sigh.

He leaned forward then, his chubby, wrinkled arms resting on his thighs. I could see his face stubble and his gray nose hairs quivering with each breath. I concluded that to come to work looking as unkept as he is probably meant his job was secure.

He was still fingering that Bic pen. He straightened up and leaned his head against the back of his brown swivel chair. He cleared his throat.

"You know," he said, "A few years ago I had a Black girl in my class, just like you. She was failing also. She came to me and wanted help and she got a B in my class.

I leaned forward.

"How did she do that?" I asked, in anticipation.

He bent his body towards me again, looking straight into my eyes.

"She didn't have to do much. All she had to do was...well...she went out with me...a couple of times..."

I straightened up tall in my chair.

"What?" I said. My eyes widened. *Did I hear him correctly?*

He started waving his hands from side to side and shaking his head.

"No, no, no. It was not what you think." He crossed his arms, nodded, and remembered. "And there was another Black girl..."

I interrupted him."I don't understand..." I uncrossed my legs. "What are you saying?" I asked, cautiously.

"I'm saying these girls got a B in my class...no intercourse was involved...just some other things...and if you want..."

I stood up. I grabbed my clutch purse off the black, scarred table.

"What are you saying? Are you suggesting...I won't do that! I will not go out with you." I said, glaring at him with tight lips and glassy eyes.

"I came here for help, not to be propositioned. I came here...this is not right..."

He sat there in his tweed brown pants staring at me. His right hand was calmly stroking his thick, white eyebrows. He leaned forward in his brown leather chair.

"They helped me, and I helped them...they got a B in the class."

I rushed to the door, grabbed the knob, and flung open the door. To my back as I existed, he yelled, "Suit yourself."

Outside, I was shaking. *What just happened?* I was just propositioned by my professor! That old White bastard turned my request for help into a nasty game of baseball! And his stories about other Black girls! He was probably lying! He thought that would convince me to go out with him for a B! *You son-of-a bitch, bastard!*

I stumbled home. I was hurt. I wanted to cry, and I was crying. Are professors supposed to talk to students like that? Who can I tell? I can't tell Sid. I wanted somebody to tell me how to punish this little disgusting monster!

I went to my room. I had a decision to make. I decided never to seek help from my other professors, especially old White ones with gray hair!

When I declared history as my major, one of the classes I took was 'History of the American West' taught by Professor Beale. He was old with brown hair peppered with gray. He was tall and lanky with an Abraham Lincoln look. He sat in a brown wooden armless chair in front of the classroom using no notes but bringing the West to life with his stories. He was a great storyteller.

In the small classroom, I selected a seat in the front row. I took pages of notes on "broken Indian treaties, White rustlers, hustlers, and backwoodsmen." He never talked about Black backwoodsmen. I guess there were none in the West.

Occasionally, I looked up from my burgundy notebook.

Professor Beale is looking at my legs!

No! I'm just being 'old White men' sensitive now.

Even if he was eyeing my legs, it was probably a once off, pure happenstance. Just in case, I began to keep my feet flat on the floor and my legs folded tight under my desk.

Professor Beale continued to spout dates and weave stories. And whenever I looked up from my notes, his eyes were on my legs! *What is with these old White bastards! Are they still glorifying slavery when they could have any Black woman they wanted?*

I should move to the back of the room. That would call attention to me. I would have to take somebody else's seat. Other students must notice. This professor is not being sly!

At least I am doing well in the class. On every quiz and exam, I can do no wrong. I get an A on everything. What is he trying to do...warm me up for the kill? You spineless bastard!

On the last day of class, everyone was milling around and chatting on the way out. I was gathering my purse and notebook when

I made eye contact with Professor Beale. I looked away quickly and headed for the exit. Before I made it to the door, he cut me off. He stood in front of me with a no-teeth smile on his scraggly face.

Oh, my goodness! What is he going to want from me? Another one wanting...he bowed slightly and said, "Have a good evening, Ms. Edwards."

He walked away. I took a deep breath and blew the air slowly out through my lips. I calmed down. I put a smile on my face and left the room.

I got an A in the class.

I failed Climate 331. I took the class again the following summer from a seat in the last row close to the right-side exit. I passed with a C.

10
PLAYBOY BUNNY

"You're so gullible...and innocent. I'm an experienced man. I need an experienced woman." And with those words, Sid broke up with me.

We were in his trailer doing our usual...listening to Gloria Lynne, Lou Rawls, and Nina Simone. We were dancing around the room pausing for hugs and kisses and sipping on Sprites from a bottle.

After the second base attempt on Mrs. Hathaway's porch swing, I expected Sid to follow up. I expected him to skip first base and head straight to second base. Instead, he did the unexpected.

When it was time for me to go home, Sid pulled me to a chair across from him at his kitchen table. With my hands in his, he delivered his farewell soliloquy.

"I love you to death. That's why I can't do this anymore. I don't want to be the one to spoil your innocence. You are so fresh...and pure. I will not take advantage of you. The best thing for me to do is to help you stay the way you are. I am not the right person for you."

I just sat there shaking my head in disbelief.

"We're so good together...and so happy. Why are you doing this? Where is this 'wanting someone experienced' stuff coming from, Sid?"

He didn't answer. He just sat there searching my face and holding my hands.

I know where this breakup talk is coming from. It's coming from his Mama. Two weeks ago, Sid brought her to Mrs. Hathaway's house to meet me.

When they stopped in front of the house, I came out to the car smiling big to greet them. Sid was all smiles in his usual blue collarless sport shirt, khaki shorts, and sandaled feet. He greeted me with a hug halfway across the yard and guided me to the driver's side of the car.

I'm always concerned about meeting mamas. Sid's Mama was 'high yellow' like him. She rolled down her window and smiled at me from behind the wheel of her big gray car. I was wearing my yellow flowered wrap around dress with my flipped hairstyle that covered the blemishes on the right side of my face.

I leaned in as we exchanged "hellos," smiles, and handshakes through the car window. Her tight smile was saying to Sid, *"She is very cute, but her skin is too dark, and she is living in a dump."* My full teeth smile was saying to her, *"I bet you're a real bitch!"*

When I heard Sid's words, I didn't cry and I didn't stutter in disbelief. I didn't wail, beg, and plead for him not to break up with me. I sat there staring back at his eyes. He was sitting there holding my hands in his, waiting.

My mind was racing. *What am I going to do tomorrow?* With Sid, I didn't have to plan...I knew the routine...the library, his trailer, and always the jazz.

He broke my spell.

"Come on, I'll take you home."

With that, we had nothing else to say. He walked me to the sorority house door, gave me a warm tight hug, turned around and left.

"Shit!" Now what do I do! Who's going to take me to the Alpha Playboy Charity Ball! I'm a playboy bunny! I was so happy to be selected. Sid had said, "They made a great choice, Little Mama!"

Now, he's not going to be my escort! I was looking forward to dressing up in a one-piece pink swimsuit with "rabbit ears," a white "cottontail" and spiked heels. I was ready to smile, strut and deliver drinks to Sid.

Did he have to exchange me and my purity for sluttiness and experience...this week?

With such a coveted role, I couldn't be seen leaving the Ball alone. I couldn't enter the sorority house all "bunnied up" under the smirking grin of Ms. Johnson!

I did what I had to do. I left the Ball alone and walked into the stillness of the sorority house. I walked past Ms. Johnson wearing my bunny facepaint, my pink bunny ears, my white "cottontail" and my black spiked heels. I strutted with focused eyes straight ahead past her smug, satisfied gaze.

I had to start planning for tomorrow.

11

SISTERHOOD

The end of the spring term was near. Everybody was busy studying for exams and writing papers. Now that I had switched my major to history, my advisor suggested that I do a term of student teaching, just in case a job at the UN didn't work out.

I made plans to spend the winter term of my senior year student-teaching at Lincoln High School in East Saint Louis, Illinois. The city was not far from our house in University City, but it was too far for me to commute. I had to find housing in East St. Louis.

Mama had kept in touch with Ms. Nora, a distant 'cousin' who moved from Mt. Vernon, and is now living in East St. Louis. She lives in the projects with her twin adolescent daughters.

Ms. Nora was a regular visitor to our house in University City. She sat in her car in our driveway, finished a bag of White Castle burgers and dragged herself into the house for a short visit. She always left behind an odor of greasy burgers mixed with hot sweat.

She was a large woman. She moved slowly. Her breathing was heavy, and she talked loudly. Mama said she has diabetes. Mama also said, "She otta stop eating so many of dem cheap burgers 'cause dey dangerous."

When I was looking for housing in East St. Louis, Mama said," You kin stay wit Nora. She say you kin stay in her 'partment for free."

It was agreed that I would stay with her during the week and come home to University City on weekends. My living in the projects with Ms. Nora was the only housing option on the table.

Daddy drove me to the projects. He parked on the street in front of three red brick high rise buildings. Through the chained fence surrounding the buildings, I saw a common courtyard filled with swinging, running, and screaming kids. Old women mostly were sitting on green wooden benches watching the running and screaming kids.

There were teens, too. Boys in white tee shirts were standing legs apart in small groups eying the teen girls. The girls in white blouses were forcing their eyes to look anywhere except at the boys.

Everybody was Black.

I entered the gate in the chain fence with Daddy and my two green, large suitcases. Two grinning teen girls with short, pressed hair rushed over to us.

"Hi. You Margaret?" one of the girls asked.

"Yes," I answered. "You must be the twins, Mable and Sable. Last time I saw you two, you were so little. Who is who?" There was more grinning and pushing as the twins identified themselves.

We made our way into one of the buildings, took an elevator to the third floor and entered an overstuffed living room. Ms. Nora lumbered over to greet us.

"Hi, y'all come on in. How you doin, Willie T? Mable, show Margaret where she gon sleep. We ain't got no fancy house. But thank God for providing us with a decent place to live."

Daddy left us.

The twins helped me organize my bed on one side of a

bedroom. Ms. Nora gave me the directions to Lincoln High school.

When I knew I was going to student-teach in East St. Louis, I contacted a sorority sister who lived in East St. Louis. Her name was Sheila. She graduated from SIU two years before me.

One day after school, I contacted her. We met for coffee. I remembered her freckles and her quick smile. She was married and living in a small one-bedroom apartment awaiting the return of her husband who was in the army and stationed in Korea.

During my first week of student teaching when I returned to the projects, the twins were waiting for me. I was trooped downstairs to "meet our friends...we made a promise."

"This here my cousin. She in college, and she teaching over at the high school."

"Hi, everybody," I said, with a wave of my right hand.

The teen boys and some of the girls looked me over. Some pushed each other around trying to position themselves to get a better view. Others circled me giving me a once over like they were inspecting a new car. I could hear whispering to the twins.

"How old is she?"

"She staying wit chou?"

"She have real nice hair."

"And she got nice legs, too."

Giggle, giggle.

I stopped coming home early. Instead, I went to Sheila's house. We talked about my teaching experiences. We talked about how to write and implement lesson plans to satisfy my teaching supervisor. We shared memories and experiences of our sorority life that brought joy to my life and hers.

One time we talked until late into the evening. Sheila decided she'd better accompany me home. I invited her up to the apartment. No one was home. She stayed a few minutes and left.

When I walked into the apartment after school the next day, I heard Ms. Nora's heavy breathing. She was yelling and crying to somebody on the phone.

"She had people in my house…I didn't say folks could come here…Cora Mae, folks steal! I can't have all kinds of people in my house. I don't allow strangers in my house. I hear what you saying…but she gon have to leave heah. I want her outta heah now...Cora Mae she got her friend. She gotta go!"

It didn't take me long to figure out that I was the one who had to go. I packed my two green suitcases and called Sheila. For the remainder of the Winter Term, I slept in Sheila's living room on a fold down couch bed.

12
FRIDAYS AT JIMMY'S

"We can create five-year plans," I said to my friends, Millie and Celia. "Just look at China. They made five-year plans, every five years, until they reached their goals. Why don't we make some plans? We can go somewhere and have some coffee and talk about our futures. That would be fun."

My friends nodded their heads in agreement. We were sitting on the floor in Celia's room. This was our last term together before graduation.

"I don't have nothing against planning my future, but I'm gonna need something stronger than coffee to do that," Celia said, laughing and stubbing out a cigarette.

"I'll drink to do that," Millie said, giggling and punching the air above her head.

Celia was lighting up another cigarette.

She said, "I know this little place on the other side of town. Jimmy's, it's called. How about we go over there on Friday?"

I like my friends. Celia is like a Mama Bear. She's in her late twenties. She came all the way from California to SIU to finish a master's degree in social work. She doesn't have a boyfriend and she doesn't seem to want one. She just stays in her room surrounded by open books, empty coffee cups and overflowing ashtrays. She is always available to listen to "problems of the heart."

Millie is a pretty, small-town girl studying elementary education. She is 'boy crazy.' She's always smiling at guys and dancing wide-legged on the dance floor. Guys just flock to her even though she has a boyfriend named Jason.

"It's hard to keep Jason happy," she said. "I know he's playing out on me. What am I supposed to do? He's an Alpha, but I'm gonna play out on him, too."

Celia ponders the issue of "disloyal boyfriends." Plumes of smoke rise above her head as she considers options for Millie. She is doing what any good social worker would do.

On Friday, we head to Jimmy's to plan and document our futures in five-year plans. I brought along my burgundy SIU notebook.

Millie parks her Beetle in front of a place with umbrella tops sticking up over a high wooden fence. We enter a courtyard. Five high wooden tables have faded umbrellas in orange, blue and red hovering over them. Four wicker stools are pushed under each table.

Attached above the doorway of the restaurant is a plank of wood. Black paint spells out the word "Jimmy's."

"This is it," Celia announces.

We are the only customers in the courtyard, so we seat ourselves at a table under a blue umbrella. I can hear the rise and fall of traffic from a nearby highway. Perched on that stool reminded me of the "sit-in' stool at another "Jimmy's" way back in Mt. Vernon. Back then, "rednecks" were taunting my sisters and me.

"Get outta here you little niggas." It took a lot of effort to keep me from falling off that stool.

There are no taunts today. We have our futures to plan.

Celia is all smiles. She is rubbing her hands together.

"They got the best 'Singapore Slings' here. You gotta try one. You're gonna love this drink."

Millie is quick to respond.

"I'll try one. Girl, you're always talking about Singapore Slings. Let me see what these things are all about."

"I'll have a 7 Up," I said.

Millie and Celia both turn and stare at me. Celia morphs into 'Chastising Mama Bear.'

"You come all the way out here for a 7 Up. Girl, loosen up! Where you think you are, still in Mt...what is it, Vermin?"

"It's Mt. Vernon..."

"Anyway, Singapore Slings ain't nothing but fruit juices with slices of oranges, cherries, and a little bit of gin. Plus, you've had more liquor than that at those frat parties!" She shakes her head and flicks a dismissive hand in my direction.

"No, I have not," I defended myself, "I always drink the non-alcoholic punch. I never..."

Celia posted her right hand in front of my face. I stopped talking. She moved her right hand to my right arm. She looked into my eyes. Millie covered her mouth to snuff out her snickering.

"I'm gonna let you in on a little secret, honey," Celia is pretending to whisper in my ear.

"Don't believe that little sign by the punch bowl that says "non-alcoholic." That sign is there to please the school administration."

She took her hand off my arm and smiled smugly.

"Shit, I poured a bottle of vodka in one of those 'non-alcoholic' bowls myself!"

She and Millie are laughing. They hold onto their sides and the sides of the round tabletop to keep from falling off their stools.

I look askance at the two of them laughing, leaning into each other and clasping hands.

All this time I've been drinking alcohol, and never realized it! How could that happen? Somebody should look into this. If a Singapore Sling is mostly fruit and stuff like Celia said, maybe trying one is ok.

"Well, I don't think it's that funny. People who don't want to drink shouldn't have to, but I guess I'll try a Singapore Sling."

While we waited for our drinks, I tore out two sheets of paper from my burgundy spiral notebook. I placed a sheet in front of Millie and a sheet in front of Celia.

"Ok, we should write down the goals we want to accomplish during the next five years. By the end of 1972, the goals we set now, will be met and then we can start all over again with new goals."

Millie is already writing on her sheet of paper.

"I know what I want. I'm not waiting five years. I want a boyfriend now, a non-cheating one."

Celia rolls her eyes. "Good luck with that."

"Well," I said. "I want a boyfriend, too."

Millie and I are busy writing.

"I also want to get my master's degree," I said.

Millie nods in agreement, "That's good."

Celia is tapping her yellow pencil on the table.

"I'm gonna think about all this goal stuff later. Right now, I just want a drink."

Our Singapore Slings arrive. The long-stemmed glasses are filled with reddish orange liquid topped with pineapples and cherries on a stick. In the middle of the liquid is a white plastic straw.

Millie and Celia remove their straws, and drink from the glass, proclaiming their satisfaction with ums and lip smacking.

I take a small sip through my straw. All those juices taste really good.

"You like it? Celia asks.

I shrug my shoulders. "It's Ok," I said, nonchalantly. I will not let her see that I am liking the taste." *Damn, this drink tastes so good!*

"Ok, guys, let's write down our goals." I said after a long draw on my straw.

"I've already got two goals," Millie said. "How many do I need? I should put down "get a boyfriend twice."

Every Friday for the next month and a half, we drove to Jimmy's. We sat on high wicker stools around a round wooden table and with black Bic pens, scribbled on a sheet of notebook paper our goals for the next five years.

My Five-Year Goals 1967-1972

- Get a boyfriend
- Get a master's degree
- Travel

13

GREEN SUITCASES

I graduated from Southern Illinois University in May 1967. My parents came down from University City.

Daddy said, "You the first in dis heah Edwards family to gradurate from college."

Daddy and Mama watched me, along with other hatted graduates rise together, sit back down together, and walk across the stage to collect diplomas.

I found them later among hundreds of parents standing under a makeshift tent smiling and clapping. I walked them to their car. Daddy opened the trunk, "We got you somethin fer yo graduration."

Mama was sniffling and wiping her eyes.

"They is suitcases. Dere's two more pieces inside dere."

"Oh, nice," I said, rubbing a hand on the large green vinyl suitcase.

"I guess I gotta travel somewhere now," I said. "Thank you. They are really nice."

My parents got in the car and drove back to University City. Two days later, I took a Greyhound bus home.

I never spent a whole summer at home in University City. One summer I took required classes to make up for my 'executive secretary' phase. Other summers, I just wanted to be away. I took a Greyhound bus home for two weeks, talked with my younger sisters and brothers, then took the Greyhound bus back to SIU.

Now that I graduated, my parents didn't understand why I was still going to summer school. I told them I was enrolling in graduate courses that would lead to my getting a master's degree.

In reality, I needed time to sort out my life. I had a bachelor's degree in history. What could I do with that? Teach school? I wanted to work for the United Nations. How do I make that happen? Who do I talk to, When? How? Where? I didn't have the answers. All I had were questions.

So, after graduating and going home for two weeks, I went back to SIU and enrolled in two graduate courses: Advanced English history, and international organizations.

I moved into a trailer with beds for four. Two girls who I didn't know shared one bedroom. My friend Jess and I shared the other. Jess came back to SIU for graduate courses since she wasn't ready to go home either.

I liked Jess. She was a Chicago girl, but she didn't act like a "city girl." She didn't mind hanging out with small town girls like me. She was tall, light skinned with "good hair," and she had a "city" boyfriend. When others gossiped about a girl who we all knew would be sent home at the end of the semester, Jess's comment was, "She probably has her reasons for going out every night."

Even when her own boyfriend dragged other "city girls" onto the dance floor, Jess was content to stand with me on the sidelines and watch. She never judged other people's behavior. I liked that.

Many times, the two of us talked about what to do with our lives now that "required classes and studying for Finals'" are over.

"Sometimes people meet at school and get married," I said. "But that is not me. I have too much to do."

Jess said, "White kids 'go abroad' to decide what they want to do. Why don't Black kids go abroad?"

"Probably because it costs money," I said. "You gotta have money."

"It couldn't cost that much. There's gotta be a way."

"I want to work for the United Nations. I don't think that's gonna happen, but I would love to go somewhere out of the United States."

Jess didn't know that 'travel' was one of my goals in my five - year plan. She said, "We should think about it."

I said, "Yeah, that would be so much fun. I think about it all the time. It just takes money. I got a set of green suitcases for graduation, so I'm ready to go!"

She said, "Yeah, I'm gonna ask my parents about it."

14
A SPY AMONG US

During our last summer at SIU, Jess and I and our trailer mates became friendly with a tall, handsome, older Black man named Bill. We didn't know anything about him except he was not a student. He just appeared on campus and always hung around with the Black students.

He played bid whist with the guys in the Student Union. He sat out on the railing leading to the Student Union and talked and laughed with the city girls and guys. To me and my summer school friends, we just knew him as the guy who took us to the local diner and picked up the check. He became our weekly "date."

One time I met him walking across campus. He was his usual friendly self, so when he asked me if I would like to grab something to eat later that day at the diner, I said, "Sure, I'll tell the others."

He said, "No, you don't have to do that...I'll see them later in the week."

After that, he and I started meeting over food three or four times a week. He always picked up the check.

When it was time for me to leave SIU after my summer courses, he offered to drive me home to University City.

I said," You don't need to do that. I always take the Greyhound Bus."

"That's crazy. I'm heading that way," he said.

So, I threw my few belongings into the trunk of his old Ford LaSalle. He had his black suit hanging from a hook in the back seat of the car.

On the two-hour trip to my new home in University City, I had a lot of questions. I asked him, "Why were you always hanging around the campus? Did you have a job?"

"Yes, I had a job."

He was never much of a talker.

"So, what was your job?"

"I was working for the government."

"But why were you on campus if you were working for the government?"

"The government asked me to work on campus."

"Did you have an office on campus?"

"Yes."

"Where was your office?"

"In the security section."

"Bill, just tell me what your job was."

It took him a minute.

"My job was to make sure there was no trouble on campus. No protests and no planning of disturbances. Students had to keep going to class."

"So, your job was to spy on the Black students?"

He laughed.

"I wasn't spying on nobody. I was there to help the Black kids. They didn't need to get involved in something that was gonna get them thrown out of school."

"So where are you headed now...to another campus?"

"To wherever I'm needed."

Spies don't talk much about their work.

"So, where do you want to go for dinner tonight?" He changed the subject.

"I don't know. I'm just moving here. I don't know."

"St. Louis has a lot of nice restaurants. I wanna take you to a really nice place. You must have heard of one nice place."

Bill's imploring me to give him a possibility. My mind is spinning.

"Well, let's see," I said. "How about Howard Johnson's."

Bill took his eyes off the road to look at me.

"Howard Johnson's!" He's laughing and looking at me and back at the highway.

"Howard Johnson's!" he exclaimed again. "That's not a restaurant. That's some kind of second-rate family motel you can find up and down any highway!"

I didn't tell him that fancy restaurants don't let you finish your food. I didn't tell him that one time I went to a really fancy restaurant after I won a writing contest in seventh grade.

We went to Lincoln's home in Springfield, Illinois and went for lunch at a white napkin restaurant. I sat with the five White parents and the other White winners in a restaurant with too many knives and forks and white napkins. I ordered a steak. I was eating slowly and pushing potatoes and spinach around just like the White people at my table. I was down to my last bite of steak. I put my fork down on my plate to finish chewing a bite of potato. The last taste in my mouth was going to be that moist, savory bite of steak.

I picked up the white napkin and raised it to my mouth to wipe away crumbs that would detract from my chewing that last morsel of steak. I was placing my napkin on the side of my plate when... what? A hand from the left grabbed my plate with my last morsel of steak! But my fork was poised! I thrust my forked hand toward that hand. But the hand was too quick. I wanted to yell, "Excuse me! I still have a piece of steak to finish."

Instead, I put my fork down and smiled just like the White folks at my table expected me to. They could not keep me from looking over at the dirty dish bin. There lay my last bite of steak crushed among rejected breads, iceberg lettuce and green beans.

To Bill, I said, "Then you pick a place."

Mama had seen Bill earlier through the picture window when he dropped me off.

She said, "Dat man, he too old to be in college."

"He's not in college, Mama. He works there."

By the time Bill came to pick me up for our dinner date, Mama had changed into a church dress and put her hair into a bun. Daddy was in the basement. My younger sisters were with me in the bedroom helping me dress. I stayed in the bedroom to give Mama enough time to settle down. I hear her saying, "How you doing? Come on in."

I heard, "Thank you," from Bill.

"I'm Margaret's mother, Cora."

"I'm Bill. It's nice to meet you."

There's that 'swishing' sound. Bill is sitting down on one of the blue plastic-covered French Provincial couches that are Daddy's pride and joy. He bought two matching couches from the people who owned the house before.

"Dese heah is very expensive couches…Franch Provanchel. I don't wont none of y'all setting on dese couches…'til we get dem plastic covers."

The air is seeping out through the plastic covers.

Mama is still talking.

"Nice meeting you. Margaret, she gon be out directly."

"Margaret...Margaret, yo friend is heah. Nice weather we having."

I made my entrance to find Bill sitting, wedged into the plastic pillow of the blue French Provincial couch near the door. He smiles and rocks forward trying to stand up when I enter. The claws of all that plastic holds him in place. He grabs the wooden arm of the couch, scoots to the edge of the seat and springs to his feet. Mama and I stand there watching him struggle to extricate himself from plastic mounds. After Bill frees himself, we watch that plastic rise back into position awaiting its next victim.

Bill's wrinkled lips smile. He looks handsome in that black suit I saw hanging in the back seat of his car. Mama is standing there smiling and my sisters are peeking from the bedroom door. Bill is still smiling as he holds open the door for the two of us to make our exit.

"Goodbye, hope to see you again," were Mama's last words before Bill escorted me down the steps and into the passenger side of the car. I know we were being watched through that picture window. They were mesmerized by his gentlemanly manners and thinking, "Too bad he's so old."

We stopped at a place with a lot of wood on the outside. The name Stan Musial's Steakhouse was flashing on a billboard out front. Bill said Stan was a famous retired Cardinal baseball player. I could tell this was a fancy place. It was new like the one in Springfield, but I could tell this place was fancier.

Spoons and forks were wrapped in white cloth napkins and placed on the right side of our plates. More spoons and forks and knives were placed with no napkin near the top and on the left side of the plate. I ordered a steak, along with a baked potato and asparagus.

I didn't know which fork to start with, so I took the one from my napkin. I didn't put that fork down. I hovered over my plate. No hand is going to grab my plate tonight. I cleaned my plate.

"You must have been hungry," Bill said.

"Yes, the food is really good," I said.

I didn't tell him that I was still hungry and that what I ate wasn't enough to feed grown people. But if a sign of a fancy restaurant is to still be hungry after finishing a meal, then Stan Musial's Steakhouse must be really fancy,

Bill walked me to my door, gave me a hug and drove away. I unlocked the door to a dark house and walked into the bedroom I am sharing with my sister, Helena. My life has come to this. I have a five-year plan hidden away on the top shelf in the closet. *I'll go to bed now and first thing tomorrow, I'll retrieve it. I've got a lot of things to figure out.*

Book II

"Wildflowers are the loveliest of all because they grow in uncultivated soil, in those hard, rugged places where no one expects them to flourish."

Micheline Ryckman

1
MAMA'S NEIGHBORHOOD

There doesn't seem to be much talk anymore about "Black folks changing our neighborhood." Mama is partly responsible for that. Her name is known to the two White neighbors across the street and to the Black neighbors on either side of our house. While Daddy is at work and my siblings are in school, Mama is working the neighborhood, making friends.

One of the Black families next door to us looked White to me, but Mama said, "Dey the Taylors…dey Black folks. Mrs. Taylor say dey from somewheah 'round Detroit where my sister Mattie Belle live. Mr. Taylor, he got some big job. Mrs. Taylor, she just stay home like me...dey all real nice though."

Mama and Mrs. Taylor are always talking over the side yard chain fence, mostly about the weather and the kids. The Taylors have two girls the same age as my siblings Joyce and Kaye. They are always running between our house and theirs.

"It is so hot here, Cora. I can't wait to go visit my Mom in Boston just to cool off. The girls run through sunscreen like water!"

"I ain't never been to Boston. I bet it real nice up dere. It don't take long to git used to dis heat. Talkin bout hot, you outta go to Missippi. All dem dirt roads an no shade trees a'tal!"

"My girls so enjoy your girls. They can come over any time. They play so well together. Cora, you can come, too and we can have some coffee while the girls play."

Mama was such a mismatch when it came to most of the neighbors on Gaylord Street. She didn't care and the neighbors didn't seem to care either. She just kept introducing herself and talking to people no matter their station.

I got my first teaching job because of Mama. One day when I was sitting in the kitchen, she said to me, "Mr. Jankins is a teacha, he kin git you a job."

The Jenkins family was one of the new Black families that had moved into a house down the street that was recently vacated by a White family. Mama was babysitting their young son until Mr. Jenkins picked him up after work.

I had seen Mr. Jenkins. He was a large man, dark and tall with an oversized head and smiling eyes. When he showed up to collect his son, I heard Mama say, "I wont you to meet my dauter. She jes finish college an she lookin fer a job. Margaret, come heah an meet Mr. Jankins."

I came out of my room so Mama didn't have to give any more information about my jobless status.

"Hello," I said as I came into the living room. Mr. Jenkins turns at my greeting. I see his face light up with a big smile like he likes what he sees. He's wearing a dark blue suit with a red and blue tie laying against his white shirt.

"So, you just finished college," he stated, smiling warmly.

"Yes," I said with a reciprocal smile. "I graduated a month ago from SIU, in history."

"That's great," he said. "And you're looking for a teaching job?"

I wanted to say, "Well no, I really want to work for the UN."

But I answered appropriately.

"Yes. I am hoping to find something soon."

Mr. Jenkins digs into his back pocket and pulls out a wallet.

"You will have no problem. We need teachers all over the city. Here's my card. You go to this office."

He moves toward me pointing out an address.

"I'm the Assistant Superintendent for St. Louis Public Schools. Just fill out the application and you can use my name if you want to."

I took the card. My heart was beating fast in my chest just thinking about the possibility of a job. I had a big smile on my face as I thanked him for his help. Mama's smile was even bigger than mine.

2

TRAINING WHEELS

Before I submitted all the required paperwork, the St. Louis Public Schools hired me. I became a "permanent sub" assigned to teach fourth grade at Lach Elementary School in downtown St. Louis. I was to report for work in two days!

How am I supposed to get to downtown St. Louis? I don't have a car. Even if I did, I don't know how to drive the streets of St. Louis by myself! I took Driver's Education at SIU, passed the test, and got my Illinois driver's license. But that was the last time I drove a car!

Last summer, Daddy tried to give me some practice. He took me out in his green Buick to drive around the streets near our house. There were no wide boulevards or four lane streets in U City, just two-lane streets. As I was slowly maneuvering the narrow, two-lane streets, I began to hear drivers laying on their horns.

Daddy said, "You gon hafta go faster dan thirty miles a hour on dese roads."

I tried but there were so many curves in the road and those horns and now those sirens were hindering my concentration. A policeman on a motorcycle started flashing his lights behind me.

Daddy said, "You gotta pull over." I was happy to get out of that noisy traffic.

The cop came to my side of the car and asked for my license. I gave him my license.

"I need your license, Sir." Daddy gave him his license.

The officer said to me, "You know you can't drive this slowly. You can cause an accident."

"Ain't that better then speedin'?" Daddy asked. Daddy knew the right questions to ask because he has gotten so many tickets for speeding.

"Maybe, but not during rush hour. I'm gonna havta give ya a ticket for this."

"A ticket for what?" Daddy wanted to know. "Dere ain't no law 'gainst slow drivin,"

"Take it up with the judge," the cop said as he handed Daddy the ticket. He rode off on his motorcycle.

Daddy stuffed the ticket in the pocket of his door.

"That son of a bitch...I ain't payin no damn ticket..."

And he didn't. The judge threw out the case because Daddy wasn't driving. I was.

I made a deal with my brother, Frank.

"If you help me buy a car and show me how to get to Lach School, you can drive the car whenever you want."

I proclaimed to my baffled household, "I can't drive down to that school unless somebody shows me how to get there first."

I know the source of my driving challenges. I'm a walker. I walked everywhere all my life, traversing up and down the country roads in Mt. Vernon and the back streets of small-town Carbondale. If I was not walking, I was being driven by Daddy or by some random bus driver or by a friend who had a car. Now in order to get to work, I have to maneuver through the narrow streets of U

City and find my way to an inner-city school through the harrowing city streets of St. Louis!

I asked my brother Frank to go with me to the car dealership. I bought a green 1967 Chevy Hatchback. I didn't care what kind of car I got, it just had to be green and small. After I bought the car, Frank drove it home, then drove me to Lach Elementary while I watched and noted every road mark, every pothole, every stoplight, and every turn. When we got to the school, I watched where he parked and how he made the reverse trip home.

It was then my turn to drive from home to the school following that same route noting every street marker, every pothole, every stoplight, and every turn including parking and the return trip home.

On Monday morning, I drove to Lach Elementary noting every street marker, every pothole, every stoplight, and every turn that I had practiced the day before. I parked in the school's parking lot. I remembered everything. Getting a degree in history and memorizing all those names of generals and dates of battles helped my driving memory.

3

PLACEHOLDER

The only teaching I had ever done was student teaching at Lincoln High School in East St. Louis. The last time I was around elementary school kids was when I was myself an elementary school kid!

When I arrived for work on the first day, I expected a tour of the school, and "a new teacher orientation." What I got was a manila envelope, a grade book, and a classroom key.

I entered a bare-walled modular classroom where twenty-six fourth graders were sitting, staring, and waiting for me to prove myself. They were all Black. The subs before me according to the kids were "so mean." That indicated I needed to let them do as they pleased if I didn't want to be run off as well. For the most part they got their wish. I wanted to stay. I wanted to give the kids stability. Also, I wanted the money.

My only problem child in class was a little girl named Reba, who came to school every day ready to fight. Anything she was told to do, she would first call me "Stupid," throw things, and when I came near her, I got the brunt of her lashing and flailing arms. I assumed I was not the source of her aberrant behavior.

I didn't see the benefit of seeking help from the office. I sought advice from another teacher who had been at the school for a year. She was also isolated in a module. She tried to help me with disciplinary issues, but she was too busy trying to get control of her boyfriend, who "doesn't want to get married" and "I think he is playing out."

Near the end of my one-year permanent sub position at Lach Elementary, I applied for a high school teaching position for the next school year.

I was hired to teach history at Beaumont High School, a predominantly Black school with over 2,000 students located in the city of St. Louis.

4

NIGHT SCHOOL

"Margaret, is dis heah word a noun or a pronoun, dis word 'voting.' I git dese thangs mixed up. Mr. Jackson, he says I'm doin so good. He the best teacha...he real handsome too."

When I came home from SIU, everybody was sitting around the dining room table doing homework, even Daddy! I expected that of my siblings, but Mama and Daddy sitting around multiplying and diagramming sentences! They were both in night school "trying to git our high skool dipluma."

Daddy said, "I got to sacon grade. I werked de farm and razed dem crops. Dere wuzn't no time to be goin to no skool. I coulda don mo thangs wit a high skool diploma."

Mama said, "I wuz good in skool. All I need now is to git my high skool dipluma. Den I kin git a betta job."

Daddy didn't stay in school. When he was in St. Louis by himself looking for a house, he learned a lot about property in St. Louis. By the time the family moved to University City, he had bought two apartment buildings. He was fixing them up and renting them out. Between the three houses in Mt. Vernon, and the newly bought two buildings in St. Louis, Daddy was too busy for school. He was either repairing or trying to collect rent from backsliders.

He said, "I don't have no time to sterdy."

But he kept taking Mama to the junior high where the classes were held. And after every class, he was there to pick her up.

Every evening before going to class, Mama went through the same ritual. She cleared away plates, glasses, leftover beans, and cabbage bowls and spread out her workbooks, pencils, and dictionary on the kitchen table.

She stood before the tall, wall mirror in the hallway and pulled her hair back into a bun. She applied a little red rouge to her cheeks and matching red lipstick to her lips. She put on an ironed white blouse, pulled on beige pantyhose and slipped on a black fitted skirt. After getting a "you look fine, you're only going to a class" comment from one of my sisters, she would sit and have a running conversation as she worked through Mr. Jackson's homework assignments.

"Mr. Jackson say I'm doing good in math and everything. Everybody like him. He ain't married neither. I say to him, 'I bet you got a lot of girls after you.' He jes laughs."

One evening I had to pick Mama up from class. She didn't know Daddy wouldn't be there, so I had to go inside to announce my presence.

A few groups of ladies, Black and White, were chatting in the hallways. Others were spilling out of open doors. I saw Mama walking with a group of women. They were all smiling too big and vying for the attention of a slim, brown skinned, tall young man. He was smiling, a hand on a shoulder here, an arm around another there. He was escorting them playfully toward the exit. Then he looked up and saw me.

5

SUMMER DREAMS

"Marge, Marge, is that you?" It was my friend Jess on the phone.

"Hi, Jess. How are you? Where are you?"

"We're going. It's all set. Everything is worked out. All you have to do is register and pay the tuition."

She was saying a lot of words so fast, I was trying to break in and ask a question.

"Jess, what are you talking about…what's worked out?"

"Marge, don't you remember? We said we wanted to go abroad, remember? Well, I found a course in London!"

"What? London! Yeah, we talked about that, but I was just…" I was stuttering and trying to remember if I had committed to anything.

"When? I'm working now and…"

"It's not now. It's during the summer. You don't have to do anything. I'll send you the information. Another friend named Sylvia wants to go too. It sounds really good. Come on, girl, let's do this! It's like a graduate school class, only it's in London!"

"Well, I don't know, we were just talking. Ok, I guess," I said. "Send me the information."

Jess didn't have a money problem. Both her parents had businesses in Chicago. One was in real estate and the other ran a touring company. There was no way I could afford to go to Europe. All that wanting to "do what White kids do" was just summer talk.

Since the trip was slated for the summer, maybe I could save enough from my permanent sub check. My only bills were the car note and gas.

I received the course description and the proposed travel itinerary. I mentioned the trip to my parents. We were sitting around the table eating brown beans, cabbage, and cornbread.

"I'm thinking about going to Europe this summer."

"You thankin 'bout goin wheah?" Mama asked.

"London and Europe, across the ocean blue."

"How you gon git dere?"

"I'm gonna take an airplane."

"You gon take som airplane over all dat wata! Dat's too dangerous!"

Mama put down her fork and stared at me. Daddy came to my rescue.

"Cora Mae, what chu talkin 'bout! Dem big old airplanes fly eveywher, over water, over tall buildings, over everything…dem pilots know what dey doin."

Daddy couldn't help reminding us of his flight to the March on Washington back in 1963.

"Dat big ole plane wuz goin hunderds of miles a hower an dat ride wuz so quick…'fore I knowed it, we was on the ground."

"Well," I said. "I don't think the trip to Europe will be so quick. Maybe about eight or nine hours."

"Eight or nine howers! You gon be flying over wata fer dat long? Dat don't make no sense!"

Daddy went back to his mantra.

"What you should be thankin 'bout is getin yo master's degree 'teada thankin 'bout runnin off somewheah in Angland. You otta be gittin back in school an gittin you master's degree. Ain't no reason fer you to keep working an not git yo master degree."

"I don't want to go back to school now," I protested. "Plus, there are no schools around here that I want to go to."

"What chou talkin 'bout? All kinda skools round heah. One ret over dere. Mossuri University...ret over deah by the airpot."

"Mr. Jackson, he so smart. He got his master's degree. You kin ast him what school he went to." Mama was obsessed with Mr. Jackson!

"I'm not interested in where Mr. Jackson got his degree, Mama. When I want to get a master's degree, I'll find my own school."

"He saw you last week and he keep talkin 'bout you, saying you talk real good. He keep asting me fer your numba, so I give it to him. He say he gon call you."

To appease Daddy, I enrolled in a graduate class in psychology at the University of Missouri at St. Louis. Two evenings a week after work, I drove to the University, sat in the back of the class and listened to the professor drone on for an hour and a half about Freud and his friends.

I hated the class. I didn't know anybody. I didn't talk to anybody and nobody acknowledged my presence. I resented spending my evenings sitting there pretending to listen and pretending to take notes. After a month, I didn't want to pretend anymore, so I quit.

6

THE DRINK

In the dead of winter's ice and snow, Mr. Jackson called me. He invited me to meet him for a drink the next day after work. We met at a cafe bar on Clayton Road.

I knew from the start that he was a married man. Who calls a decent young lady out in ice and snow for a drink at 4:30 in the afternoon, unless he has to get home to his family in time for supper?

I tried to make the "drink" worth his while. I wrapped myself in a long black wool coat over my green wool skirt with a white blouse. I covered my blouse with a matching green vest and a white neck scarf. I covered my flipped hair with a black crown hat to match my knee-high black boots.

I sat across from him at the table. I removed my hat and gently ran my right hand through my flip. I unwrapped my neck scarf. I placed my hat and scarf on the empty chair to my right.

"It's warm in here," I said.

I slowly peeled off my coat and let it hang on the back of my chair. I loosened the top buttons on my blouse.

I saw Mr. Jackson's dancing eyes piercing through my outer

garments. I heard him trying to control the speed of his breathing. I saw his lascivious smile. He couldn't wait to compliment me.

"You know, you are nothing like your mother. You are so…so articulate. I love your mother and she is doing so well in class. And when I saw you, I said to Miss Cora, 'Is that your daughter?' and she said, 'Sho is.' You know how your mother talks. She is such a special lady, and…"

"Well, she thinks a lot of you too, and she so enjoys your class." I was trying to expose his ploy, so I asked, "Do you always have drinks this early in the day?"

"No, I have a class tonight. I had put off so long calling you, and I wanted to see you as soon as I could. What would you like to drink?" *Um, he's smooth!*

I wanted to keep his impression of me going, so I said, "I'll have a whisky sour."

He catches the eye of the waiter wearing all black. He orders a beer for himself and says in a take charge voice "a whisky sour for the lady." He sneaked a peek at his watch. *Another sign of a married man.*

"So tell me about yourself. How do you like working at Lach Elementary?"

"Oh, it's fine. I'm looking forward to moving up to the high school next year. That's where my comfort level is."

I don't want this 'drink' to be about me.

"What about you, Mr. Jackson? What do you do besides teach my mother?"

I was trying to add some levity. He grinned, then laughed out loud as the waiter sat my whisky sour in front of me. I picked up the plastic stirrer and swirled the contents a couple of times. The waiter placed a brown bottle of beer in front of Mr. Jackson. He picked up the cold beer and wrapped his white paper napkin around the bottom half of the beer bottle. *That's what's done for a small child to prevent frostbite. Another married man sign. And he has kids too!*

"Oh, come on now, none of that Mr. Jackson stuff. My name is Al."

He flipped his left hand toward me in a dismissive gesture. He took a small swig of beer from his iced bottle with the white paper napkin covering the bottom half.

"Ok, Al, what is your day job?" I asked with a smile.

I don't like whisky sours. But I must finish this drink.

I lifted the fluted glass, closed my eyes, and took a small sip. My lips contracted.

Al was toying with that white paper napkin.

"I do what I love," he said. "I love the English language."

I'm looking at him with squinting eyes, trying to feign interest. I got some of what he said.

"I'm a coordinator. I work with the English teachers in our district helping them implement new teaching guidelines and methods. It's fun and keeps me busy. And you know what I do in the evenings."

I close my eyes and sip. Al takes a swig out of his brown beer bottle with the white paper napkin covering the bottom half.

"But I want to know how you spend your time."

He looks at me with dreamy eyes.

"What have you been doing since you got to the big city? It can't be all work and no play."

"Well."

I take another straight faced, closed eyes sip before I answer.

"At this point, that's the way it is. I don't get out much...just trying to get my footing."

I splayed my hands in an open gesture then placed my left hand on the wooden table. I picked up my fluted whiskey sour glass with my right hand for another straight faced, closed eyed sip.

I heard Al's chair screech, and I felt his knee brush mine.

I opened my eyes to witness him slide both his hands onto my left hand. His hands were unexpectedly soft. He was leaning into me with eyes fixed on mine. He had moved his brown beer bottle with the white now soggy napkin to the side of the table. With my left hand covered with both his hands, he began to speak.

"You know I like you. I was so taken with you the moment I laid eyes on you. You are just beautiful. Your hair, your speech, your personality. I'm just blown away. I want to be the guy who gets you out of the house."

I smiled shyly. He continued.

"You can't be sitting home. There's a lot going on in St. Louis. We have a lot in common. We're both from Mississippi!"

He smiles big. I nod in recognition.

He turned my left hand over and used the middle finger of his left hand to trace my finger veins like he's a fortune teller. That tickled.

"So, what part of Mississippi are you from?"

I take back my hand and reach for my fluted glass and take a sip.

"I don't want to talk about the past. I want to talk about you."

He is leaning in making eye contact.

"So, tell me what makes you tick. We're both adults."

"Yes, that's true," I said.

I didn't want to waste my time or his.

"I don't see any future for me here in St. Louis. I somehow don't feel I belong here. I'm not getting what I want here in this city so far." I didn't want to insult him.

"Well, that's what I'm trying to say to you. Give me a chance." I am turned off by his insincerity. *We just met and you're asking me for a chance to do what?*

"I'm really interested in going back to school," I said. "Maybe going into some type of theater or maybe just being in a place where I can go to plays and see shows." He straightens his back. As he listens, the look on his face evolves from incredulity to smiling satisfaction. He spread his arms out before him.

"Everything you want is right here!" He knuckles the wooden table twice. "I can't think of it right now, but there are live shows here in St. Louis all summer. And there is that big theater downtown with big name people coming in all year!"

Yeah. So why am I sitting in a restaurant that I had to drive myself to? Why am I stretching my whiskey sour and you're stretching out a Budweiser? Why don't you just come out and say "I'm a married man with kids. I just want a little side job!"

I said, "I think there are so many more opportunities in a bigger city to just walk out my door and be in the middle of shows and music and people walking to shows." I'm smiling and my wide eyes are picturing my version of Broadway. My hands are circling in midair.

Al is staring at me. He shakes his head. He has a smug smile on his face.

"Has anybody ever said that you want too much? You can't have everything you want, you know. No place in this world is going to have exactly what you want, especially some big city."

He leaned forward looking at me with pleading eyes.

"St. Louis has a lot to offer. You just gotta find it."

"Yes, there probably are a lot of things here that I don't know about, but…" He interrupted me.

"What if you don't find what you want in your 'bigger city'?"

His eyes are glaring. He raises his shoulders and splays his hands.

"What are you going to do? What are you gonna do then? Huh?"

Why are you getting agitated? We're sipping a drink in a plebian restaurant and you're telling me to accept my fate because this is all there is!

I didn't answer him.

He insists.

"What are you gonna do? Move to another place, and then to another place? That's what wildflowers do! Is that what you want to do? You want to live your life like wildflowers?"

Wildflowers? *They used to grow all around our pig pen in Mt.*

Vernon. We used to stomp them down, but they kept coming up in a different place. We just couldn't snuff those things out!

Al is looking at me with wide eyes and flared arms. He is waiting for an answer.

"Well," I said, "I just think it's important to be open and ready for whatever comes my way." *I didn't answer his question.*

Still glaring at me, he picks at that soggy white napkin covering the bottom of his brown beer bottle. He drops little soggy pieces on the table. He took one last swig from his beer bottle and looked at his watch.

"Well, it's been great talking to you."

He gives me a no tooth grin as he pushes back from the table.

"And if you ever want to, I'm ready to show you the city."

"It was nice talking to you as well. I guess I'm just still trying to find my way!" I said, with a tight smile.

"Ok. Well, good luck with that."

He left to go teach Mama's English class.

Mama never asked me about my date with Mr. Jackson. She continued going to her classes and continued to "love" Mr. Jackson. He never called me again. I guess it was something I said.

7

FIRST TIMER

I understood better what the trip to London entailed. SIU was offering an extension course, Shakespeare 471 in London during the summer of 1968. The course was to run for eight weeks from mid-June through July and into early August. The University collected all the fees for tuition, airfare and provided housing. Students taking the course would be responsible for food and incidental travel expenses.

Jess's parents made all the arrangements for us to travel around Europe during August after the course ended. Our itinerary included touring Madrid, Rome, Florence, Venice, Grindelwald, and Paris, by train, boat and plane.

I was so excited. I paid my fees. I requested my birth certificate from Mississippi. January 4 was typed in as my birth date. *That's not my birth date. That's the wrong date!* I don't need a mix-up now. I interrupted Mama as she was doing Mr. Jackson's homework.

"Mama, why is this birth certificate saying my birthdate is January 4? My birthday is February 5."

Mama just looked at me. "If your birth serrtificate say Janrary foth, your Daddy musta wrote down de wrong date in the Bible."

The University told us to pack for fall and summer weather. An umbrella was a "must." My two large green suitcases my parents had given me for graduation were ready to go. My new movie camera and film were tucked away in my green carry-on. Frank dropped me off at the St. Louis airport a few miles from our house.

I spotted and joined a group of about fifteen White students excitedly waving SIU/London signs. I didn't know anybody. I signed in and collected my travel documents. Together, we proceeded through security and boarded the TWA 707 enroute to New York.

The thought of flying made me nervous...very nervous. I exchanged smiles with some of my travel companions trying not to show the tale-tale eyes of a "first timer.'

I smile and make small talk with my seat mates while fastening my seatbelt and listening to how to save myself in an emergency. When I hear the roaring of those big engines speeding that plane down the runway, I fix my eyes on the faces of the stewardesses. They are chatting and smiling like all that roaring and speeding mean nothing. I don't trust their smiling faces. Smiling is part of their training. They are trained to smile in the face of impending tragedy.

We are going up and up and up. I stop breathing. My hands gripping the arm rests expose every vein. *At least I'm sitting in an aisle seat. That's good, just in case I have to make a quick exit before we get too far off the ground!*

Daddy lied to me. I'm supposed to like flying. I'm supposed to hope for a long flight and regret a quick landing. *I want to get off this thing now!*

One of my seat mates is reading a book. The other is leaning forward to see better out of that little window. I close my eyes, tighten every muscle in my body and pretend to sleep. If worse comes to worse, at least I won't see it.

The plane finally lands in New York. We locate the noisy SIU group assembled in a corner of the airport. They are waving signs, smiling, and talking excitedly among themselves. Everybody is White, except Jess and Sylvia. The two of them are all smiles as we approach each other with enthusiastic hugs. I don't know Sylvia, but she seems friendly and excited to be included. She is taller than Jess and me and dark skinned like me with long hair like me. She seems shy and reticent like she is from a strict household like mine.

The two-hour flight from St. Louis to New York readied me somewhat for the flight to London. I settle in for the ride but keep an eye on the faces of those stewardesses.

8

BRUNO'S GAME

I don't know how we made it to our hotel on Upper Berkeley Street without crashing. There were so many cars in the streets, and everybody was driving in circles and on the wrong side of the street!

The hotel was a three-story walk-up with beds for two. The three of us wanted to room together, so Jess and I shared until an additional bed was delivered.

Our classes started the day after we arrived. We had lectures four mornings a week at the University of London and in the afternoons, we visited a Shakespearean site or a play. Weekends were open for us to explore the city on our own. Exploring to us meant shopping at Marks and Spencer, eating at Indian restaurants, and stopping in a tea shop in the late afternoon to have a cup of tea with milk and sugar.

Halfway through the course, we relocated for three days to Stratford-upon-Avon, the birthplace of Shakespeare. There, we were immersed in everything Shakespeare. We went to performances indoors and outdoors, to museums and monuments. We went to his house, church, and burial grounds. We got to know Shakespeare.

But for me, this trip is about freedom! Here in London for the first time in my life, I'm not living under anybody's curfew or anybody's watchful eyes. Nobody in America is watching me here in London!

The students, male and female, who eventually become our friends are enrolled in the summer session at the University of London. They are mostly from the continent of Africa. They say they are from North Africa, places like Morocco, Egypt, Sudan, and Libya. Some are married and some are single. They all seem to live on campus in Lillian Pension Hall. One White girl named Lynn from Pasadena, California, is among our group of friends.

Just being around the North Africans was a unique experience for me. The females with their heads covered made the food. We all spent many evenings sitting on the floor eating sauces, meat, and salads from large trays the women had prepared.

The guys were always available to chauffeur us around London in their cars or on the underground. We were tourists to them who had to see Buckingham Palace, the Tower of London, Big Ben, and Trafalgar Square. One weekend the single guys, Baha, Ali, and Essa drove the three of us to Scotland. We stayed in the home of their friend, a Black professor of biochemistry who was teaching at a university in nearby Stratford. We visited the sites in Perth and looked out over the city from Edinburgh Castle.

Every day, there was traffic between our Upper Barkley apartment and Lillian Pension Hall. With a limited amount of time before we moved on to the next country, I was determined to take advantage of my freedom. I was open to overtures from interested suitors.

Jess pushed any and all suitors away with, "I have a boyfriend back in Chicago waiting for me."

Sylvia flirted, but she had made her position clear to Jess and me. "I'm saving myself for my wedding night."

Being in London was my best opportunity for the right guy to score a "homerun."

My main player is a tall, thin, brown-skinned, curly haired guy named Bruno. He spent the last five years studying in Germany. That's where he got his name Bruno.

He is in London for the summer visiting his younger brother, Amal who is studying political science at the university. Being in London is Bruno's 'last gasp' before he has to return home to run the family business. His father has summoned him.

"Home" is a place Bruno labels "hot, dusty" and "not Germany." The prospect of returning to that place after living in Germany for five years causes him to have bouts of melancholy. Sometimes he won't talk. Other times he refuses to join the group dinners. He mopes around and tears up at any mention of going "home." He only ceases wallowing in his fate when I am around! My presence brings a smile to his face. He becomes talkative and socially engaged.

Seeing this change in Bruno's mood and behavior, Amal and his White girlfriend, Lynn, start engineering 'meetings' between me and Bruno. We find ourselves next to each other at our group dinners, on car trips and even walking around town. They encouraged Bruno to "take Marge out and have some fun."

The five weeks that Bruno and I were together in London were intoxicating for me. I was short of breath. I couldn't eat. Bruno was on my mind constantly. I felt the same way with Roland at the church conference when I was in tenth grade. I lost my chance at a boyfriend back then because Daddy said "No." Daddy is not in charge now.

Bruno is not shy. I knew right away that he has spent a lot of time around baseball fields. With me, he spent a lot of time going between first base and second base and one time he almost stole third but turned back. I understood. It takes time and nerve to "make a steal!"

The end of July means our Shakespearean study is coming to

an end. It is time for us to leave England for other parts of Europe. I spend the final days of class pecking away on a borrowed typewriter trying to crank out a paper analyzing "King Richard III and his Horse." *I wish I had taken the course for Pass/Fail, but to appease Daddy, I went for a grade.* I never missed a chance to say to him, "I'm in graduate school getting my master's degree."

Jess, Sylvia, and I want to show our appreciation to our friends for their generosity and their friendship. So the evening before we are to leave London, we organize a good-bye party. The party is to be held in the party room at Lillian Pension Hall.

We overspend on platters of sausage rolls, egg sandwiches, cheese and pineapple sticks, grapes, and chips. Everybody brings their own drinks. We are swaying to the music of The Temptations "I Wish It Would Rain," The Beatles "Hey Jude," Tom Jones "Delilah," and James Brown's "I'm Black and I'm Proud."

I am wearing my newly bought long sleeved green crepe dress with the v-neckline and a bow that exposes a hint of cleavage. The bow is loosely tied under my neck to block the full view. The flared skirt accentuates my legs. On my feet are my newly bought multicolored sandals that have a touch of green to compliment my dress. No pantyhose for me tonight!

Last week Bruno and I were in the playoffs. Tonight is the final. Tonight, Bruno has to hit a homeroom!

I am ready. My hair is straight and flipped and pulled to the right side of my face to cover a couple of outbreaks. Bruno is wearing his usual brown slacks, checkered brown jacket, white shirt, and brown sandals.

Everybody seems to be in on the game. Bruno has a light in his eyes. His friends are encouraging him to get me away from the party.

"Hey, you dirty old man. Marge looks so pretty tonight. Where you taking her?"

"I bet you're not gonna get any sleep tonight!"

"It's getting late, but that's not gon matter to you."

Bruno just grins.

Anticipation is in the air.

We are practically pushed out of the door. Bruno has an old beat up dark blue car with a smashed in door on the driver's side. It has a big couch seat in the front.Bruno said it is a German car.

I climb onto that big bench seat and squeeze in tight next to him. During our drive I am getting nervous and anxious about what is going to happen. I can't stop talking.

"And I spent so much money shopping that I had to have my parents send me some more. I just love English tea with milk, don't you? I only bought one souvenir, a red double decker bus for my brother, Anthony. I shouldn't spend so much. They have really good stuff here, though."

Bruno's response to all my ramblings is to smile and pepper his silence with an occasional "oh" or "ah."

He parks the car somewhere near the Thames River in a spot that reminded me of "Lover's Lane" back in the park of my childhood in Mt. Vernon. We both know that tonight is the night for him to make the steal. Tonight is the night for me to say "Yes!"

Bruno wastes no time. He is like a well-seasoned chef. He is good with his hands. They are moving to the right spots. First base is for amateurs. Bruno expertly unties the bow under my chin and exposes second base. As he feasts there, he begins to murmur, "oh," "ah," "oh."

I am encouraged, I am relaxed. I am his for the taking. His body is shaking. I'm thinking, *"This man is about to cause an earthquake or is he about to have a heart attack!"*

His murmurings become whimperings...my neck…is that water? *Is there flooding with earthquakes?*

My chest is wet. His hands stop seeking. His arms release me. I open my eyes. Tears are glistening on his cheeks, around his nose and his mouth.

"Bruno," I query, trying to steady my breathing and my heartbeat.

"What's the matter? Did something happen? You feeling Ok?"

I search my clutch purse and find a Kleenex. Bruno is face down on the steering wheel, his arms covering his head. His body is trembling. I fix my hair and straighten my dress just in case I have to seek medical help. At the same time I am mopping up some of his dribbling.

"Bruno, talk to me. What's the matter?" The slobbering and whimpering continue.

"Do you want me to go get help? Is this because I'm leaving tomorrow? It's all right. I'll be coming back. It's Ok. We can keep in touch. I'm gonna miss you, too."

I get on my knees. I put my left arm around his back as he is face down over the steering wheel.

He is trying to speak. The tears and the slobbering make it hard to understand his mumblings. I pry his head up long enough to hear, "I just can't..."

"It's Ok, Bruno. We don't have to…it happens sometimes." I rub his back and run my fingers through his wavy hair, speaking soothing words like, "No need to cry," and "Don't worry about it."

Bruno continues his utterings. He turns his head to the side towards me. "I can't go…I won't...I…I…won't go back to that damn hot, dusty country! I won't go back!"

He is screaming. His words are clear now.

"What? Bruno, are you talking about your country now! Is that what you're crying about?"

I get no answer, just a renewed surge of tears and mumblings.

This night is about me, about us! This night is not about your hot, dusty country!

I retrieve my hand from his back. I watch his tears run down his face. I don't care that slobber is dripping onto his brown slacks. I move away from him to the passenger side of the bench seat. I take a deep breath.

Game over!

The next morning, we left for Madrid.

9

MY BROODING BED

Our young tour guides ushered us around Madrid on trains and buses. We went from flamenco dance performances to rein-led horseback riding to prancing matadors waving red flags in the faces of wounded bulls.

When we were out touring on our own, we were always followed around by young Spanish men, smiling and pointing toward buildings and statues. After "Hola" and "¿Cómo estás?" we decided, "Ok, let's hangout with this trio."

Jess and Sylvia spoke a few words of Spanish from their high school days, so they were our interpreters. Through smiling teeth and quickly spoken English, Jess reminded us of our standing rule, "Never go anywhere with anyone alone."

Jess was good at navigating. She pulled out her map and one of the trio pointed to where we were, and the monument we were viewing.

We got comfortable with the smiles, giggles and gesturing of the trio. One of them pointed to the Philip IV monument as our next destination.

"We go," he said. We boarded a bus.

I had my movie camera case slung over my left shoulder and my green purse hanging over my right shoulder. I was sitting next to a trio, exchanging smiles and nods.

When we got to the monument, we exited the bus and walked to the statue of Phillip IV sitting on the back of a rearing horse.

"Jess," I said. "You and Sylvia go walk around and stand in front. I want to get you on film."

I reached to my left hip to retrieve my movie camera. My eyes followed my reach. *My camera must be on my right hip.* My eyes and my hands moved to my right hip.

I screamed. The eyes of bystanders, tourists and the trio pan to me.

"My camera! Where's my camera? My camera is missing! I just had it. Who took my camera? Somebody took my camera!"

I am screaming and gesticulating to the trio. The three of them are looking at me with confused eyes.

"No comprende!" They are raising their shoulders and their arms.

Jess and Sylvia run to me and follow me around, peppering me with questions.

"Did you take the case off on the bus?"

"Did you drop it?"

"Did your strap break?"

"No...no...no." I am running around in circles holding my head and screaming, trying to remember.

"I know I had it on the bus, and it was on my...Where is my camera?" I am screaming at the trio. My hands are directing them to go search for my camera.

The trio take turns throwing up their hands and shrugging their shoulders while speaking Spanish too fast for Jess or Sylvia to understand. Their words "No see...lost...no see!" are clear.

I dump the contents of my green purse onto the grassy plaza. I pick through hard candy wrappers, tourist brochures and movie cartridges. I yelled for Jess, Sylvia the trio to empty their bags onto the concrete pavement. Each fumble through bubble gum wrappers, bottles of lotion, extra clothing, and tourist pamphlets. No movie camera is revealed.

I am weak-kneed. I am distraught and in tears. I wander among tourists and sightseers looking at faces for signs of guilt. We push aside shrubbery and meander around the base of the statue of Phillip IV sitting on the back of a rearing horse. I am wandering around, blurry-eyed in a zombie-like state.

"Autobus!" I announce to the trio. I pantomime driving a bus. I point to my eyes with my pointer finger while screaming at them.

"Where is that bus? Find that autobus! I need to look in the bus. Which way did it go?"

"Policia!" One of the trio screams back at me. "Policia!"

We board another bus and arrive at a building that is the police station. The trio rattles off quick words to two men in uniform. Between gesticulations and scribblings on notebook paper and a comforting hand on my shoulder, my loss is recorded. We take a bus back to the hotel. That's when I take to my bed.

What else can I do? I can't face my loss. Recordings of my time in London were for naught, lost. Recording memories to come? Not possible! Money I spent on a top of the line movie camera? Wasted!

For the next two days, I rose from my bed only for breakfast. I can't pass up the crusty rolls, orange marmalade, butter, and tea that are brought to our door. I have to claim my two rolls before they are claimed by Jess or Sylvia. I can't suffer another loss.

I drag myself to the table, take my two rolls and tear each in half. I spread butter on each half and spoon a small glob of marmalade on top of the butter. I sit back taking small bites of crusty bread, butter, and marmalade with intermittent sips of tea with milk and sugar. I allow myself a quiet chewing moment of ecstasy. Then I crawl back into my bed.

Before I "lost" my camera, we had plans to have dinner with Sylvia's cousin. He is a serviceman stationed at the U.S. Air Force base in Madrid. I force myself to rise from my bed to honor that outing.

We took a taxi to his apartment in downtown Madrid. Her cousin along with two other young men met us at the door. The three of them looked like they were in heat. Their smiles were too big, their chest hairs were exposed and they were wearing long shirts to cover their "desires."

At the dinner table, I was seated next to Sylvia's cousin, Jeremy, in his red and blue striped shirt, his horn-rimmed glasses and his short army haircut. He gave me a warm side mouth grin as he caressed my left hand. I was still harboring loss, as I retrieved my hand. My grin back to him was labored. I was wearing my red and white checkered dress with a flared skirt. I needed the whimsical colors to lift my spirit.

Jess, with her hair up and supported by a white headband, was seated next to Will with the army blue shirt and no glasses. She was talking about her boyfriend and saying, "He didn't want to come along, but maybe next year." She was gently removing Will's hand from her arm.

Sylvia was at the head of the table wearing her high neck collared blue dress. She was staring at Ben across a spread of green beans, fried chicken, white bread and a can of Hi-C. He was seated at the other end of the table. He was licking his lips like he couldn't wait to get his hands on the zipper of her high collared dress.

After dinner, the music came on loud and the lights went down low. Jeremy dragged me onto the dance floor. He held me close. He whispered in my ear, "It has been so long since I held a sista in my arms. This feels so good. How long you gon be in Madrid?"

I nudged his head out of my neck so I could speak.

"Not long. We're leaving for Italy tomorrow. It was so nice of you guys to have us over."

I was pulling away, looking for Sylvia.

"Wait a minute." Jeremy was pleading and trying to give me a backrub.

"Come on now," he said. "The evening is just getting started. He was hanging on to my arm. I was moving and speaking toward that high white collar, which is all I could see in that dark room.

Sylvia and Ben were standing close with Hi-Cs in hand. Ben was fingering that white collar with the hand not holding his Hi-C. Sylvia was giggling while attempting to remove his fingers from her collar. When I reached her, she was trying to distract him.

"You see, my parents wanted me to go to school in Chicago, but..."

"Sylvia," I said. "We have to get up really early. Shouldn't we be leaving?"

We grabbed our purses, thanked the guys for being great hosts, and left the three of them, standing in the doorway still in heat, staring at our backs.

10
BLACK ANGELS, FRESH AIR, BAREFOOTING

In Italy, we visited three cities. In Florence, we visited the Da Vinci Museum, Michelangelo's David, Giotto's Bell Tower and climbed the Leaning Tower of Pisa. In Venice, we hung out in St. Mark's Square, took a gondola boat ride on the Grand Canal, and crossed the Bridge of Sighs.

In Rome, when we had free time, we allowed young men to be our guides and companions. I had no movie camera to lose.

Language was no barrier. We were welcomed as "Black Angels," which turned out to be the only English words our friends had picked up from the movies. We smiled back unoffended. We were Black and we accepted "Angels" as a compliment.

Pointing, gesturing, and smiling, we re-visited Vatican City, the Pantheon, the Coliseum and the Trevi Fountain.

We were three young Black women in Italy on a budget. We took busses and ferries to move between cities. We encountered rich White men in white shoes and suntanned White women in wide-brimmed hats boarding small planes. One time, when a storm was brewing while we were in Florence, a rich American couple solicited us to join them on a charted plane back to Venice.

The small plane was there, waiting for boarding. The couple was all smiles when we said "Yes, thank you."

"Wonderful," said the blonde lady in her black straw Gucci sun hat. "It will be so much cheaper with five people instead of two."

Wait...are we expected to pay for this plane ride? I thought we were getting a free ride! I see the same question and thought on the faces of Jess and Sylvia.

For the sake of being polite, Jeff asked, "What is the cost...for the plane…I mean, how much do we each have to pay?"

The blonde lady in her black straw Gucci sun hat said with a dismissive smile, "Oh, it'll be no more than a hundred dollars or so. We're just lucky to beat this storm."

Sylvia and I both nudged Jess. She knew what to say.

"You know, we have changed our mind about taking the plane...we already have train tickets...but thank you anyway."

We didn't stick around to hear the rich American couple voice their haughty disgust at our penury status.

We preferred traveling on the ground.

Grindelwald, Switzerland was a different experience. We met no young tour guides as our companions. We were on our own. We watched and waved to skiers in chair lifts, walked and breathed in the cool mountain air and enjoyed the scenery. It was a breath of fresh air.

Paris was my favorite city. I could speak the language. We met people, ordered food, and enjoyed croissants daily. I felt comfortable there; I felt comfortable barefooting in the streets.

We met Guy and Dennis, two Black Frenchmen who took us to sites around Paris. They wined and dined us. With them, we visited the Palace of Versailles, the Eiffel Tower, the Bastille Monument, the Notre Dame Cathedral, and the Louvre. They took pictures with us with Sylvia's and Jess's cameras. We took pictures of them and us with Sylvia's and Jess's cameras. I had no camera to take pictures of anyone.

On August 15, we flew back to New York City. I knew I was

back in the United States. I was stopped at immigration and my green carry on was searched. They found two wrapped crusty rolls. I had taken them from the dinner tray on the plane. That discovery led to the agents rummaging through my two large green suitcases in search of more contraband. They found nothing.

The three of us finally sat together on a bench at Kennedy Airport relishing our European experiences.

"It was so freeing," Sylvia said as she was waving her arms and looking around at the people traffic racing past us. "We ran the streets with Black boys and White boys and nobody raised an eyebrow!"

"Yeah," I said. "I knew I was not in the United States since we weren't met with wide-eyed stares. I kept waiting for somebody to come up and tell me how happy they were to see me and thank me for showing up to visit a museum! It felt so good that nothing like that happened anywhere we went."

"Well," Jess said, checking her watch. "Now that we're back, it's going to be hard for me to just accept things the way I used to. I feel smarter. I see things differently now. We'll have to see. But we're not in Europe anymore."

"Yep," I said. "I have a lot of things to think about. I now see possibilities. There's a whole lot of world out there, and I want to experience more of it. Until then..."

With goodbye hugs all around, we vowed to keep in touch.

11
TIA

I met Tia during the new teacher orientation at Beaumont High School. We were both young, new, and hired to teach in the history department. She is White.

The last White friends I had was when I was in junior college back in Mt. Vernon. That was strange given all the White folks at SIU and all the White folks living on our street in University City.

Tia and I were destined to become friends. We had a lot in common. I lived in the suburb of University City, and she lived in the suburb of Creve Coeur. I lived at home with my parents; she lived at home with her parents. I had an attractive body, nice legs, and nice hair, and so did she, for a White woman. More than anything else, we both had skin problems. I had acne, and she had psoriasis. Everyone could see my skin problem. Hers was hidden under long sleeves and long hair. It was our fight to control our skin condition that cemented our friendship.

We did have one difference and it had to do with driving. Tia was audacious behind the wheel; I was cautious behind the wheel. I had my brother Frank do a "show me" drive before I drove myself to the orientation at Beaumont. I watched attentively every stop sign, turn and lane change. Once again, my history degree helped me remember everything I was shown, such as the streets, building markers, lane changes and parking places.

Daddy asked me, "Why you need somebody to show you where dat school is. You kin go all de way ov'r to Angland and all dem places an you can't drive to a skool a mile from heah. It don't make no sense!"

Tia could drive anywhere and fast. When we had a late meeting or a night event, she picked me up in her little gray Chevy. She took Interstate 70! She merged into traffic going sixty miles an hour while talking about "going out" and "new medicine" she's going to try. I never responded to anything she said when she was driving. I wanted her to keep her eyes on the road. I just sat there holding onto my seat praying that we would reach our destination alive.

My relationship with Tia was different from those of my White girlfriends back in Mt. Vernon. Our relationship was reciprocal. Tia came to my house and I went to hers. When we went to parties or to evening events at school, Tia was always the driver. She would come to my house and wait for me to finish dressing. We would then go to her house, and I would wait for her to get dressed. She let me know if I needed to add more makeup to cover my acne, and I let her know if she needed more cream to cover her psoriasis. We looked out for each other.

12
BLOWING SMOKE

After Jess, Sylvia and I arrived back in the United States, we each got on with our lives. I lost contact with Jess, but Sylvia and I kept in touch. She wrote me letters and sometimes called me "just to see what you're doing." I always said, "I'm not doing anything. Just going to work and teaching history."

One time she said, "I want to come visit you. We can just talk and go out and stuff."

I didn't quite understand why a Chicago girl would want to come to a town like University City. She knew I was just working. But, if she was coming to visit me, I felt obliged to try to show her a good time.

Before she arrived, I contacted a friend in St. Louis, and asked her if she knew any place that would be safe for single women to go, and maybe meet eligible men. She recommended a bar in the suburbs called Randy's. I asked Tia to come along and do the driving.

I have never been on a "manhunt" before, and I know Sylvia hadn't either. I decided to wear my green London dress with the fitted waist and A-line flare. That always accentuated my legs. I loosely tied the neck bow. I heard that it was always cold in bars. My long sleeves would take care of that.

I expected my London dress to also be an enticing conversation piece. When a guy's pickup line was, *"Hey, Beautiful, that green matches your eyes,"* I would follow with, *"Thank you. I can see you have a good eye."* I would finger the neck bow while explaining, *"I picked this little thing up in London a few weeks ago."* He would be impressed. He would ease onto the bar stool next to me and lean in to hear more.

While we were dressing to go to Randy's, I asked Sylvia, "Do you think I need to put on more rouge?"

I was standing in front of the mirror dabbing my cheeks with a makeup sponge.

"You shouldn't put on more," she said, sounding like a scolding Sunday school teacher. "You don't want to look like a lady who walks the streets." Sylvia didn't believe in wearing any makeup, except lipstick.

I said, "I think I'll part my hair to one side to show off my eyes." I was fiddling with my flip.

"And I'm going to wear my London flats. If my dress doesn't get any manly attention, my shoes surely will!"

I was laughing and twirling around in front of the mirror. I was watching Sylvia. She was putting on that dark blue pleated dress with the big white collar. I stopped twirling and asked, "Don't you want to wear something a little more sexy? Why don't you wear your pink blouse and black skirt? It's got a split, a nice little tease."

"Oh, I don't think so, it's too revealing!" Sylvia was covering her chest with her hands.

"It is not," I said. "We want to attract a man or two, right?"

Sylvia changed into the black skirt and the pink long-sleeved blouse. She buttoned the blouse up to her neck. I assisted by unbuttoning the top two buttons.

Her hair was flipped to her shoulders like mine, but her face was flawless, unlike mine. She finished her look with pink lipstick.

We waited for Tia to pick us up.

Tia lived in a townhouse. Her parents were in the small living room watching television when we arrived. We exchanged "hellos" and smiles before we headed off to Tia's bedroom.

She settled on black flats, a dark blue skirt, and a white blouse. I checked to make sure she had used enough cream to cover any visible psoriasis. She checked my face to make sure I had used enough makeup to cover my blemishes. Proper dressing and coverage were very important aspects of this manhunting expedition.

We passed through the small living room on our way out, exchanging good-byes with Tia's parents who were still sitting and watching television. They kept their eyes on the television as we passed. I wonder what they thought about Tia going out with two Black women.

Tia and I had agreed to make a stop at 7-Eleven to pick up a pack of Kool cigarettes. They could come in handy if we needed an additional dab of sophistication to put one of us over the top. She put them in her purse and away from Sylvia's prudish eyes.

We drove around and around at Randy's, looking for parking. "That's a good sign," Tia said. "This place must be hopping."

We entered the bar to low lights, loud music, and lively chatter. Three young White men were standing near the long bar facing the entrance. They sipped from a glass in one hand and scissored a cigarette in the other. Their eyes glanced over Tia as the three of us entered. I gave Tia a little nudge.

I put on my 'city girl' face and glided over to an empty bar stool. Tia and Sylvia appeared next to me.

"Tia," I said loud enough for the guys sipping from glasses and scissoring cigarettes to hear me. "Do you want a drink?"

That was the cue for one of the young men to saunter over, blow smoke in Tia's face and put a drink in her hand.

No one sauntered over. No one was looking our way. We were not in Europe anymore.

I whispered just among the three of us.

"I wonder if they have Singapore Slings here. Tia, would you mind ordering our drinks? Can you ask if they have Singapore Slings. How about you Sylvia?"

"How about me, what?" Sylvia was wrapping herself tight in her black sweater.

"What do you want to drink?"

"Oh, I don't drink…I'll just have a 7 Up."

Tia said, "Usually when you come to a bar you drink something with alcohol in it."

"I didn't know we were coming to a bar." Sylvia was standing looking defiant with her arms folded across her chest.

I had never been to a bar like this before either, but at least I was willing to pretend.

I said, "If they don't know what that is, just get me a white wine and tell the guy to put soda water in it."

"That's called a Spritzer," Tia said. "I'm gonna have a whiskey sour. Did you decide yet, Sylvia?"

I was sipping, smiling, and looking around. There were not enough seats at the bar for the three of us, so I let Sylvia hold my seat while I worked my way through the crowd. I was looking for Black guys. I saw two in different corners smiling in the faces of White girls. Neither looked my way.

I walked back to the bar and joined the others. The two of them were now sitting and standing in the same spot looking around and sipping their drinks. Tia was talking too loudly, waving her free hand too much and smiling too big. She always does that when she has a drink in her hand.

I said, "Why don't we spread out and mingle? Tia, can I have a cigarette, please?"

Sylvia was facing me, sipping her glass of 7 Up. Her pink blouse was buttoned up to her neck.

"What are you gonna do with a cigarette?" she asked.

"Smoke it, of course," I said.

"I didn't know you were a smoker!"

Sylvia's eyes were wide and her mouth hung open. I watched as her surprised eyes morphed into squinting disapproval. She crossed her arms again, staring me down.

"I'm not a smoker, Sylvia." I said. "I just hold it in my mouth and blow out the smoke. Where're the matches?"

"Nobody uses matches anymore. You need a lighter," Tia said as she left for the bathroom.

"Where am I going to get a lighter?" I said out loud to myself.

Sylvia is looking around like she wants to be somewhere other than standing with a smoker!

"You wouldn't need a lighter if you got rid of that cigarette."

Sylvia sounded just like Mrs. Johnson, my dorm mother from college. Both were always making snide remarks about any slight deviation from a norm.

"If you insist on smoking, why don't you ask for a light from just any guy in here with a cigarette hanging out of his mouth."

I watched Tia coming toward us pulling down on her skirt and realigning her hair to cover exposed redness near her left ear.

I asked the bartender for a light. I wasn't sure if I should suck on the cigarette or blow on it during lighting. I did a little bit of both, until I got a light. I perched myself on the bar stool, crossed my legs, faced away from the bar. I scissored the lighted cigarette.

I blew on the cigarette and produced an impressive plume of smoke. I was bound to get some manly attention from this display. Sylvia coughed a few times, fanned at the smoke a few times, and walked across the room. I was alone listening to chatter, laughs and slurps. I held my Spritzer in one hand and a lighted cigarette in the other. I waited for at least one gentleman to approach.

The three of us left for home shortly before midnight. Sylvia was still coughing and fanning.

~

I don't quite understand Sylvia. She is a Chicago girl, but she doesn't act like one. Those Chicago girls at SIU, they knew a lot. They knew about different kinds of coffee, soda pops and what pills to take to stay awake to study. They knew how to sneak into the dorm after hours and they knew all the latest dance moves. They knew how to get a boyfriend when they wanted one, and they knew how to let a guy know when they were not interested. They walked through situations with their heads held high and were not concerned about what other people said. I learned from those Chicago girls. Sylvia was a Chicago girl, but she had a lot to learn.

But we were alike in some ways. When we were in Europe away from parental eyes, we let our guard down, me more than Sylvia. I was open to some "base running," but she had to have a wedding ring on her finger first.

Before she left to go back to Chicago, we both agreed that we liked the freedom we felt in Europe. We wanted that feeling again. Researching to find another venture abroad became Sylvia's calling.

13

PDA AND ABOVE AVERAGE

"Hey Margaret, I found one! I found one! It's in Africa!"

Sylvia was screaming into the phone.

I am having a very stressful week at work. I had no time to talk about Africa.

"Sylvia, I can't talk to you now. I'll get back to you next week. But Africa sounds good."

I have hall duty. I am scanning dimly lit corners and stairwells near my classroom. I am on the lookout for students engaging in PDA: public displays of affection. My job is to remove the hands of boys from the butts of girls and to chastise the girls who seem to enjoy the touch. My ears are poised to weed out boy-talk about girls' body parts.

"Look at that fat ass."

"Hey baby, we gon git it on tonight."

I am here to break up entanglements and to send girls off to class.

"Jerry, I know you're not doing anything, so take your arm

from around her waist. Sandra, please go, you're gonna be late. Just go to class. No, do that after school...not here."

I usher the last students off to class.

I hate hall duty.

"Miss Edwards." I turn around when I hear my name. I look down the hallway. Nobody is there, except Mrs. Combs. She is coming toward me.

Tia and I have a running commentary about Mrs. Combs. She is a special education teacher. To us, she is strange. Black is her color. She always wears a black skirt, a black blouse, and a black vest. It's hard to tell what kind of body she is hiding under all that blackness, but I can tell she is not fat. Her face is framed with cropped black hair and her feet are fitted with black socks and black loafers.

Whenever I spot her coming toward me in the hallway, she never has a smile on her face. She would say, "Good morning," or "Good afternoon" and her eyes would travel from my eyes to somewhere on my body below my neck. I would always look away.

Today, she called my name. She is wearing that same stoic face and her usual black attire. Why is she calling my name? Her eyes are meeting mine.

"Oh, hello?" I say, cautiously. I can't move my feet. I wait for her to reach me. I push back my hair as I wait. Her eye contact is piercing. I want to look away. This time I make my eyes confront hers.

She moves in close to me. *Move, feet!* They don't. She puts her right hand on my left arm just above my elbow. She gently strokes my arm. *What is she going to do to me?*

My muscles stiffen. Her hand is dry.

"I have something I've wanted to say to you for a long time," she said. Her voice is monotone, lacking in emotion.

I stopped breathing.

"What is it?" I ask.

I look past her. We are standing in an empty, quiet, dim hall, looking into each other's eyes. *What if she...*

"You have a beautiful walk. Don't you *ever* give up that walk."

She removes her hand from my upper left arm, lowers her head into a slight bow, walks around me and goes on her way.

I am left standing there staring down that long, quiet, empty hallway. I couldn't turn to look after her. I just stood there with my mouth open. I grinned. She spoke to me! She touched me! Wait 'til I tell Tia!

For the remainder of the day, I focused on 'keeping my walk'.

Did she engage in PDA?

The twelfth-grade girls insisted on talking and passing notes and wanting to get out of my class to 'go see the counselor.' The assistant principal was doing an unannounced visit this week to see why so many of my students needed a counselor.

I tried for days to get those girls to take notes and understand the importance of the Gettysburg address.

"Betty, turn around please. Everything we talk about today and the rest of the week is going to be on the test. So, you may want to write down the questions and the answers. Who here is going to college?"

"Ok, most of you. That's great. Then you better get a good grade on my test. So listen and take notes. Ok. Who wrote the Gettysburg address?"

I'm looking around the room at the twenty or so students to see who I should call on.

"Betty, who wrote the Gettysburg address?"

"The President?"

"That's correct, Betty," I said. "It was a President."

I knew it was important to give her some positive feedback for the partially correct answer.

"Now which President was that?"

There was silence.

"Who would like to help Betty out?"

Hands are waving all over the room. I have total student engagement. I capitalized on that enthusiasm. I thought of Mr. Roland, my fourth-grade teacher at Washington School. I remember him looking for the student who he was sure had the right answer. I'm walking around the room looking to engage every student, especially the ones not raising a hand.

Johnny does not have his hand raised. I walk to his desk and in a conversational, personalized manner I ask, "Johnny, which President wrote the Gettysburg Address?"

He looks at me with anxious eyes, wanting to please me with the correct answer.

"Jefferson?"

I clasp my hands together and smile at him. I place a hand on his shoulder.

"That was real close, Johnny! Let's see if someone can help you out. Johnny, who would you like to call on to help you out?"

Johnny is all smiles now. He gets to play teacher. He gets to call on someone. He is empowered. He gets to call on anyone he chooses to name the President who wrote the Gettysburg address!

Everyone is attentive, anxious, hopeful, and ready for the spotlight. Who will he choose?

Johnny is toying with the class. He is smiling. He is enjoying seeing his classmates squirm under his power.

I'm smiling. I'm enjoying my clever engagement methodology. A little anxiety is good. *Keep them talking to each other. Keep them waiting and wondering, Johnny. They are thinking about history. I'm on a roll.*

When the assistant principal enters my classroom and sits in the back of the room with her stern face, her clipboard and her busy pen, my students know the drill. They refrain from having side conversations, passing notes, and needing to see the counselor. She rated my teaching "above average."

I saw Tia later in the hallway. She was wiping tears from her eyes with her fingers and heading toward the bathroom.

"What's the matter?" I asked, touching her shoulder, and following her into the bathroom.

"She gave me just 'average' on my evaluation. I…I" sniffle, sniffle "work so hard," sniffle.

"I deserved better than that. She knows I" sniffle, nose blowing, eye wiping, "work hard. It's just not fair!"

Tia is my friend. I listen to her. I want to support her.

I said, "Oh, maybe she was having a bad day. Sometimes principals see a little something like one of your kids not paying attention and you get marked down for that. It probably had nothing to do with your teaching."

Deep down though, I didn't feel that bad about Tia's 'average' rating. It felt good that I was 'above average.' Girls like Tia had always prevailed over Black girls like me.

For once, a Black person did for me what White people had been doing for White girls since elementary school. I was a good teacher. I engaged my students in their own learning.

I wonder if Tia was able to do that.

14
GOING HOME!

I called Sylvia back a week later to get more information about Africa.

"I told you, I found a summer program in Africa. My friend told me about it. It's like our Shakespeare class, we go to the university and..."

I interrupted her. I had to bring my knowledge of geography into this conversation.

"Wait a minute, Sylvia. Where in Africa is this? North, South, East, West? Which country is this program in?"

She was raising her voice now.

"What difference does it make which country it is? It's in Africa and I want to go! Do you want to go or not?"

"Yeah, I want to go. I just need more information about where I will be going, and how much it's gonna cost."

"Ok, I'll send you the information, but we need to register now."

The information I received was from The American Institute for African Studies. The brochure said participants were going to be "introduced to the history and culture of African people through our experiences in Ghana." We were to gather at the Union Theological Seminary in New York City for our orientation and final instructions before our flight.

I was ready to go. I didn't hesitate.

I told Mama, "I'm going to Africa!"

Mama said, "Afica! What in the world you goin ta Afica fer!"

In June of 1969, one year after my trip to Europe, I was on a plane to New York. This time I was more relaxed. I looked out the window instead of trying to read signs of panic on the faces of stewardesses. I met Sylvia in La Guardia airport. Sylvia told the taxi driver to take us to the Union Theological Seminary.

The driver said, "So you going to Columbia University."

"No," Sylvia said, showing the driver the paper with the directions. "It says Union Theological…"

"Miss, I been drivin a taxi in New Yok City fer thirty yeahs. I know where Union Theological is. It's Columbia University."

We sat quietly then, hoping the driver was not directionally challenged.

We entered a large lobby and were directed to place our luggage in a holding room.

A tall Black woman in African dress handed us a packet of materials and suggested we 'mingle' while awaiting introductory words from the trip leader.

I didn't know who to mingle with. I just looked around to see what kind of people I was going to be spending a whole summer with in Ghana. There were Black men and White men and Black women and White women. Some looked like undergrads and some looked like graduate students. Some were dressed in African garb. Others were running around chatting and directing people and acting like educators.

One woman passed our way and whispered out of the side of her mouth, "That's the widow of Malcolm X over there in that green scarf."

We looked through the crowd at that green scarf. "Wow," I said to Sylvia. "I wonder if there are other famous people on this trip."

All together, we were a cohort of about thirty people sitting and listening to the Institute Director provide answers to some of our questions.

"We are on our way to Ghana. Why Ghana? This country was the first West African country to gain its independence. Under the leadership of Kwame Nkrumah, Ghana freed itself from Great Britain. There is a lot of African history you will learn as you immerse yourselves in African culture. Our base is the University of Ghana in Accra. They are our hosts. Housing is provided on campus in the dorms. Meals, lectures, and cultural activities are available at the University.

"Everybody on this trip is an adult. This program has no participation or class attendance requirements. You can choose to follow your own interests and even make your own travel decisions. There will be scheduled excursions to villages and castles. It's up to you if you choose to participate. Other than that, you are on your own to discover the wonders of this African land."

Looking out the window as we were landing in Ghana, I was in awe of the landscape. Everything was so green! The trees, the grass, the bushes, everything was a virgin green—deep, lush, and seemingly untouched. I had never seen such foliage before.

We arrived at the university, and we were ushered off to our military style dorms. There was a male dorm and a female dorm. Sylvia took the upper bunk. I took the lower.

I am in Africa. I am in a Black, independent country! Black people are everywhere. I walked around with my head up, proud to be Black. I attended all the lectures. I took pages of notes on tribes, wars, Kings, and Queens. I took notes on British colonialism and their immigration policies. I learned that the British had invited immigrants from Lebanon to promote Ghanaian goods. That British policy was still evident every time I went to shop in any indoor store. A Lebanese always stood behind the counter.

When African dance lessons were offered at the university, I was there waving my arms and stomping my feet. When vendors appeared offering to dress me up in African attire, I selected red, black, and yellow material. I stepped out in a long skirt, a cape top and a matching headdress.

I walked the dirt roads and covered my fingers with 'gold' rings made by a lone metal vendor sitting on a roadside stump. I pounded fufu with the cooks, much like I had churned buttermilk as a kid back in Mt. Vernon. I joined others and feasted on plantains, cassava, and fish stew.

But because participation in lectures and cultural activities was not required, some participants spent most of their time socializing with the many African students who were willing escorts. Very few rose from their beds to attend lectures or to participate in cultural activities. I was disappointed by this behavior. Sylvia was appalled and aghast!

The group leaders had to have side conversations with some of the young female students about "protection." They even provided free condoms in abundance at the entry and exit doors of the dorms.

The level of participation in university offerings increased when away trips were announced. Everybody was geared up to go even if they had not been to the lectures about the trip.

One time we went to the Ashanti Region, and to the capital, Kumasi. The trip offered a shopping opportunity. I went to a small shop to buy souvenirs. I bought Ashanti dolls, an Ashanti headrest, Ashanti beads and a dashiki for my brother. Because I had been to all the lectures and knew the history, all my souvenirs were bought from shops owned by a Lebanese.

After that trip, all the guys, Black and White shed their college tees for multicolored African dashikis.

~

The most anticipated trips were those scheduled to the slave castles, Elmina, and the Cape Coast. I knew the role the Dutch, the Portuguese and the English had played in the slave trade. I knew how millions of my African ancestors had been held naked in cold, dark dungeons before being shipped out to the Americas and the Caribbean. I was prepared for an emotional rollercoaster when I entered the somber walls of the castles. We were warned that "this experience may be difficult for some of you."

I was among a large group of Black and White tourists being led through the dark corridors of Elmina Castle. Most of us Blacks in the group saw ourselves as descendants of the captured souls who had trudged along these same corridors. Some Whites among us were assumed to be descendants of slave traders who sent our Africans ancestors to the dungeons destined for America. Other Whites among us were assumed to be the slave owners who kept our ancestors in bondage in America. There was palpable distrust and suspicion in these corridors.

It was hot. The lighting was dim. Bodies were touching mine. I heard breathing. Out of the masses, I heard a wail and a prayer, "No, God, don't let this happen. Help us forgive those who did this."

In front of me, a body faltered and fell onto the brick corridor. Young Black men in dashikis with stoic faces rushed to extend strong arms and shoulders.

Is this a reality show? I want to turn back, but I can't.

There is slow, forward momentum. I am being pushed along through narrow openings, pushed along over rough brick pavement, and pushed along where I didn't want to go. I can't move my arms. There is too much sobbing, sniffling, wailing, and praying.

The crowd halts in the dark. A voice alerts us, "You have reached the Door of No Return." I crane my neck trying to see what is happening up ahead. There is an eerie silence. Then there is light.

I am standing in the light of a tall open door. I am looking up at the blue sky. I hear water pounding the rocky shores of the Gulf of Guinea! This was the same blue sky my African ancestral fathers saw before they were chained in the bowels of ships. These are the same corridors my slave ancestral mothers traversed before being chained on the upper decks where they were easily accessible to the lascivious desires of their captors.

There was silence as we stood there with our thoughts, until one lone wail pierced through the sunlight.

15

DASHIKI JUSTICE

After the Castle visits, some dashiki-wearing young Black men became protective of our African homeland and culture. They were on the lookout for signs of 'disrespect.' That's why a White male participant named Adam was put on trial.

All mail and packages arrived for us at a small post office very near the university. Once when some of us were milling around checking for mail from home, a young White man could be heard yelling to one of the local postal clerks. His brown hair was hanging over his ears and he needed a shave.

"I have been coming here every day and you keep telling me my package has not arrived. What do you mean, you don't know? What is wrong with this place? Can't you do something as simple as check to see where my package is?"

He was pacing and jamming his hands into the pockets of his blue shorts.

Walter, a dashiki-wearing Black student, tried to intervene.

"Hey man, why you talking to the young lady like that? She's just a worker trying to help you out."

The young White man was throwing up his arms to emphasize his point.

"These people should be able to tell me where my package is. Nothing is working in this country. This is a simple question!

"Wait a minute, man."

Walter moved closer.

"Do you know where you are? Do you realize you're in Africa? Ghana, a Black country! You don't come to Africa and disrespect the people here."

The young White man started walking away.

"I'm not disrespecting anybody. They should be able to keep track of..."

Walter yelled after him. "You can't just walk away from this situation. What's your name?"

Walter was following behind the young White man, trying to engage him in conversation. "What's your name, man?...I'm talking to you."

A bystander yelled, "His name is Adam."

Walter did not back off.

"Adam, you went too far. We got to get to the bottom of this situation. You gonna have to explain yourself. We gon put you on trial...today!"

The mention of a trial attracted more dashikied young men with folded arms to stand with Walter.

Adam stopped, threw his head back and laughed out loud.

"Trial? Are you nuts? Who are you to put me on trial? This is ridiculous."

Walter and his 'prosecution team' did not laugh. Walter said to Adam, "Be in the meeting room at five this evening for your trial. And don't be late!"

I was in the meeting room at five o'clock with Sylvia. About twenty other people were there, too. The room was set up like a courtroom. Walter and two of his 'assistants' in their dashikis were standing at the 'counsel table' talking and writing on note pads.

The jury of three Black men and two Black women were seated in the 'box.' Everything was ready for the trial to begin. Adam, the accused, was missing.

The 'prosecutors' were talking among themselves and looking toward the door. Seated onlookers began to murmur.

"That guy's not coming."

"Somebody go find him."

"He better show up."

Adam appeared in the doorway. He looked around the room.

"What is this?" He queried. "Are you all nuts?"

Walter walked from behind his table and with the wave of his left hand stated, "Please, take a seat in the witness chair."

"I'm not sitting in that chair. Who do you think you are?"

"Adam, you are being put on trial for disrespecting this country and you will answer for your behavior. Now, *sit in the chair*!"

I was beginning to think I should not be in this 'courtroom.' Everybody got quiet. Adam was looking around at all these mostly Black faces with a confused look on his face. It was like he didn't know if he should sit down or run.

He moved slowly to the chair and landed heavily with his legs spread apart and his arms folded. He was shaking his head back and forth.

Walter began the questioning of the slouching accused.

"What is your full name, please?"

"You know my name. My name is Adam Singer."

"Mr. Singer, earlier today after we returned from seeing and listening to the atrocities inflicted upon our African sisters and brothers, our ancestors, did you inflict a similar atrocity upon a worker in the post office?"

"I didn't do anything, I didn't say anything. You are taking out on me what happened three or four hundred years ago."

"Are you saying you don't care about what happened to my African ancestors? Are you saying you are better than the African people 'cause you are White?"

Walter was directing his questions to the audience. His back was to Adam.

"That's not what I'm saying. You're making stuff up. Whatever I said, I'm sorry. I am sorry. Now I am leaving."

Adam stood up and took a few steps in the direction of the door. He was rushed and restrained by a wall of dashiki clad Assistants.

I elbowed Sylvia.

"Let's go."

We put our heads down, circumvented the "lawyers" and "prosecutors" and made our way back to the dorm. I queried my dorm mates who stayed to observe.

"Nothing happened. It was just a lot of loud talking. Everybody left, after Adam said he was going to apologize to the clerk, and that was it."

16

KELVIN'S EPIPHANY

I was focusing on learning African history and trying to see how it felt to be "home." I accompanied some group members to villages with rounded straw huts scattered along grass bare paths.

Some of the older female group members were crying and hugging barefoot village mothers. Other group members were seen falling to their knees in the village dirt and reaching to the heavens declaring "Ohhhh, I'm so blessed to be home. I can feel the sun, the air, the dirt under my feet. Oh, Lord…I'm home...I'm home!"

I guess I am a fraud for not declaring these villages "home." I had never been to Africa before, and neither had these women. I loved being in Africa with my 'sisters and brothers,' but it didn't feel like I could call it 'home.'

Sylvia and I were always in the company of two guys, Kelvin and Greg, who were students at Queens College in New York. They were our sightseeing buddies.

Kelvin was young. He had just finished undergraduate school and was about to enter graduate school. He was tall, thin, blinked a lot and tended to force air out of his nostrils when he got excited. His flaring nostrils reminded me of the wounded bulls fighting for their lives in the rings in Madrid. He was an intellectual, a philosopher and an aspiring professor and minister. He was really smart.

Greg was also slim, but taller than Kelvin. He was dark, quiet, and was a teaching fellow at City University in New York. His camera was his constant companion. He photographed "things of beauty" from African artifacts to village scenes to faces of local women and children. When he focused his camera on me, Sylvia intervened. She had her eyes on Greg.

"Chicago is so much like New York, such fantastic nightlife. Greg, you and I have experienced big city life."

One time, the four of us were in a village strolling the dusty paths among mud plastered huts making our way toward a local schoolhouse. I was walking with Kelvin.

I was wearing my newly tailored red, black, and yellow African skirt with a matching cape. Kelvin was wearing tan church pants, and a red, white, and blue plaid short-sleeved shirt. A white pocket protector inserted into his left shirt pocket held his black Bic pen and a small notepad. He was holding a small black Bible up to his chest with his right hand. He and I were walking ahead of Sylvia and Greg.

"Why are we here?" Kelvin asked me.

"Why are we here?" I asked in return. "You know, we want to see what an African school is like."

He was breathing noisily through his nose, holding his thin frame erect and looking at me askance.

"I'm talking about life," he said. "What is life? Is happiness the goal of life? If you ask most people..."

I stopped listening, wishing I was on an outing with somebody who talked about normal things. If I was talking to Greg, he might say, "You wanna go out later? We can catch a mammy wagon and check out the happenings in the city. Would you like that?"

It could be exciting to be squeezed in next to Greg on one of those local busses. Greg had potential, but Sylvia closed down that lane. She cozied up to him and he believed that behind her coquettishness was an experienced 'baseball' player. Just walking through this village in front of them, I could hear her persistent, "No...no," followed by childish giggles. I am sure that when Greg drops those bedroom eyes on her and just tries to hold her hands, she would scoot away. He will find out soon enough that she has never played baseball and has no intention of playing "until my wedding night."

I had played some baseball and had memorized the behaviors of real Chicago girls. I could have been with Greg, but was stuck with Kelvin, who quoted scriptures and searched for answers to unanswerable questions about life.

Near the end of our trip, the group leaders decided to thank our African hosts by having a celebratory party. We decorated one of the school's large auditoriums with flowers and African kente cloth streamers. We had food, drinks, dancing, and stage performances.

I volunteered to perform a song as part of the program. I dressed in a short sack dress with big red, purple, and black flowers on a white background. Togetherness, laughter, hand slapping and brotherly hugs permeated throughout the hall. I was caught up in the moment.

When my name was called to perform, I grabbed the hand mic, took to the stage, and belted out my version of Nina Simone's "You Can Have Him." I pranced across the stage, swaying my hips with subtle gyrations. The whistling and applause during and after my performance seems to have tugged at the hearts of some in the audience who had barely given me a "hello" before.

"You were great!"

"Are you a professional singer?"

"Where you been hiding?"

Kelvin even had a glimmer in his blinking eyes. With a glass of Coke in his left hand and his nostrils flaring like he had just run a mile, he guided me off to the corner of the hall. I expected him to question the meaning behind my song choice. I planned to tell him to 'loosen up and enjoy life.'

He was blinking rapidly and pushing breaths through his nostrils. He took both my hands in his. He was yelling something at me over the chatter and the loud music.

"...graduate schools in New York? I want you to."

"I can't hear you. What did you say about graduate school?" I asked, putting my left ear closer to his face.

"I want you to come to New York." he said, accenting each word.

"You want me to come to New York? Is that what you said?"

"Yeah," he said, yelling into my ear.

"What would I do in New York?" I stepped back from him, spreading my arms and shrugging my shoulders.

"I think It would be good. We would both be in New York, going to graduate school."

I threw up my hands. I started stammering.

"I can't go to graduate school in New York! I don't know anything about schools in New York? I have a job I gotta go back to. No, no, I can't do that."

Kelvin was standing tall now. He was calmly sipping from his glass of Coke. He stepped to a table, placed his empty glass on it and retrieved the black Bic pen and his notepad from the pen protector in his plaid shirt pocket. He was writing as he spoke.

"These are the schools you should apply to, Fordham University and Columbia University, Teachers College. They are both really good schools. When you decide which program you want, just ask for an application."

"Kelvin, this is crazy. I don't even know what program to apply to." He handed me his written note. I tucked it inside my green purse.

Kelvin smiled at me and nodded his head a few times.

"Yes," he said, as he cradled my hands in his, "This could be good."

On the plane back to the States, all I could think about was Kelvin's crazy notion of graduate school in New York. He kept visiting me on the plane, smiling, nodding, and pushing air through his nostrils. He whispered to me through hot air during one of his meanderings, "Why don't you two stay a night or two in New York...See how you like it. You can stay at my place."

Sylvia was offended initially, intrigued next and finally giddy at the possibility of bedding down at a guy's place.

She whispered to me, "We can't spend the night at a man's apartment! I'm not that kind of person...but Ok...as long as the guys sleep in a separate room."

We spent two nights sleeping in the living room on the floor and on couches along with other random 'daytime guests.' We saw a bit of Queens and our virginity remained intact.

17

GROWING SEEDS

I was intrigued by the idea of schooling in New York. And having a friend like Kelvin who knew the city would make the transition easier. He had definitely planted a seed. I left Ghana with the names of two New York graduate schools in my purse. What harm could come from my requesting information about their programs?

Teaching had never been high on my list of careers. That was my fallback profession. After giving up being an executive secretary, I wanted to be a historian, working for the UN, and traveling the world. I never wanted to be stuck in a high school teaching American history to uninterested students! And yet, I don't mind being around kids.

My senior girls always want to see the counselor.

"Miss, I need to go see my counselor."

"My counselor gonna help me find a college."

"My counselor...a *counselor...*counseling!" *What about...I can be a counselor! The counselors at Beaumont...they don't know what they're doing...telling failing students to apply to college. I can fix that! That's it! I'll apply to graduate programs in counseling!*

I squirreled away in my bedroom and wrote to Fordham University and Columbia University, Teachers College requesting information about their graduate programs in Counseling.

According to the brochures I received, Columbia University, Teachers College, was introducing a two-year master's degree program in school counseling. They were recruiting a cohort of thirty students to pilot the program.

Fordham University's program was offering a one-year master's degree in school counseling.

I couldn't stop now, I was encouraged. I completed the counseling program applications from both schools. When I was a senior at SIU, I wrote an autobiography in my social psychology class. The teacher, Mr. Russell, gave me an A+ and commented, "This is a thoughtful and clear analysis. If you are still undecided about your life plans, why not go on to graduate school? Need a letter of recommendation?"

It took forever to hear back from both schools regarding my acceptance. I rushed home every day to get the mail. Old high school fears of not being selected by either university crept into my mind. My nails were down to mere stubs.

A letter arrived from Fordham first. It was a thin white envelope. 'The thinner, the better' did not put my trembling hands at ease.

I closed myself in my bedroom, ripped open the thin white envelope and scanned the one-page letter for words like "congratulations," "admitted," and "financial aid." Those words were all there! I wanted to scream for joy. But screaming for joy over the possibility of leaving home would be unacceptable.

I put "controlled excitement" on my face and I walked into the family room. Everybody was bent over plates of spaghetti with white bread. Mama and Daddy were sitting at the dining table. My older siblings were scattered in chairs with plates on their laps. The little ones were relegated to a small table in the kitchen. This was the perfect setting.

To no one in particular, I announced, "I got accepted to Fordham University."

"You got accepted where?" Mama wanted to know. She was picking at her spaghetti trying to get strings to stay on her fork.

"To graduate school at Fordham University," I said, casually. "It's in New York."

Daddy cleared his throat.

"Why you have to go to skool in New Yok? You got all dese skools ret heah in St. Louis. You don't need to go to no New Yok to go to skool."

My sister Lena weighed in. She was studying at St. Louis Junior College.

"Every city has good programs. But getting a good education is more than just going to school, it's meeting other people in different..."

Daddy cut her off.

"I don't care wat chou say. You don't need to go to no New Yok to go to skool."

I was less anxious when the thin envelope arrived from Columbia University. I already had an acceptance under my belt. I scanned the one-page letter again for words like "congratulations," "admitted," and "financial aid." Those words were all there! I didn't bother to tell my parents about my acceptance to Columbia. I mentioned it to Lena and Helena.

I had to figure out which university I wanted to go to. I had to consider which was offering me the most money and which would best suit my need to get a taste of 'life.'

I called Kelvin to give him the news and to get his opinion on which school I should choose.

"I did it!" I was talking too loudly and laughing too much. "I got accepted to both universities! I can't believe it! Now what do I do?"

He gave himself credit first. I could hear his breathing. "I knew you would get in. What kinda money are they giving you?"

I told him what I knew.

"Fordham is a one-year program, and they are offering me some reduced tuition, but I have to get loans. Columbia is a two-year program, and they will give me free tuition with loans also."

Without hesitation, Kelvin said, "You gotta go to Columbia. That's the best school. You'll be so close to everything, and it's basically in Harlem!"

"Harlem!"

I'm yelling now.

"I can't live in Harlem. I've heard about all kinds of stuff..."

"Don't worry about Harlem," he said. "That's just White folks talking. That school's been there for years."

There was a pause in the excitement.

Then he said, "You know what I've been thinking..."

Wait a minute! Is he thinking something is going on here? No! That's not possible. After almost two months of "What is life" and "What does it mean to live forever?," I have no interest in Kelvin beyond friendship. And besides, I don't think he has ever even been to a baseball game!

"What?" I asked, hoping he wouldn't say anything crazy.

He said something crazy.

"I've been thinking...I wanna come down there to see you. We can celebrate...and talk about New York. I've never been to that part of the country. I'd like to see St. Louis."

He was blowing air again.

My worst nightmare is to host another big city friend coming to a small midwestern city looking for a good time. Only this time, it's a guy!

I hated the idea. But I had to grant his wish. Just like with Sylvia, I feigned enthusiasm.

"Oh, that would be great. It will be lots of fun! When are you planning to come?"

He came at a very, very bad time.

18
FIRST DATE

Gerald came to my classroom early in my second year at Beaumont. I was sitting at my wooden desk shuffling papers trying to decide what to take home. I heard my door open. I looked over to see Gerald wearing that wide mouth grin that exposed a gold filling in his molars. He was wearing a wide legged gray suit with a purple shirt and a red tie.

"Hello, Miss Edwards. How you doing?"

He fingered a flip chart of world maps as he came to stand in front of my desk.

"I'm doing just fine. How about you?"

"Great. Great. I was just wondering if you are free this Friday night? There is a new cabaret place, I think it's called Gemstones. Everybody says it's very nice. There's a singer and everything. I'm just wondering if you would like to go and check it out?"

His hands were leaning on my desk. Then he jabbed them into his pants pockets and stood up straight, still talking as he inched backward toward the door.

"I'm going, if you would like to go."

I smiled just thinking about the possibility of listening to live music. I also smiled just watching 'Mr. Jokester' squirm.

I said, "If you're asking me to go with you to a place where I can hear a live singer, the answer is 'yes.' I'd love to."

He exhaled.

"I'll pick you up at seven."

I had seen Gerald in the hallways and in the cafeteria. He was a math teacher. He was dark skinned with a short crew cut, of medium height and well-built for a thirty-something-year-old man.

He had never registered with me as an eligible bachelor. I knew him as a jokester. Some other female teachers even referred to him as a clown. He talked too loud, he laughed too loud, and he dressed too loud. Everything about him was loud. A pink or purple shirt with a red necktie was his trademark. I don't like loud.

He also had other foibles that were very noticeable. He had a yawning problem. And he was not discreet. Each yawn was accompanied by his right hand attempting to cover his wide-open mouth, but an audible "Ahhh" announced his presence.

Gerald also had a leg problem. When he walked, his right leg seemed unable to bend. So that right leg kicked out to the side before coming to join his left leg. I assumed that leg issue was the reason he wore such wide legged suit pants.

He didn't know I had been to Europe and to Africa. The only person at school who knew of my travels was Tia. When I got back from England I wanted to talk about my trip. I wanted to tell my students about my being on the London Bridge and my riding on the top of double decker buses. I wanted to talk about my hanging out with Middle Easterners and Italians.

When I got back from Africa, I wanted to tell my students about African music and dance. I wanted to tell them about African schools and villages. I wanted to tell them about Elmina Castle and the Gulf of Guinea. I couldn't tell them anything about my travels. None of this was part of the curriculum.

My travels did not seem exciting to most people I talked to, including my own family. So, I just retrieved my burgundy spiral notebook from the top shelf in my closet, turned to my five-year plan and wrote "England, Europe, Africa/Ghana" next to the word 'Travel'.

Gerald was my first date in my almost two years of living and working in and around St. Louis. I was excited. I told Tia. She was not impressed.

"He's not your type," she said. "He's too much of a clown, don't you think?"

"Well, yes, but it beats sitting home every weekend."

I never discussed my goings and comings with anyone in my household. When they hear me asking, "Which dress do you like?" or, when I pin my hair up in the middle of the evening, they know I am going out with a man. The expectation of a "gentleman caller" is an exciting event in our household.

When Gerald parked his car on the street in front of the house, Mama and my younger sisters joined me in looking out the picture window to get a first impression.

He got out of the car and walked up the steps with that right leg kicking out to the side.

Mama said, "Margaret, he hansom! He dress real nice, too."

What! Where's the clown suit! I expected to dismiss him at first sight. Now I have to rethink this. Is this the same Gerald! He's in a dark gray suit and the pant legs are 'normal.' The purple shirt and red clown tie are replaced with a white shirt and a gray and red striped tie. Is this Gerald?

I am glad I took the time to prepare myself for this outing. Since Africa, I am sporting a neat, tight Afro. My sisters agreed that my peach one-piece flimsy dress with long sleeves, a deep cleavage and a flared skirt is an eye-catching choice.

I shooed everybody out of sight and opened the door.

Gerald's eyes betrayed his rehearsed confidence and nonchalance. His eyes fixed on me: my face, my cleavage, my legs. I smiled. He wiped his forehead. He was breathing rapidly. He was standing in the doorway saying nothing.

So, I said, "Hi Gerald. Do you want to come in or shall we just go?" He moved his eyes from my body to the screen door that was holding him upright.

"Oh," he said. "Yeah, we should go."

He rushed ahead of me down the steps and opened the car door. I seated myself. He closed my door, rushed around, and pulled open his door and got into his seat. He reached toward the ignition panel.

"Oh, where did I put the keys. Oh, they must be in my pocket. Let me see, I gotta get out. Hard to find things in my pockets."

He stepped out of the car, dug into each pants pocket, and pulled out a set of keys.

"There. Got 'em," he announced.

He starts the car. He finds his voice.

"We're going to a place called Gemstones. I don't know what the name stands for but it's supposed to be pretty nice. Good atmosphere I hear, with the music and all."

The place is nondescript. It is on the ground floor of a low-rise office building. It is embedded between two banks, Citizens Bank on one side, and Wells Fargo on the other. Gemstones Cabaret flashes in neon lights above the clear glass door.

Once inside, the space is quite large, longer than it is wide. There is a small, raised stage at the front of the room. A piano is stage left. A microphone stands center stage. A small table holding a tambourine is left of the microphone. The back wall of the stage is surrounded from ceiling to floor with strings of silver glitter. The lights are low, but I can make out large abstract designs covering the walls. The space feels cozy and warm.

We stood at a small wooden round table for two in the middle of the room near the front. I looked around. Tables for four were further back. I wanted to be able to see the singer when she took the stage.

Gerald pulls out a chair and adjusts the table to ensure that I have an unobstructed view of the stage. When we are seated, a young woman with long brown hair wearing a long skirt approaches to take our drink order. Gerald defers to me.

"What would you like to drink?"

"I'll have a Singapore Sling," I said.

"Can you say again? I didn't hear you. It's getting noisy in here," the waitress leans in closer.

I raise my voice, "Singapore Sling."

The waitress repeats my request, "Singapore Sling." She writes something on a notepad.

"And how about you, sir?"

"I'll have a glass of Sauvignon Blanc."

With that done, I relax. Ordering a drink is not something I have done lately. I feel like my college days are still upon me especially when the waitress returns apologizing.

"I hope the bartender got your drink right. Singapore Sling is a new one for him."

She sat my drink down in front of me. It looked familiar, the tall bowl-like glass, the orange-colored liquid, accented with a fruit filled toothpick lying across the top. A cherry with a long stem dangled inside the rim of the glass.

To ease her mind and Gerald's, I remove the fruit to a saucer and take a sip. I purse my lips and close my eyes knowing I need to show that I can be flexible in my tastes and appreciate the possibility of human imperfection.

"Perfect," I said.

There are smiles all round. I had passed the 'hard to please bitch' test.

We talk about school stuff. I speak first.

"So, how long have you been at Beaumont?"

"Eight years, nine with this year."

"Where did you go to college?"

"University of Maryland."

"You must like teaching math."

"Oh, not sure how much longer I can teach math. I think I want to do something else."

The stage lights up. The back wall tinsel shimmers in the light. A pianist emerges and begins to play "Fly Me to the Moon." I am relaxed, loose, smiling and allowing my left hand to tap the table to the beat. The rise and fall of chatter, the clinking of glasses, the piano music, and the ensuing applause. This atmosphere resonates with me. And the calming effects of my Singapore Sling helps me to really like this place.

The pianist introduces the singer, a young, tall White woman wearing a long shiny gray dress with a slit on the side that exposes her leg up to her upper thigh. She grabs the mic from the stand and throws her head back, and swoons into her version of "How Can I Be Sure."

I have never heard the song before, and it doesn't matter. I am appreciating her performance, how she moves around the stage and how she smiles and toys with the audience. She is a confident performer. I am enjoying her enjoyment.

When I got home, I took down my burgundy, spiral notebook. I turned to my five-year plan and with my Bic black pen I wrote: Become a Nightclub Singer.

Almost every weekend, Gerald asked me out. He knew I loved the performing arts. We went to outdoor MUNY opera performances. We went to plays at a local college and we went to dinner at fancy white napkin restaurants. But most weekends, we ended up at Gemstones Cabaret. Our drink orders were always the same, a Singapore Sling for me and a glass of Sauvignon Blanc for him.

19
DECIPHERING GERALD

After about a month into my relationship with Gerald, I got suspicious. He had changed. At work, his loud, jokester personality no longer announced his presence.

He no longer acted like the 'clown.' He began to wear white shirts and tailored suits.

Whenever he was around me, he laughed with his mouth closed enough so I didn't see the gold fillings in his molars. He yawned less often and without the accompanying "Ahhh." He was respectful, chivalrous, and sometimes too accommodating. He routinely bought $100 seats at the MUNY when I said I wanted good seats.

The problem was that he never seemed interested in playing baseball. Never did he make a move toward first base! When we arrived at my house after a date, Gerald would come around the car, open my door and guide me up the steps to my door. Each time we arrived at my door, I anticipated something. A peck on the cheek, a "I enjoyed the evening." Something. Instead, I got a no-teeth smile, a little bow, and a definitive "goodnight."

Yes, I am a "catch." I have perfectly styled hair, beautiful legs, articulate speech, and a college degree! I also have a brain.

He is a catch too, for somebody. I was trying to figure out why he kept his feelings and desires locked away. Why was he deliberately avoiding any physical contact with me beyond a hand to guide me to a chair or through a door? Our conversations were never about 'us.' He kept it mundane, always about school politics or his plans to do some advanced degree.

He did divulge one time that he is working nights at the airport to make extra money to support his future educational plans. That answered the yawning question.

He asked me about my plans. My answer was always the same.

"I don't know yet, but I will be getting my master's at some point." *That's in my five-year plan, and so is 'get a boyfriend!'*

One time after work, he invited me to his apartment which was very near the school.

Maybe this is it!

We entered his living room. I was gobsmacked! *I walked into an old person's apartment! This is Big Mama's living room.* It was dark with an overstuffed brown couch, an overstuffed brown chair, and a big brown television as the centerpiece in the front of the room.

"Come in. Come on in."

Gerald threw his satchel on the brown chair and hurried to turn on the lamps on each side of the brown couch.

"Come on sit down. This is my little piece of territory." He spread his arms out wide. My eyes follow the direction of his arms. I tried to show delight.

"Nice," I said, walking around in the tight space picking up bric-a-brac, examining it and placing it back on the brown end tables.

"How long have you lived here?"

"About six years. It's nice enough, very convenient to get to work to both jobs. Speaking of jobs, I have to work tonight, so I need to get a little shut eye, for about an hour or so. Do you mind?"

"No, no," I said. "I'm fine. Just turn on the TV for me."

In the middle of a muted, hand covered yawn, he switched on the TV and lowered the volume. The familiar music of *Leave It To Beaver* filled the room.

"Do you like this show?" he asked. "It's my favorite. I watch this all the time."

"Yeah. I like it. It's really funny."

"Ok, I'm gonna take a nap now."

He turned toward me and looked at his watch.

"How about waking me up in an hour, around 5:30?"

"Of course," I said, with enthusiasm, trying to sound as if this request was perfectly normal.

"Great," he said as he disappeared through a door on the left side of the living room. He didn't offer me a drink of water.

I perched myself on the edge of the brown couch and gazed in the direction of the television. I couldn't concentrate on how Beaver's antics and misbehavior would be resolved by his stay-at-home mom or his hard working, problem-solving dad.

I kept going back to what to do about Gerald. How do I approach this relationship which is not a relationship? No attempt at baseball? Is this normal? As far as I am concerned, that makes us just friends. Does he just enjoy taking me out and spending money on me because it makes me happy? Or does he have a more sinister plan that he will reveal at a time and place of his own choosing?

Tia thinks he is trying to make himself irresistible.

"No man is going to spend money on you unless you give him something in return," she said.

"But it's been almost two months and he hasn't asked for anything! Something is wrong with him. Any other man would try something!"

I am a twenty-three-year-old woman sitting in the apartment of a thirty-three-year-old man. The man is sleeping behind a closed door. I need to wake him for his second job in about ten minutes. Something is strange about this.

I look around at dingy beige curtains and touch the saggy, worn, velvety brown couch. The end table near me is scarred with a water stain on the right side. This living room furniture needs an upgrade! Can I be interested in a man who lives like my grandmother?

Gerald upgraded his behavior and his appearance. But Mama said, "No matter what you try to do, you ain't ever gon change no man!"

At 5:30, I knocked gently three times on the closed door on the left side of the living room. I waited for a response. Nothing. I turned the doorknob, pushed the door open gingerly and peeked inside.

The light from the open door revealed Gerald sprawled out on a brown sleigh bed. His big clean-shaven head is facing away from the door. He is wearing a white undershirt. A dark colored sheet is wrapped around him from his waist to his feet. There is a tall brown chifforobe near a white shade-covered window.

I can hear him snoring lightly. How to wake up a snoring man in his own bedroom is something new for me. I have to think about this. I decide to walk up to him, lean over and gently shake his shoulder.

I whisper, "Gerald, Gerald. It's 5:30."

He rolls over towards me, moans, stretches, and yawns. I straighten up and step back. Waking up and yawning and moaning should be private business.

"Hey," he said through mumbling lips. "I didn't want you to shake me. I wanted warm lips all over my face. You know what I mean?"

He closes his eyes and starts stroking his face and shoulders.

I turn and walk through the open door back into the living room. I stand in front of the television just looking at the *Leave It to Beaver* credits. I hear the bedroom door close. Gerald enters dressed in a light blue shirt and dark blue pants.

"Well, time to go," he said.

He grabs keys off the table, switches off the television, and directs me toward the front door with an exaggerated flair of his right hand. I head to my green hatchback; he heads to his black Chevy.

"See you tomorrow," he said, before getting into his car and driving off.

20
LEANING LEFT

When I got back to the U.S. from Africa, I was energized. I was emboldened. I was optimistic. I felt in charge of my life. But after a couple of months, I developed a pain in my ass.

At first, I dismissed the pain as just soreness from sitting too much. That soreness soon turned into a tiny lump mostly on the right side of my butt crack. I mentioned the lump to Mama and Daddy.

Mama said, "That ain't nothin but a old boil…it will go away by itself."

Daddy said, "You jus hav to set down real hard and bust dat thang."

I still had to go to work. Once I got to my classroom in the morning, I stayed there until it was time to go home. I taught my classes either leaning slightly over my desk or sitting and putting my weight on my left buttock. I then gingerly switched sides when numbness set in.

When the pain didn't go away by itself and the lump got a bit larger and more painful, Daddy said, "Go see dis Dr. Randell. He a real good doctor. He Black. We oughta be supoting Black doctors."

I went to see Dr. Randell. He didn't take appointments. His office was downtown near Lach Elementary where I used to work. It was on the ground floor of an old brownstone building. The name, "Dr. Randell" was etched on a worn brass plate tacked on the door. I pushed open the door and was hit by the sweaty odor of twenty or so men and women sitting on brown folding chairs, dozing, or staring off or coughing. Some were leaning against the wall and sitting on windowsills. I was the youngest person in the room. Everybody was Black.

Watery eyes observed my entrance. I found an empty wall and leaned against it to get some relief from the pain in my butt crack. A man with a cane leaning against the same wall caught my eye and pointed with his cane toward the front of the room. My gaze followed his pointed cane to a small school desk. He demonstrated in the air that I needed to sign in.

The pain in my ass was throbbing now, but I had to straighten up. It was a long walk to the sign in desk. I weaved slowly around brown chairs, sprawling feet, and stuffed bags. I picked up the clipboard, retrieved the dangling yellow pencil and scribbled *Marge Edwards* on the next open space. I counted nine names scribbled ahead of mine. I worked my way back to the wall, leaned against it and waited.

This doctor must be very popular with all these folks waiting into the evening just to see him. I made my way here after work, so I was dressed for work: gray, burgundy and blue pleated skirt, burgundy sweater, two-inch black pumps and ample right-side coverage for my acne.

After about an hour of standing and looking around trying to imagine what was ailing most of these people, I heard "Marge Edwards." The receptionist led me back to an office containing two well-worn red leather chairs and a scarred wooden desk. I eased into the chair across from the desk. I was given a clipboard with a form attached. I filled in personal information like my name, address, and phone number. I also completed information about my past illnesses. Where it asked for *reason for visit,* I just wrote *pain.*

The office was the size of an ample closet with white Venetian blinds raised to cover half the one window in the room. There was an examination table covered with white paper. Three glass jars with lids sat on a counter. One was filled with cotton balls, another with thin wooden popsicle sticks and the other with paper clips.

The walls were faded. I think they were painted yellow once. The wall over the desk in front of me was covered with framed degrees from...*what is that*? I leaned forward on my left buttock, squinting, trying to read the small print. The door opened. I sat back, felt a jolt of pain, leaned left, and crossed my legs at the ankles. My behind felt better.

In walked a medium height, light brown skinned man with a muscular build and wavy black hair brushed back from his forehead. His white doctor's coat was open in the front. He had a stethoscope dangling from his left shoulder. He smiled as he walked over to my chair. He extended his right hand.

"Hello, I'm Dr. Randell. How are you?" *Nice warm hands.*

I smiled back as I responded. "Just fine, thank you."

I uncrossed my ankles as I leaned forward to accept his hand. He gave me three firm shakes.

He crossed to the desk, picked up my clipboard, scanned the information and leaned in toward me.

"How can I help you?"

I tried to find the right words.

"I'm not sure. I mean I have a pain back here. I think it's called a boil?"

I was leaning forward and pointing toward my behind. He stood up and leaned over me trying to see where I was pointing. *Awkward!*

"I'll need to take a look," he said, standing up straight and putting a soft hand on my shoulder. *Good bedside manner...*

He left the room. A few minutes later his female assistant walked in with a white sheet. She instructed me to remove my skirt and lay on the table, my backside up. She adjusted my undergarments to expose my butt crack.

She remained in the room. Dr. Randell returned.

"Now let me take a look."

He fingered the exposed area with warm hands applying varying degrees of pressure.

"Is the pain here?"

"How about here?"

I answered "Yes" to each question and each touch.

He extended the perimeter of his examination from the pain area to the surrounding areas. His questioning continued.

"Is the pain here?"

"How about here?"

I answered "No" to each question.

He covered my behind with the corner of the sheet and returned to his desk.

I raised up slightly on my elbows.

He turned in his chair to face me.

"What you have is called a boil in layman's terms. The only way you will feel better is to reduce the inflammation by inducing drainage or shrinkage. I may be able to do that with a series of injections. And if that does not dissolve it, then it will have to be lanced. What do you think? Shall we proceed with the injections?"

"Yes," I said. "I think so."

He proceeded with the injection.

Back in his office, he scheduled a follow-up appointment for the next week.

21

MOVING UP

When I arrived for my appointment the following week, his receptionist ushered me to his office immediately upon my signing in. I was puzzled. There were ten names signed in before me. The brown folding chairs were again filled with older Black people. They were dosing, coughing, and nodding, their feet spread wide into the isles. *Why am I jumping the line?*

After my second injection, I was ushered by his assistant into Dr. Randell's private office. He was sitting in a brown leather chair at a large metal desk looking over reading glasses at papers in a yellow manila folder. He was still dressed in his doctor's whites. I sat down leaning left in the blue leather chair across from him. He didn't look up when I sat down. I scanned the office. He had two windows with seat cushions in red, white, and blue patterns. There were framed pictures on a tall built-in bookcase and a pair of hanging files arranged on the left side of his desk.

The sun was going down. I am not a night driver.

I have to get on the road before dark.

I asked tentatively, "Is there something you want to see me about?"

He looked up then, his eyes feigning surprise as if he didn't know I was there.

"Oh yes. You are going to need a few more injections in order for this protrusion to dissipate. So, I scheduled another appointment for you next week."

"Ok," I said. "How many more injections do you think I will need?"

"It is hard to say. You should be feeling less pain soon."

"Good, I hope so. Also, Dr. Randell, I am just wondering why I was called before some other people. They were here before me. I don't mind waiting my turn."

He looked at me. I looked at him also, waiting for an explanation.

He closed the manila folder, carefully placed it to the right on his desk, took off his reading glasses and leaned in toward me.

"I like you," he said. "I liked you the first time I laid eyes on you. You know that, don't you?"

I pushed my shoulders back against that blue leather chair. *Ouch, that hurts. Should I get up...slowly...and hobble out of this office?*

Instead, I started stuttering.

"I like you too. I get good service here, and everybody is so nice."

He ignored my fumbling for words.

"You are so poised, so articulate, so different from other people I have met. I want to get to know you better."

He leaned back in his chair.

I shifted my behind more to my right hip.

"I just don't want to be called out of turn," I interjected.

"I also know that what I'm saying to you is unprofessional, and I shouldn't be saying it. but I would never say or do anything unethical when I am examining or administering medical services to you. You understand that, don't you?" *He's ignoring my concern!*

"I guess so." *I do not like this kind of talk! What's with these men? I came for help.*

"Yes, I moved you up on the roster. I wanted to see you. Most of my other patients are regulars. They don't mind waiting. But I will never move you up in the line again, if you'll honor me by having dinner with me."

He's smiling now and leaning back in his brown leather chair, regarding me.

I'm just sitting there, leaning left, and staring at this man with my eyes furrowed trying to figure out what to say.

"You don't have to tell me now. I'll call you, but I'll call you only if you give me permission. Your number is in your folder." He taps the manila folder on his desk.

I blurt out, "I'm sorry, but I don't go out with married men."

He didn't hesitate.

"I'm separated...and have been for two years. I'm working on making the separation official, and I have no children."

22
SPICY WORDS

Dr. Randell was not having success shrinking that lump in my butt crack. My appointments turned into half hour sessions in his office chatting about his plans to "move out of this neighborhood and get attached to a hospital. "

"That would be great for you," I said. "But these people here need a good doctor in the neighborhood. What will they do if you leave?" I felt like his therapist.

In spite of reminding him of my discomfort with "jumping the line and having people wait, his response continued to be, "So go to dinner with me. Anyway, they're fine. They're used to waiting."

"Ok. I'll have dinner with you, Dr. Randell, you know my condition."

"Yes, I do. By the way, my friends call me Keith."

Keith called a week later. I met him in Target's parking lot in University City. He pushed open the front door and I gingerly slid into the seat of his big black Mercedes. He headed out of town "so we can have some privacy."

I felt uneasy sitting next to him on my left hip trying to avoid putting pressure on that lump festering between my butt crack. He looked over at me and smiled. "You all right?"

I smiled back and used both my hands to help me shift in my seat.

"I'm fine."

I crossed my legs at the ankles. I was trying to relax in my checkered brown, beige, and burgundy A-line skirt with a complimentary beige sweater. I substituted knee highs for panty hose.

Dr. Randall looked so good and confident in his striped blue and white shirt with the sleeves rolled up to his elbows. He seemed slimmer without that white coat.

At first, dinners with Keith were almost like going out with Gerald. Both took me to expensive steak restaurants, opened doors for me, guided me to my seat with one hand, and pulled out my chair. Differences began to emerge.

Gerald avoided any sign of affection toward me, no hand holding, no hugging, no attempts at first base.

Tia said, with dramatic flair, "He wants to deprive and starve you into submission. He wants to be in a position to pounce when you become weak-kneed with desire!"

Keith knew the limits my butt crack pain placed on my movement. But that didn't stop him. Married men are like that.

One time after an expensive dinner at a Ruth Chris Steakhouse restaurant in nearby Edwardsville, he lost control.

We were sitting in the parking lot, talking about my wanting to go to New York for graduate school. I was not wearing my seatbelt. I was sitting as usual leaning on my left butt cheek.

"I want to get out of teaching." I cut the air with my hands. "The woman who counsels kids at Beaumont has problems telling kids how to prepare for college. I think I could..."

I heard the click of Keith's seat belt. I turned as he leaned across the center seat, and with both hands grabbed my face including a handful of my hair. He pressed his lips on mine.

I groaned gibberish, "Ooooh, watchudoin?" I pushed him away

with my left hand and lifted my butt off the seat with the other. Maybe he thought I was suffocating. He sat up and threw up his hands.

I lifted my butt off the leather seat with my hands. I closed my eyes. I continued my pain mantra.

"Oh, oh, oooooh. That hurts. What are you thinking? Oh, oh, oooooh, that hurts."

Keith went into a sorry mantra. "I'm sorry, I'm sorry. I wasn't thinking. I apologize. I'm so sorry. I wasn't thinking. You are in agony, and I furthered your pain with my capriciousness. I lost myself in the paroxysm of..."

There he goes, another "P" word. One thing I like about my conversations with Keith is his use of new vocabulary, especially his "P" words. He uses words like 'precocious' and 'pomposity' and 'pithy.' He sometimes throws in "F" words like 'fecundity' and 'fractious' to add variety. He encourages me to 'spice' up my vocabulary.

One time when I was complaining to the counselor about one of my students, I used one of his 'P' words on her. I said, "I worry about Jennelle. She is too precocious for her age."

Holding my butt cheeks off the seat was exacerbating the pain. I opened the door on my side of the car. Keith stepped out of his side of the car and rounded the front to help me exit.

I pushed him away. There in the parking lot of Ruth Chris Steak House holding onto the open car door to give me balance, I raised my skirt and squatted with my knees spread apart. I looked like I was taking a piss. *Am I poised now, Dr. Randell? Just look at me!*

I held my head high, closed my eyes and remained in a squat with knees spread apart until the throbbing in my butt crack subsided. To stop Keith from pacing around me like a lap dog, I reached out for his hand to help me slowly rise to my feet.

"I am so apologetic, but I can't eradicate this desire to express my affection. You are so alluring." *Oh, stop it, Keith!*

I knew what I had to do. I had to get this lump in my butt crack looked at by a doctor with hospital privileges.

23
RELIEF STORIES

Mama got a job working in the kitchen at St. Mary's Hospital. Her job was to put food on trays for patients.

She said, "Dis a good job. I ain't never gon clean no White folks house no mo. Mr. Jackson said I kin work in nursing at a hospital. He say they always looking for peeples to work dere. He was right 'bout dat."

Mama had to wear a uniform. White dress, white stockings, white shoes, and a blue smock to cover that white dress. Before she went to work, she fussed daily over that uniform.

"I need to wash my uniform."

"You can't use dat washing machine now, I need to wash my stockings."

"Margaret, kin you iron my uniform?"

"I can't go ta work looking like a bum!"

At dinnertime at home sitting at the kitchen table, she couldn't stop telling work stories. Daddy never said much. It was hard to tell if he was listening because he just kept eating his white bread, white beans and drinking water after every few bites.

I took my plate of white beans, white bread, and a glass of Kool Aid to the table in the family room. I could still hear Mama talking.

"Maggie, she been working dere ten yeahs."

"Francis, she big and fat, she walk real slow, but she kin put dat food on dim trays. She always talking 'bout her kids."

"Dim White doctors real nice. Always sayin "how y'all doin ladies...dat food smells so good."

When I decided to see a doctor with hospital privileges, Mama made arrangements for me to meet Dr. Fletcher, "a real nice doctor." I met him in his office. I didn't tell him about Dr. Randell and his boil diagnosis. I just laid on his table and let him figure out for himself what the problem was.

He said, "You have a pilonidal cyst. It seems to be infected and needs to be lanced. You can see my assistant and schedule a time for the procedure. You will need to be hospitalized, probably just overnight."

Based on my school breaks and time needed to recover, I scheduled the procedure to take place during the Christmas break. Until then, I did what I could to keep pressure off my butt.

In my classroom when I needed real butt pain relief, I resorted to dropping things on the floor near my desk. I dropped papers, pencils, chalk, erasers, anything so I could bend to pick up the item. I needed a deep bend from my waist to get maximum butt crack pain relief.

One time in class after talking, leaning, and pointing in class, the pain was excruciating. I sat down behind my desk, took the 'left hip leaning, right leg over left' posture and waited. My butt pain was still throbbing. I needed immediate relief.

I dropped a yellow number two pencil on the right side of my desk. Bending to pick it up would give me immediate relief. I was just beginning my maximum relief bend and looking forward to the joy of a butt crack spread when one of my star students jumped up from his seat. I saw his hand reaching for my pencil. I grabbed his hand, my head almost touching the floor. *What a relief.*

"You didn't have to pick it up, Jet," I said, smiling. "I need the exercise, from sitting too much."

I did two 'fingers to toes' exercises to drive home the point. *Bonus relief!*

Gerald was going to be a problem. My excuse for not going out with him over the past few weeks had to do with "lots of papers to grade" and "spending the weekends in Mt. Vernon." And I told him also that I would not be available to see him during the Christmas break either as I was having a minor, one day medical procedure. I expected him to understand and say, "I'm sorry. Hope you're Ok. Let me know if I can help."

Instead, he pissed me off with his questions.

"What's the matter?"

"Can I help?"

"What hospital are you going to?"

They put me in a room with an old, overweight White woman with scraggly gray hair. She was in the bed across from mine. She was lying on her back propped up with pillows all around. She was watching me and holding a television remote. The television was off.

From the moment I settled in with my three pillows propping me up on my right side, she never stopped talking.

"What ya in for?"

From the way she talked. I could tell she was a redneck.

I kept my answers short.

"I need to have a cyst lanced."

"Oh, is dat all...dat ain't nothin. First time in a hospital?"

"Yes."

"You ain't got nothin ta be scared about, honey. I been in here a lot. This my third time!" She chuckled.

"My gut keep falling out and they keep puttin it ret back in." She chuckled again.

I smiled.

"My name is Sheila. What's yours?"

"Marge."

Sometimes I give people who I will never see again a made-up, shortened version of my first name.

"When you goin under?"

"Tomorrow morning...early I think."

"Well, don't you worry. You gonna be fine." *I'm beginning to like Sheila.*

She was right. I was back in my room in time for a late breakfast. I was propped up with pillows. A wad of gauze-like padding was tucked between and around my butt cheeks which were resting comfortably on an innertube shaped pillow. I was enjoying the relief from pain. I was enjoying my solace. Sheila was away. I was sucking orange juice through a straw.

My door opened. Who could be disturbing my peace? Mama had already made her stop by, and it was not time yet to collect my breakfast tray. I couldn't see who opened my door. I waited for them to round the corner. I heard voices.

"Oh my goodness. Who dey from?"

"Cora Mae, dey beautiful."

I heard Mama's voice, "I don't know. Dey sho is butiful."

Mama entered. Behind her were three other Black ladies. They were hidden behind a big, giant bouquet of red roses, topped off with four or five balloons with words like "Get well," "Love," and "Happiness" stamped on them.

I thought this florist shop display was for Sheila. But the group stopped at my bedside.

"What is this?" I asked. I sat up and got a reminder-pain in my butt.

"These are for me?" I asked. "I didn't...nobody knows I'm here."

One of the hidden ladies answered.

"Well, somebody out dere know you heah. Ain't nobody ever sent me no flowers lak dis."

The ladies couldn't contain their enthusiasm for this display.

"Ooo whee."

"Set 'um over dere."

"Let her see de card first."

While they were fussing over the placement of the twelve long stem red roses with three heart shaped balloons reaching almost to the ceiling, I asked Mama, "Did you tell anybody about my being here?"

"I ain't said nothin 'bout you to nobody."

Mama was smiling. The ladies were beaming. One lady in her blue smock handed me the card. She stepped back cupping her cheeks in her hands. Eyes were wide, bodies leaned in, waiting. I opened the card and scanned the contents looking for the name of the sender. *Damn it! Gerald!*

For the ladies, I smiled big as I placed the card over my heart. A collective exhale of congratulatory sighs filled the room.

"I told you."

"Didn't I tell ya it had ta be somebode special?"

The heavy set, blue smocked lady leaned over to me.

"Honey, you lucky to have a man like dis."

She spread her fat arms toward that extravagant display on the windowsill. "Ain't no man gon spend dat kina money on you unless his nose is wiiiiiiide open!"

"You rite 'bout dat, girl" and "Sho nufs" were heard all around, even from Mama.

I smiled. I nodded my head shyly and fingered the card with my eyes closed. I opened my eyes and eyed the flowers. I indulged the ladies' need to have these expensive twelve long stem red roses with three get well white heart shaped balloons be a love story. I put on a show for Mama in front of her friends.

When I got home, I took down my notebook from the top shelf in my closet. I opened it to the page entitled *Five-Year Plan*. Gerald's name was printed in my handwriting under 'get a boyfriend.' I put a line through Gerald's name with a black Bic pen.

24
FRIENDS

On Friday, I am meeting Kelvin. He is getting a room at the Quality Inn near the St. Louis airport. The only person who knows about his visit is Tia.

"Why are you going to bed with a guy if you don't like him? That's crazy."

It is Thursday and she is driving me to work, a habit left over from my butt pain days. She is still talking too much and driving too fast. I take charge of making conversation.

"I didn't say anything about going to bed with him. We are just friends. He just told me about a school that I happened to apply to, and happened to get in. People help each other like that all the time. I am not saying 'thank you' by going to bed with him. Kelvin understands that. Anyway, I don't like him like that. He's just a young man wanting to see a bit of St. Louis, a city near the south that he has never been to before. Plus, he's a deep thinker, a philosopher, and he likes to talk and..."

We arrive at school in one piece.

"Ok," Tia says, walking into the building. "Tell me about it on Monday, if you can get out of bed."

Kelvin's plane arrived at about one-thirty in the afternoon. I knocked on the door of his hotel room at about three. He opened the door with a big smile, a drawn out "Hellllllo," and a big hug.

"Come in, come in. How you been?"

He was directing me to the one soft chair in the room. He sat in the straight-backed brown chair at the desk. He talked about his flight.

"There were so many people, and the weather, there were storm clouds."

He was talking about getting to the hotel.

"I had no problem getting a taxi, much easier than in New York."

I was not listening. I was looking at this young man sitting before me. He was the same as when I met him in Ghana a year ago. He is slim, taller than I remember, with a light brown face and a short, cropped haircut. He sits now with his eyes shiny. He's still blinking. *He should check his contact lenses.*

His fingers are long and expressive as he talks. His dress, the same. He's wearing khakis and that short sleeved multicolored button-down shirt with the pencil guard inserted in the front pocket.

He's excited. Air is being pushed out through his nose as he speaks. I can tell he can't wait to move beyond just conversation. His eyes had widened when he noticed the change in my appearance. I am no longer sporting a large, wiry Afro. My hair is straight with a Mary Tyler Moore flip. It bounces with the slightest turn of my head. The skirt of my slim-topped burgundy dress flares and lays just over my crossed legs, exposing just enough thigh to increase the speed with which he pushes air through his nostrils.

I want him to feel comfortable. He is my guest.

I stood up, walked to the window, and looked out at hotel signs, parking lots and fast-food restaurants. I turned around to face him. He was on his feet looking at me. I moved the conversation to food.

"So, what would you like to do? Take a walk to one of the restaurants? There's a Howard Johnson's across the street, and that looks like an Italian place over there...a diner over there...I like restaurants with lots of choices, don't you?"

I was moving from one end of the large window to the other, scanning the scenery for signs of food offerings. I stopped.

Kelvin's body is next to mine. He is hovering behind me. He wraps his arms around my waist and buries his head in my bouncy, flipped hair. He is mumbling words. I have a hard time making out what he is saying. I stand there like a statue, hoping he backs away, stops messing up my hair and answers my question. I try to wiggle free with "I didn't hear which restaurant you like."

He lifts his head out of my hair, still pressing his body against mine. He starts gnawing at my left ear and my neck and whispering words that sound like "to stay in...get to know each other..." I had a hard time hearing what he was saying with all that air being pushed out through his nose.

I untangle his arms from my waist and step aside. I chastised him. My hands are flying up and out to emphasize my points.

"Kelvin, you just got here. We've got the whole weekend to get to know each other. Right now, why don't we talk about New York and about Columbia...and..."

I was searching for anything except pursuing what "getting to know you" meant.

He walked around the coffee table pushing air and staring me down. He takes my hands in his like we were about to do a "do-si-do."

No strength in these hands, too soft, bet these hands never chopped wood.

"Ok," he said, looking at me with those blinking, shiny eyes. "Let's just walk around and see what we like."

Thank goodness! This guy can never be more than a friend to me. I can never put his name under 'boyfriend' in my five-year plan.

I don't like holding hands, but I allow Kelvin to take my left hand in his. I was open to anything to get him out of that hotel room. I feel the creases on his fingers. He is annoyingly rubbing and caressing my fingers.

We chose the crowded diner. Johnny Cash's "Daddy Sang Bass" is blaring over the speakers. I like Johnny Cash.

This is just the kind of atmosphere I need tonight. We squeeze into a small booth and yell across the table to each other. We each order a 7 Up.

"How are your studies coming? Did you finalize your major?" I ask.

He is sipping his 7 Up from his glass through a plastic straw. I take a sip from my glass.

"I'm still taking courses in theology and philosophy. I like them both, so I'll probably get a double major and then start a doctorate in philosophy."

"Wow, that is impressive. You are smart enough to get that done. Well, good luck with that. So, what happened to Greg?"

"Oh, he graduated and got a professorship at City University. He is getting his doctorate over there. He told me that Sylvia is moving to New York, too."

"Oh, my goodness, that would be great! An African reunion!"

I enjoyed the conversation and the food. He asked me about my work and my friends. I told him about people at work, like Tia, and about students not liking to work hard. I told him about girlfriends from SIU.

"Do you find time to go to church?" he asked.

"I sure do...almost every Sunday. I have a couple of friends there. How about you?" *He probably has his Bible in his suitcase.*

"Yes...every Sunday and sometimes on Wednesdays...I'm still deciding on my majors."

He wanted to know about fun places to go in St. Louis and said, "Surely you have friends besides Tia and your students."

"Yes," I said. "I go out with other teachers sometimes. I have a doctor friend who likes steak, so we go out when he's free. What about you?" I asked. "What do you do for fun?"

He wipes his mouth, his eyes glaring.

"I have too much work to do. If I'm not reading or writing papers, I'm home." He's pushing air through his nose.

"Anyway, I don't need to go out. I have you." He reaches for my hand that is on the table. I smile and cringe but allow him to finger the creases in my palm. I pull my hand back and point my finger at him in a chastising manner. *This guy needs scolding like he's a little kid!*

"Oh, you shouldn't put all your eggs in one basket, Kelvin. You're a young college man. You should be going out and having fun. You know people in New York better than you know me."

"That's why I'm here," he said. "I want to get to know you better."

Shit!

I took my leave for home right from the diner's parking lot. Kelvin gave me a peck on the cheek. We agreed that I would come again to his hotel at around ten on Saturday.

By three p.m. on Saturday, Kelvin was packing his bag and heading back to New York.

I arrived at the hotel as planned. I was wearing my yellow wrap-around dress and my multicolored sandals from my London trip. I held a black clutch purse.

I stood at the hotel door, took two deep breaths, then knocked lightly. Kelvin opened the door wide. He was wrapped in a white hotel robe. I was smiling and in the process of saying "Hi," when he pushed the door closed behind me with his foot. He swept me in his arms and began kissing me anywhere he could, my hair, my neck, my ears, my eyes. He gave me no time to deposit my purse on the soft orange chair!

I turned my face and and tried to push him away. He was suffocating me with his noisy breathing and excited mumblings. He smelled of Aramis. *That was good.*

"Kelvin, stop it. Stop!" I was bending, turning, and pushing. He dragged me and my purse to his queen-sized bed. I still had my black patent leather shoes on! With one hand he loosened the ties on my yellow wrap-around dress. I was trying to push him away. *He has strong arms for a boney guy with soft hands.* His lips were still searching for mine. With one hand, he was tugging at my bra.

I screamed and started hitting him with my clutch purse.

"Kelvin! Stop! Stop it right now." He was smothering my words and screams with his lips and pinning my clutch purse arm down with the hand not tugging at my bra. "You want the hotel staff to come up here? I will keep screaming until they do. Now get away from me."

He stopped. He swung his legs off the bed and stood up. Air from his flaring nostrils are quite audible now as he fussed with the belts on his white robe. I slipped off the bed, re-wrapped my dress, ran my hand over my hair and moved to collect my purse from the bed. I stood next to the orange chair holding my purse with both hands.

In a pleading and sympathetic voice, and with my hands reaching toward him, I said, "Kelvin, there must be some misunderstanding. I don't know what's going on. We're friends, good friends. I don't go to bed with my friends."

He had wrapped himself in his white robe and moved to look out the window during my pleading. His head was down, his breathing was noisy. Something I said caused him to spin around and began to yell and gesticulate wildly. "You don't go to bed with your friends. You think I'm naïve. You think I don't know what's going on here!"

Well...yeah to both!

He leaned over the bed and jabbed the air towards me with his forefinger. He stabbed each word with emphasis. "You're sleeping with those guys—your 'doctor friend' and your 'teacher friend!'"

Satisfied with his conclusion, he returned to staring out the window at hotel signs, passing cars and restaurant billboards.

"What?" I was shaking my head in disbelief while maintaining my position near the orange chair. I yelled at his back.

"I'm not sleeping with anybody! Where did this come from? My doctor? He has nothing to do with what's going on here. In any case, none of this is your business."

He turned around smirking and puffing. His tone is patronizing.

"You're sleeping with this doctor. You're sleeping with your teacher friend. Who else are you sleeping with? Huh...Huh? You couldn't stop talking about your 'friends' and you don't sleep with 'friends'? You think I came all the way down here just to see a 'friend'? I don't have that kind of money. "

His eyes are shining darts, his noisy nose puffs permeating the room. He was yelling now. "Why do you think I wanted you to come to New York? Huh? Why? So I could have another 'friend?'"

I maintained my position near the orange couch chair as I continued to try to ease the tension.

"Kelvin, I'm sorry that you think I don't want to sleep with you because of my doctor friend or my teacher friend. I don't want to sleep with you because we are friends! Kelvin, you have never even held my hands, except last night. All that time in Africa, we just talked and went sightseeing together. Never did we do anything beyond that! And you know why that's all we did? Because we are just friends. Maybe something could happen later, but..."

"Forget it. I'm leaving." He grabbed his suitcase off the floor near the window and placed it on the side of the bed nearest the window. He hurried to the chest under the television, opened the top drawer and took out two neatly folded multicolored collared shirts. He placed them in the brown suitcase on the bed.

"Kelvin, I don't know what to say. I was looking forward to seeing you and I'm sorry about the misunderstanding."

I moved toward the door and maintained a stance at the door with my right hand on the doorknob. He continued his trips between his suitcase and the chest of drawers pushing air in both directions.

The tension in the room is heavy. I pull open the door, turn to look at Kelvin who is bent over his packed brown suitcase and breathing heavily through his nostrils.

"Goodbye. Kelvin. I'm really sorry to lose your friendship."

I closed the door behind me.

There was silence in the hallway.

25
CUTTING TIES

Dear Margaret Edwards,

"...no on-campus housing is available at this time. We have arranged temporary housing for you at the YWCA. You will be contacted when accommodations become available on campus."

—Columbia University, Teachers College, Residential Services

No housing on campus! What is the 'YWCA'? Where's that!

I had to talk to somebody. Surely not my parents...about living in New York in some place I never heard of!

I called Keith. We're sitting in his car in Gimbels parking lot in Ladue.

"I'm sure you're not the only student at the Y. You'll be fine."

He looked over the letter.

"Lower Manhattan. That's not a bad spot."

He reached over and gave me a long hug.

"Stop worrying," he said, smiling. "It's temporary. Just think, you're a student at Columbia University!"

I was not convinced that my housing situation was sorted out, and neither was he.

Mama called Uncle Pete and his wife Wilma about my coming to New York and got their phone number.

"You call Pete if you need anythang...he been in New York fer yeahs. He knows everthan 'bout dat place."

She didn't know that I wanted no family involved in my life in New York. I had no intention of calling Uncle Pete for anything. *I am starting a new life in New York.*

I had no intention of returning to work in Missouri either. I resigned from the St. Louis Public School system and collected my fifty dollars from my retirement fund.

I made one last check in the bedroom that I shared with my sister for the last three years. No visible trace of my life remained there. Everything that was mine, clothes, souvenirs, college papers and college books was gone. Clothes I didn't want, I gave to my sisters. Everything else was dumped in the garbage can. I even finally discarded my London tapes from my video camera that was lost in Madrid.

I tucked my burgundy spiral notebook containing my five-year plan into my small green carry-on. *Cecelia and Millie...where are they now with their goals?* That was three years ago. Time is running out.

My two large green suitcases that had gotten me through Europe and Africa were waiting at the front door. They were scuffed and scarred even after being scrubbed down with Comet and Lysol. Arriving in New York with shabby suitcases would give the wrong impression.

My brother Frank drove me to the airport. I exited my green Hatchback. It belonged to him now.

Book III

"May your life be like a wildflower, growing freely in the beauty and joy of each day."

Native American Proverb

1

GENTLEMAN CALLER, SEQUINS, AND HARLEM

I dragged my suitcases to the taxi line. A round stubbled-faced driver opened the taxi door and stepped aside.

"Where to?" he asked.

I opened my letter from Teachers College Residential Services.

"The YWCA," I said.

His eyes scanned my body from head to toe.

"Ok," he said.

We pulled up in front of a tall building with a red brick front. All the buildings around were tall. Lots of mostly White people were walking by like wherever they were going, they had to get there fast. I followed the stubble-faced taxi driver with my suitcases up the steps and into the small lobby of the building. I gave him a dollar tip. He stared at my tip and his eyes again scanned my body from head to toe. He left the lobby.

"Hello. Welcome to the Young Women's Christian Association."

I followed a woman's voice to a small window with bars. I felt like I was talking to a bank teller. The head of a brown-haired, pleasant, faced woman appeared behind the bars.

"Oh, hello, I said. "My name is Margaret Edwards and

Columbia University said..."

"You're all checked in Margaret. Just sign here and you're all set. A few house rules are in this packet along with your room key. Elevator is around the corner. Ok?"

"Yes. Thank you," I stammered. "But I was wondering if there are any other Columbia University students staying here."

"Sorry," the woman said. "I'm not at liberty to discuss other guests in our facility. Enjoy your stay."

Upstairs I knocked lightly on the door that matched the number on the key in my hand.

The door was opened by a smiling, blonde, White girl with brown roots.

"Hi, I'm Hanna. I guess we're roomies."

She extended a manicured, red nail polished hand. I took her hand in my unpolished and unmanicured hand.

"I'm Margaret. Are you going to Columbia, too?"

"Columbia?"

She had a confused look on her face.

"Oh," I said. I was just wondering if you were also staying here until a room opens up at Columbia."

"No way!"

Hanna was helping me pull my suitcases to one of the two small beds on either side of the room.

"I'm not smart enough for college. Columbia? No way! I'm a working girl! This is your bed, and your dresser is this one. This is a small pad, but the location of this Y is great. Restaurants, hamburger places, hot dog stands. Anything you want right here. You'll see."

I took a few necessities out of my green carry-on and placed them in my assigned drawers. I took out the rules from my packet and laid them on my bed.

"You don't need to read those rules," Hanna said from her prone position on her multi-pillowed bed.

"All you need to know is 'No men past the lobby.' Break that rule and you're outta here."

Around six p.m., the phone rang. Hanna flung herself off her bed and grabbed it.

"Hello? Yes. Ok."

She sounded disappointed. She hung up the phone and turned to me.

"A gentleman is waiting downstairs to see you."

I look up from the rules.

"What gentleman? I don't know any gentlemen. I just got here."

Hanna is staring at me from her perch.

"Well, people get to know you pretty fast around here."

I picked up my purse from the blue blanket and headed downstairs. From the elevator, I strolled to the bank teller window to inquire...

"Margaret!"

I turned toward that voice. Keith was walking toward me smiling. I threw both my hands over my mouth to keep from screaming.

"Keith, what are you doing here? You didn't tell me you were coming!" I buried myself in the comfort of his arms. I felt the strength of his embrace.

"You know I wouldn't let you come to this place by yourself. Let's go to dinner," he said, pushing me away at arm's length.

"You look like you made it here without a scratch."

He hailed a taxi to take us to a steakhouse some distance from the Y. He ordered wine for himself and sparkling water for me. I was anxious to get answers to my questions.

"Why are you here. Why didn't you tell me you were coming? The Y is nice, don't you think? It's not bad at all. I have a roommate who…"

Keith stopped me. He covered my left hand with his.

"I'm here because I wanted to look in on you to help you make a smooth transition to this big city. If they had put you in Columbia housing, I would have stayed in St. Louis. I'm sure the

'Y' is a safe place for young women when they are inside, but there are some sleazy people and sleazy things going on right outside your door. The sooner you're out of this area, the better." *So he was here to look after me! I had planned on a clean break from him and Gerald and Kelvin...*

"What about your patients? How long are you going to be here?"

My questions kept coming.

"My patients are fine, and they will be fine until I get back. Right now, it's you that I care about. I'll be here a couple more days, until you get settled in University Housing."

The next day, we took the 'underground' to Columbia.

Keith said, "In New York, just call it a train."

We walked from the train down Broadway. We entered the tall gates of Columbia University and strolled along the walkways of the campus. We turned left on Amsterdam Avenue and walked to 120th Street where Teacher's College is located.

My eyes were searching for Whittier Hall. We walked past a tall brown building with steps on two sides leading up to glass double doors. Engraved into the concrete between the steps were the words *Whittier Hall.*

I stopped. I controlled my urge to scream. I pointed instead.

"Keith, this is my dorm! Whittier Hall. This is where I'm gonna be living. Look at the size of this building, and they don't have a room for me?"

"Um, interesting location," Keith said, looking up at the building and then gazing down the street. "You may as well be living in Harlem."

"Where's Harlem?" I asked, as I was slowly walking and peering into the shops next to Whittier Hall, a sandwich shop, a key and shoe shop and a drug store. Across the street is an appliance store and a dress boutique. *Perfect location!*

"Where's Harlem?" I asked again.

"Next block and you're in it."

We walked down Amsterdam to 125th street.

Keith announced, "This is Harlem. This is 125th Street."

I heard bad things about Harlem from Daddy, even though he had never been here.

"You going up dere to New York to go to skool. You ain't got no business bein 'round dem peoples in Harlem wit dem drugs and dranking wine all time a nite. Dey jes like dem peoples in Milwalkee. Dey never go ta bed."

Kelvin had told me not to worry about Harlem.

Looking up and down 125th Street from one end of the street to the other, Black people were everywhere. I had never been around so many Black people in America before. Men in green and red dashikis and women in African dresses with matching head wraps mixed and mingled with other men and women and kids dressed in white shirts and short skirts and short shorts. Everybody was walking, talking, laughing, leaning in doorways, pushing strollers, carrying over-stuffed shopping bags, eating from paper bags, and waiting. A lot of people were just standing, looking, and waiting.

I didn't spend much time in the room at the Y. When I got home from outings with Keith, Hanna was always away. When I left in the morning, she was snuggled under her bed covers. With all those sequined tops and tall, spiked heels on her side of the closet, I began to wonder what kind of work she was doing that kept her out most of the night.

I mentioned my concern to Keith.

"I never see Hanna. She's always out when I get home. I wonder where she works."

Keith looked at me askew.

"What do you mean, 'you wonder where she works'? What do you think she does for a living?"

"She sorta said she works down the street, maybe in a bar or something."

He leans toward me pushing his unfinished steak to the side.

"Have you seen any black skirts and white blouses in her closet? Have you seen black patent leather shoes and collared dresses in her closet?"

Keith was staring at me, waiting for an answer. I tapped my right pointing finger on the white tablecloth while staring into space trying to recall Hanna's wardrobe. He answered me.

"The answer is 'no.' That girl is a working girl, all right. She's a prostitute! That school put you in a whore house. And that is reprehensible!"

"Oh, Keith, stop it. Columbia wouldn't do that...be reprehensible. Anyway, it's the Young Women's *Christian* Organization. They have all these rules about safety and men in your room and…" *I have to look up reprehensible.*

Keith pulled his steak back.

"Margaret, stop being so naive. Why do you think I came up here? This is New York. Rules are broken with impunity in this city."

He cut into his steak.

I appreciated and noted the new word, *impunity.*

When I got home that night, there was a folded piece of paper on my bed.

Margaret Edwards was written in black on the outer fold. As usual, Hanna was not in the room. I looked around. Who's been in this room? My heart started racing.

I picked up the folded paper, opened it slowly and read out loud.

> *We have a room for you at Whittier Hall. Please check in at the front desk tomorrow by 12 noon.*
>
> *— Teacher's College, Residence Housing Office.*

My thought processes were incoherent. Maybe this is a trick. I read the note again. How did they know my name? Who put the note on my bed? It must have been Hanna. I've been in her room for two nights. She's trying to get rid of me. Where is she anyway? *Oh, yeah, she works nights.*

I grabbed my black clutch purse and my key and rushed to the downstairs payphone. I dialed Keith's number.

"Hello." *Right number. That's his voice.*

"Keith," I said breathlessly, clutching the phone tight to my right ear with my right hand and fumbling to open the folded note with my left hand. The note fell to the floor. I bent and retrieved it.

"Margaret? Is that you? What's the matter?"

"Yeah, it's me. I'm just not sure. I got this note. It was on my bed."

"And what did the note say?" His voice was calm like he was talking to one of his patients.

"It said I have a room in Whittier Hall, and I'm supposed to check in tomorrow before noon!"

"Ok. So, we will go to Whittier Hall tomorrow, before noon and you will check in."

He said it in that 'know it all' voice.

The next morning, I was expecting Hanna to spring from her covers and admit that she had forged that note. She did not even come home last night. *I think that's against the rules!*

When I came down the elevator with my two green bags and my carry-on, the woman behind the bars yelled out to me.

"Miss Edwards, I see you got my note. I had to let myself in. Hanna signed out last night. Room's empty now. Sign right here. Good luck to ya."

We took a taxi uptown to Whittier Hall. I wanted to take the train. I needed the practice. But my bags were too big.

We were sitting in the back seat of a yellow taxicab with seat belts tight around our laps. *I'm going to be living in New York City. I'm going to be living in a dorm with people like me, men and women who want something different...*

"I can go back home to my practice now that you are safely ensconced in University Housing." Keith reached over and patted my left hand.

I gave him a no-teeth smile hoping to hide my thoughts. *What do I do and say when the taxi stops in front of Whittier Hall? Is he gonna try to kiss me and say stuff about 'missing' me? Is he going to want to keep in touch and visit me in New York from time to time? Or is he going to see this as an opportunity to exit my life and lift his chest with pride that I was able to break free?*

The driver pulled to a stop in front of Whittier Hall, got out and opened the curbside door. He walked back to open the trunk. I heard the click of Keith's seat belt. I fumbled with mine before it released me.

Keith slid out of the open curbside door and extended a hand to me. He instructed the driver to deposit my suitcases on the landing up the steps. The two of us were left standing near the closed curbside door of the taxi. I was holding my small green carry-on bag on my shoulder with my right hand and clutching my black purse to my chest with my left hand. No hands were left for hugging.

I watched students walking in and out of the tall doors of Whittier Hall. *What if somebody saw me talking to or even hugging a man twice my age? Entry and first impressions are so important.*

Keith said, "Coming to New York for school is a momentous step for you, and your life. You'll do well."

He leaned in, gave me a dry peck in my right cheek, turned and took his seat in the taxi.

Through the window, he said, "Give me a call when you get settled in."

I stood there on the curb watching his taxi pull away.

Such a classy guy!

2

IVY LEAGUE ENTRY

I met a potential boyfriend before I had even seen my room! I was dragging my heavy suitcases into the lobby of Whittier Hall, when this good-looking, thirty-something Black man appeared at my side.

"Let me help you with your bags," he said. *I guess suitcases are called "bags" up here in New York.*

"Oh, thank you," I said. You're very kind."

He lifted both 'bags' and placed them around the corner near an elevator. Across from the elevator was a long, chest-high counter. The man disappeared through a side door and reappeared behind the counter.

"Let's get you checked in." *Such a professional voice.*

I watched him gather forms, search through index cards, and get a ballpoint pen from a desk drawer. He was wearing a pressed collared white shirt with the sleeves rolled up to his elbows. *Nice, slim body. He must spend a lot of time in the gym. He's probably part of a work-study program. I admire a man who works to pay his way through school.*

"What's your name?"

He looked up at me from a clipboard with papers attached.

"I want to make sure I have the right person."

"Oh, I'm Margaret Edwards. I was staying at the YWCA, just until a room opened up here."

I leaned into the counter so he could hear me and to help him find my name on the clipboard list.

I followed his manicured finger down a list of names.

"That's my name," I blurted out. I pointed a finger in need of a manicure on the clipboard next to my name. I stepped back and waited not wanting to appear too aggressive, that first impression thing.

"Ok, let's get you settled in."

He reached under the counter and took out a room chart. He placed it on the counter. I watched his blue pen move across the chart.

"You're in…let me see...room 7G on the seventh floor...um, you got a very nice room."

He looked up at me and flashed a set of white teeth that were too big for his mouth. *That's disappointing.*

I gave him a no-teeth smile.

"There is no cooking in the room. If you need to heat up food, you can do that down here. The floors are divided. Men's floors are two, three, and four. Women's floors are five, six and seven. All the information you need is in this information packet."

He handed me a blue folder.

"Any other questions, just ask at the desk. My name is Bill. Here's your key. Sign here and you're all set. Any questions?"

"No, not yet," I said through another smile that said, 'don't mess with me…yet…I know all about fresh meat.'

He appeared on my side of the counter from the side door. He walked past me and pushed the elevator button.

I could feel his eyes on me as he made me an offer.

"Let me help you with your bags." *And what else do you want to help me with?*

He walked around me to my bags.

"Thanks, Bill." I said. *I know your game.*

"If you could put them on the elevator, I can manage from there."

He lifted the two bags and placed them on the right side of the elevator. I stepped in and stood on the left side of the elevator. I pushed the close button. I left him standing in front of the closing door, eyeing my legs.

3

BLACK DEARTH

What a room! Big, high ceilings and so clean! It didn't look anything like my dorm room in the sorority house back at SIU. This room is private, and off the hallway in the corner near a stairway.

A closet was on the right side near the entrance. There was an oversized twin bed on one side of the room covered with a blue quilt with two pillows covered with white pillowcases propped up against the back wall. A large center window with white blinds and white curtains provided a view of 120th Street and Amsterdam Avenue. A built-in desk surrounded by shelves covered the wall across from the bed. There was a blue-cushioned chair at the desk and a blue couch chair near the window. *Somebody must really like blue!*

I was standing in the middle of the room, mesmerized. *This will be my home for the next two years!*

I looked under the blue quilt at clean white sheets. I looked out the window at White students jaywalking across 120th Street. I ran my fingers over the shelves looking for some flaw.

I heard a light knock on my door. I opened the door to a smiling, brown-skinned woman, dressed in a gray and white uniform. She was holding a blue feather duster. She looked like a cleaning lady.

"Hola," she said. She was looking around me and pointing into my room. "You hav bery nice room. Me Bela...I clean yo room...two days clean Monday...Thursday." She noted the days on her fingers.

"You clean my room?" I asked.

She laughed and spread her arms wide.

"I clean everything."

I was standing in the doorway. The door to the room nearest to mine opened. I heard a voice say, "Hola, Bela? I thought I heard you out here."

Bela waved and scurried down the hallway pecking at the wall with her blue duster.

Still holding open my door, I looked around the corner and saw a small doll-like figure with a big, reddish-brown Afro. She was smiling and coming toward me with an outstretched hand. She was wearing a white button-down blouse in need of ironing and a pair of brown bell bottom jeans with fraying hems.

"Hi, I'm Layla. Welcome, neighbor!"

"Thank you," I replied, returning the smile. "I am so glad to finally be here. Would you like to come in?"

Layla was about my height, small-framed and light skinned. She smiled a lot, but she seemed lethargic. She dragged herself around my room looking out the window mostly until she settled into the blue couch chair. I sat on the padded desk chair.

"What's this about cleaning my room?" I asked.

Layla's face became slightly animated as did her hands.

"Oh, girl, you don't have to worry about cleaning or changing your sheets. Bela does all that. All you have to do is go to class and pay your tuition. But I don't know how long the maids are gonna keep their jobs. The University says having all these cleaners is costing them too much money. They voted to get rid of them all. I don't know what is gonna happen...we have been protesting...and marching all over the school. . .students are mad."

She dragged herself to her feet.

"Listen, let me go so you can unpack. If you want, I can drop by later and we can go get something to eat and walk around a little bit."

"Oh, that would be great." I walked her to the door.

"Thanks for dropping by. It was so nice meeting you," I said with sincerity.

Layla left with a, "See you later."

As I unpacked, I wallowed in my good fortune. This is what I hoped for, to be at Columbia University among smart Black people, and especially smart Black men!

I just met a Black girl, somebody to hang out with and learn from. And I just caught the eye of this guy Bill at the desk! Me, the great-granddaughter of slaves. I'm at Columbia University, and I have a cleaning lady! I wonder if the University is trying to get rid of the help because Black students are here.

I took my burgundy, spiral notebook from my carry-on bag and put it on the top shelf of the sliding door closet. I left my toiletries in the bag. I hung up my dresses, skirts, white blouses, and my hooded long black coat. I filled the three closet drawers with sweaters, underwear, pantyhose, and socks. I lined up my church shoes, my London sandals, and my black loafers on the closet floor. I stood back and surveyed my belongings.

I gotta get some new clothes!

When I met up with Layla later in the day, she was still wearing that white shirt in need of ironing and those same fraying brown pants. On her feet were a pair of strapped sandals. I was wearing my most casual outfit, a multi-striped button-down shirt with brown pants. I wore my black loafers on my feet.

We took the elevator down to the first floor and walked toward the information desk. Bill was there shuffling papers, but he looked up and smiled at us with his big teeth.

"Hey, guy, any mail for me?" Layla asked.

Bill regarded me, but walked to the back slotted wall, took envelopes from one slot, and flipped through each envelope.

"Not today," he responded, with his back still toward us.

He returned to the counter and looking at me, he asked, "Where you ladies off to?"

I gave him a no-teeth smile but deferred to Layla.

"Just to the sandwich shop," she said as we were exiting.

I said nothing, but I could feel his eyes on my butt as I rounded the corner.

We went to a small sandwich shop a block from Whittier. The place was busy with students yelling out their orders to two guys behind a high display case. One guy had a White face, the other a Black, good-looking face. Layla seemed quite friendly with the Black guy and he with her. She yelled over the noise.

"Jay, this is Marg. She just arrived. We'll have two of the usual."

I gave Jay a wave, but he kept his head down. He made and bagged the 'usual' and handed it over the top of the display case to Layla.

"How much do I owe?" I yelled to Layla as I was unzipping my black clutch purse.

"Nothing," she replied.

She guided me past the lines and out the door. I didn't see her pay for the sandwiches and the drinks. Maybe she has some kind of 'line of credit' system going on.

I was trying to take everything in. I have a great room and I've met two good-looking young, Black men on my first day! I couldn't wait to ask Layla about what's going on with them. I held out and talked about other things first.

We walked back to Whittier and sat at a table outside in the courtyard. The 'usual' for both of us turned out to be overstuffed cold cut sandwiches with a Coke and chips on the side. As we ate, I told her about my stay at the YWCA, but leaving out the parts about my roommate being a prostitute and about Keith and his showing up to help me settle in. I told her about my coming from teaching in St. Louis to Teachers College to get my masters in guidance and counseling.

I learned that Layla was in her second year at TC as a music major, concentrating on piano. She was from Atlanta, the only daughter of a doctor. Her plans were to move from TC to Julliard.

She was picking at her sandwich, tearing off small pieces and chewing slowly. I finished half my sandwich and wrapped up the other half for later.

"So," I said coyly, "What's the story with Bill and Jay?"

She just looked at me.

"What do you mean?"

"I mean, they are really handsome guys. What's their story? What are they studying?"

"Wait a minute," she said. "You're talking about Bill who works at the desk and Jay from the sandwich shop?"

She started laughing and tapping her slim fingers on the table.

"Those guys! They aren't students. They're just working for a living. That's funny. You thought they were students! No, those guys are nice, but they were doing these jobs when I came here a year ago."

"Wow," I said, trying not to sound deflated. "So, who are the Black guys on campus or in Whittier?"

"Listen," she said leaning forward, "I don't know where the Black men are. I have not seen or met any at Columbia. And for sure none are living in Whittier Hall. I've seen a few undergraduate guys running around, but graduate guys, forget it. The only Blacks in Whittier are a couple of girls. And they keep to themselves mostly."

"Wow, that's disappointing," I said.

I didn't want to sound desperate, so I changed the subject slightly.

"So, what do you do for fun?"

Layla didn't have to tell me about her well-to-do upbringing, I saw it for myself. She never asked the price of anything, never finished her food, and never wrapped it up and saved it for a later meal. She was as out of place as me. She was trying hard to fit in with her frayed brown bell bottoms and big Angela Davis look-a-like Afro. But I have an eye for privilege.

Her room was small but looked like a magazine picture. Her bed cover was store bought. It was a cotton terry cloth white bedspread, not the University issued blue blanket. There were pink stuffed animals perfectly sitting upright on the back of her bed. Her desk and shelves were covered with silver framed pictures of smiling family and friends. A pink fluffy large rug pulled everything together into a perfect bedroom for a fifteen-year-old who loves pink.

After about a week, I was able to confirm what Layla had said. "There are no Black men in Whittier Hall." I turned my attention to Black women. I counted five, including Layla and me.

The women in the dorm included an older woman from Dallas who was finishing a degree in social work, a quiet, pretty young woman from North Carolina working on her doctorate in French, and a tall, pretty Maasai-looking woman who is in my counseling program. It was good to meet the social worker and the French student, but I hope the Maasai woman and I would have a lot to talk about since we were the only Blacks in the counseling program.

4
MEET, DRINK, MUNCH

The Counseling Program participants gathered in a large upstairs classroom in Russell Hall. Classical music was being piped in, drinks were being poured and mingling and smiles were all around. I felt comfortable being among my classmates and drinking 7 Up from a plastic cup.

I surveyed the participants. Most seemed to be recent college graduates and seemed to know each other. The Masai-looking Black woman was in a chatty conversation with the two young counseling professors. The three had drinks in hand.

The meeting began with Professors Jake and Conley welcoming us as the first "select group" for this pilot program. They gave an overview of the thinking behind this two-year Master's Program in Guidance and Counseling.

Jake started to explain. "You will be immersed in the theory and the practical, lectures and interactions with experts, and..." The words were not flowing coherently. He couldn't control his laughter. Conley took over explaining that they started celebrating early because, "We are so delighted that our idea for this program has come to friction...I mean fruition."

The individual introductions began.

From the young group, there were names like Julie, Isaac, Tammy, and Sarah. They didn't live in Whittier Hall. They lived on the 'outskirts of New York City.' I imagine their bedrooms were like Layla's. I saw privilege in their ankle high brown leather boots and their collared short jackets with attached fur-lined hoods. They didn't carry clutch purses.

There was a young married couple from South Carolina with a heavy southern accent. They smiled a lot and wanted to "come to Columbia to this great program."

I didn't trust them.

There were a few other nameless young brunettes and faux blondes all vying to be more scintillating than the next. I took note of one such blonde named Cami. She was tall, handsome, and flirtatious. But it was her long, blonde hair that was the 'head turner.' She especially turned the heads of the doctoral student and Professor Conley. They gathered around her, groveling for her attention. I found the two of them disgusting.

The Maasai look-alike was next to introduce herself. According to our class list, her name was Grace. She is tall, thin, lanky, and very dark with a short, trimmed Afro framing her pretty face. She is smiling big. She opens her mouth to speak.

Is she speaking? I hear squeaking. Her voice is like that of a meowing kitten! Shame! She squeaked something about being from upstate New York.

During my introduction, my voice was strong when I announced my hometown, University City, Missouri. I received a round of applause for having come the furthest away to be a part of this program.

"Bonding activities" seemed to be a priority for Jake and Conley. I was hoping that Grace would give me a sign during these early days of activities that we had something in common. But from where I was sitting or standing alone most of the time, all I saw was her laughing and chatting with the two professors like they were her best friends! Maybe they were. Maybe she had been recruited by them so they could check the "diversity" box.' My acceptance into the program must have been a bonus!

The students who lived on the outskirts of New York City were always too ready to host a bonding party. They arranged the carpooling, and we traveled forty minutes from New York City to one of their homes. The setting was always the same: a big backyard, a covered pool and enough leftover space to accommodate stations for drinks, burgers and hot dogs, barbecued brisket, and other things that Isaac said were canapes.

Once I stood on the manicured lawns with my flowered paper plate, I always settled for brisket and a hot dog. There was no one to talk to so I wandered toward the stations closest to the lighted patios. I wanted to see inside the houses. I saw long white draperies, big glass chandeliers and long tables with armless chairs.

The students who lived "on the outskirts of New York" hosted two or three more bonding parties. I chose not to attend.

5
THE HANDLER

When I first got to Teachers College, I was open to going to parties off-campus where Black men might be present. News of these parties always came from an Afro-centric young couple from Chicago. They lived in an apartment somewhere in Harlem. They were enrolled in the social sciences at Teachers College.

Sometimes, they told us about a party in Brooklyn. Layla and I would board the night train with them to check it out. None of us were familiar with Brooklyn so walking unfamiliar streets in search of a party proved to be a fool's errand almost every time. After a few weekends of that, we decided to party closer to home.

One Friday, Layla and I went to a get-together at the International House where most foreign students lived. The House was located a few streets over from Whittier.

I was comfortable among foreign students. I had lived with and partied with them in Europe and in Africa.

This gathering was held in a cavernous, low-ceilinged hall. A table with two bowls of punch was at one end of the room. The students, mostly males, were mingling at the other end. Some of the guys were in colorful dashikis and sandals. A few Black and White girls were wandering around the middle. Foreign music was being piped loudly into the room. Somebody had forgotten to dim the lights.

I was just wandering around the middle of the room wearing my London-bought green long-sleeved dress with the A-line flare and my London-bought multicolored sandals. I wandered over to the punch table, picked up a flowered paper cup, looked inside and decided I didn't want any punch. I put the cup down on the white tablecloth. Two foreign guys were watching me. I smiled in their direction. One was tall, dark, and slim. The other one was medium height, light-skinned and muscular. I had my eyes on the muscular one. He looked like he would be good at playing baseball.

My smile led the two of them to smile back at me. Both were sipping from cups. Both sauntered over to my spot in the middle of the room.

"Hello," I said.

The tall one said, "Hi."

I waited for a follow up.

The tall one continued after taking a sip from his cup, "You live here?"

I was familiar with how foreign students talk, so I clarified what he was trying to ask. I spoke each word slowly and clearly,

"I don't live *here.*" I pointed in the direction of the floor. "I live in Whittier Hall. Do you know where that is?"

I got no answer. The three of us were standing together smiling. I was clutching my handbag and surveying the crowd. The two of them were speaking foreign words and sipping from their paper cups.

The tall one spoke again.

"My friend wants to visit you."

I took the conversation back to essential information.

"What is your name? And your friend's name?" I directed my right hand toward the muscular friend.

"My name is Marge." I placed my hand on my chest.

The tall one spoke again to his friend. I waited patiently with an understanding smile on my face. Finally, he turned and spoke to me.

"My name is Eso, he's Musa."

He taps his chest and gestures toward Musa.

"Nice to meet you." I said, bowing slightly at the waist.

"Where are you from, and what are you studying?" I directed my questions to Musa.

Musa looked at Eso. Eso responded.

"We from Ethiopia. We study engineering. "We come to your house tomorrow," Eso announced.

I just said, "Ok," hoping they would not. Most young students on the Columbia side don't know where Whittier Hall is!

Eso and Musa showed up at my door the next day smiling and wearing their same party clothes.

I invited them in.

Eso sat in my blue couch chair and Musa sat in my wooden desk chair. They were just sitting on the edge of their seats looking around my room.

I tried to engage Musa in conversation. Afterall, if we ever got around to playing baseball, it was important to talk first. "Musa, would you like some tea?"

He looked at Eso who shook his head.

I was getting a little frustrated. But I said with a smile, "Eso, I would like for Musa to speak. He must know how to speak English!"

Musa had such a good-looking innocent face. Layla saw him in the hallway one time.

"My goodness, that guy is so good-looking. Y'all make such a cute couple." She didn't know he was mute and had a handler.

I sat on my bed and looked directly into Musa's eyes.

"Musa tell me, how long have you been in the US?" He seemed startled that I was talking to him. His eyes moved from me to Eso.

Eso saved him.

"He can speak English. He don't like to speak."

I put on my counselor hat.

"Eso, Musa needs to practice in order to get comfortable speaking…it will help him in his classes."

My advice always ended with Eso's, "We will come again."

I allowed them to come again because I was allowing myself to experience new things and new people. I had been at Columbia for almost two months. I didn't want to end this relationship too soon. I wanted to see where it was going.

One time the two of them came over and as usual took their seats and refused tea. Eso announced, "Muso like you."

Muso was sitting at my desk in the blue cushioned wooden chair smiling. I was sitting on my bed thinking, *This experience with these two is not normal, foreigners or not.*

I saw Eso give a nod of his head toward Muso. Muso rose from his chair, walked to my bed, and sat next to me with his hands resting on his thighs. His face had that same flat line smile.

Is this a puppet show? I was smiling, watching, and waiting to see what was going to happen next. Eso gives another nod of the head. Muso takes my right hand in his right hand. Eso gives his right hand a flipping gesture. Muso puts his left hand around my waist.

I am no longer a participant. I am a participant-observer. I am doing research on these two and their mating habits.

I hear kissing sounds coming from Eso. Muso leans his body into me, pushing me down on the bed. He is leaning on me waiting for Eso's next direction!

I am lying on my side, inhaling the smell of sweat and stale breath. I am picturing what it would be like to play baseball with three people, me, a base runner, and a coach. I am repulsed by the vision.

I push Muso off me and stand up. I straighten my blouse and skirt. I run my fingers through my hair to ensure my flip had the proper bounce and swing.

"Well, guys, you should go now."

Eso's face furrows with confusion. He stands and spreads his arms.

"You don't like Muso?"

"Yes, I like Muso, but I have to study now."

Muso is still sitting on my bed, wide-eyed, waiting for further instructions.

I open my door and wave them out with both hands. As I close the door behind them, Eso says with confidence, "We will come tomorrow."

I went downstairs and told Bill to cross Eso and Muso off my visitors list.

6

LAWMAN

My eyes met those of a White guy looking hopeless and hoping to be rescued. We were both leaning against the back wall of the party room at another one of Columbia's student get-togethers. I didn't look away fast enough, so he took that to mean he had permission to approach me.

"Hellwo," he said.

I didn't want some drunk White boy talking to me. I looked away.

"You a thudent heah?"

I looked at him through the dim lights. He was tall and skinny with scraggly straight brown hair. He looked like one of the Beatles. He didn't have a glass in his hands, but he was running his hands through his hair, shifting his weight from foot to foot and slurring his words.

I smiled at him.

"Yeah...I'm in a master's program at TC. How about you? What are you studying?"

He leaned his skinny frame closer in so I could hear what he had to say. He was shouting words into my left ear.

"Thuding law…my hole family lowyers...gonna wok in my daddy firm. We...lowyers in town...Misthsissippi."

"Mississippi?"

I didn't move from my spot. Maybe there could be something here.

I shouted excitedly into his ear.

"You're from Mississippi? Me, too. What part?"

He continued shouting over the loud music.

"Yeah, I'm Leonard. Ya gotta name?"

"I'm Marge," I said, smiling big and showing too many teeth.

"And a pone number? I wont ta call ya…too mush noise in heah..."

He called and showed up the next day. In the light of day, I saw that he was young, had a cleft palate, and was not White.

I soon soured on our relationship. I didn't like writing daily briefs! His review of "speedy trials" was especially off-putting. I said to him on a number of occasions, when he was sitting in the blue couch chair in my room, having tea with milk and sugar, "Leonard, let's get out. Let's go get some food from Sylvia's."

His response was always, "I gotta wite a brief dis week...lisen ta dis, 'Amendment four says evyone is entided ta a peedy trial. Dat means the accused has to be brout to twawl queckly or released. The healtf..."

I stopped listening and started watching him. His long legs stretched out from my blue couch chair. His face was youthful, and his hair was unruly. Sheets of yellow lined paper were scattered on his lap. His eyes were focused, his hands were quivering as he transferred words from scattered sheets to a lined yellow pad of paper.

He came to my room night after night, had a cup of tea with milk and sugar and practiced his "'peedy trial briefs" on me. Leonard probably never played baseball. It was acceptable that he was using me as a sounding board for a few more weeks. I had plans to go home to University City for the Christmas holidays. Before I left, I put a line through his name under 'Boyfriend' on my Five -Year -Plan.

7
RUNNING WATER

One cold evening before my night class, Introduction to Measurement, a class I hated, I was walking on 120th toward "the best fresh bread store in New York City." I wanted to get some honey wheat bread to make me a creamy peanut butter sandwich before I went to class. Class was in an hour.

I was wearing my ankle length black coat exposing my brown lace up boots. I had a brown sock hat pulled down over my flipped hair. I had prepared for that gust of cold air that was going to hit me in the face when I reached the corner of 120th and Broadway. My head was down, and I was forging fast against the cold.

"Hey, you better look up...lots of traffic out here."

I stopped. It's a man's voice, a Black man's voice. All I could see were black boots. Army boots. No, they were galoshes.

My eyeballs were frozen. My fingers were fumbling trying to unwrap my mouth so I could speak. I willed my eyes to move from the boots to a knee-length black coat to a red neck scarf to a beautiful brown face under a black sock hat. An ice-laced moustache covered his smiling mouth. *My Prince! I knew there must be Black men on this campus, and I just found one!*

"I wuz goin to de bread stor." *I sounded like an idiot.*

"Looks like you can use a cup of tea," he said, smiling down at me. *Tea...a tea lover too! We are meant to be!*

He took my left arm and guided me with his strong confident right arm through Russel Hall to the cafeteria. We sat at a table for two. My eyes were following his every move from the shedding of his black coat and sock hat to his long strides to and from the tea station. He was tall and thin with a packed down black Afro. This is a man, not one of those boys just out of undergrad school. But is he eligible? I decided to enjoy the moment. We just met!

"Better?" he asked.

"Yes, much better," I managed to reply.

So why am I still wrapped up like a mummy?

I slipped out of my coverings, my coat, my scarf, my gloves and finally my hat. He was looking at me, at my face. While he was off getting tea, I manipulated my hair for maximum acne coverage.

"I'm Richard, by the way, and you are...?" He reached his right hand across the table. I slipped my right hand into his.

"I'm Marge. Nice to meet you." We laughed together over one handshake. His hand was warm. My hand was cold.

We exchanged stories about why we chose to come to Columbia. Richard shared that he was an assistant principal back in Colorado and had come to TC to earn a degree in Teaching and Learning. As he was talking, I was watching his mouth push out into a kissing motion as he puckered up to sip his tea.

When it was my turn to share, I left out the part about Kelvin and focused on the "good school" and the new two-year counseling program. I was also thinking how beautiful it would be if he were single. But I never met an Assistant Principal who was not married.

We met again two days later for tea. One time we even walked down Broadway, taking in all the undergrads drinking beer and chatting too loudly. He never suggested or asked me to go out on a date. He never made a move toward first base.

After running into each other for about two weeks and grabbing a cup of tea in the cafeteria, I never expected him to show up downstairs at the desk. I got a call from Bill requesting me to, "come down and collect your guest."

When Richard saw me exit the elevator, he stood upright and retrieved his sock hat from the counter. He was wearing khaki pants and a black turtleneck that matched his patted down black hair. His red scarf and black coat were slung over his right arm. He looked so good. I should have taken off this old green shirt and changed into my orange sweater.

He was smiling big and trying to make light of his unannounced visit.

"I was in the neighborhood so I thought I would drop by," he said.

"Oh, no problem," I said. "I'm glad you did. Come on up and have a cup of tea."

Bill was watching me as the elevator door closed.

I kept my word about the tea. As he slung his black coat over my desk chair and made himself comfortable in the blue couch chair, I started the hot water pot. I sat across from him on my bed, waiting for some clue about the purpose of this visit. He talked about how cold it was outside, about his looking forward to having a break during the upcoming holidays. He didn't say what he was doing for the holidays. I didn't ask but I bet he would be going home to Colorado to see his family.

I busied myself making tea with milk and sugar for me and black for him. I pulled my two-shelved plastic table between us. This was a good find. I had retrieved it from the curb. It is perfect for having tea for two. I switched the radio on low. Sammy Davis Jr. was in the middle of "Candy Man."

It's a Thursday night. Somewhere around eight o'clock, small talk had run out and our teacups were empty. I had a class on Friday morning. Richard's head was moving to the beat of The Bee Gees now. He gave no indication of leaving or that he was planning to engage me in a little baseball. I needed him to either wrap me in his arms or ask for another cup of tea. He just leaned forward spreading his arms in the air and talked about music and musicians.

"I have all the Bee Gees music. Those guys just know how to sing...."

I felt compelled to join him. "Yeah, they are so good, but I think James Taylor is just as good. I just love his voice and I also like Neil Diamond and Harry Chapin."

"Why you so into all these White dudes. What about Bill Withers and Lionel Richie?" He's jabbing his pointer finger at me playfully and accusingly.

"Oh, those guys are a given," I replied with a little giggle and a dismissive wave of my left hand. "No need to brag about them...."

We sat there listening to Carole King. *It is now getting to be nine p.m., my bedtime.* I needed to change the trajectory of this encounter. I smiled.

"I'm going to go wash this stuff and get ready to turn in. I'm one of those early-to-bed people."

He responded, "Ok."

I stood up, gathered the two saucers and two cups, and went to the closet for my pajamas, robe, and bag of toiletries. I closed the door behind me and headed down the hall to the bathroom. I washed the two cups and two saucers and laid them to dry on a towel. I took a longer than usual shower with my special occasion rose soap, put on my green silk pajamas, and covered myself with my long pink terry cloth robe. I gathered my teacups, saucers and my toiletries bag and headed back to my room.

I opened the door gingerly. I expected to see Richard's smiling face sitting in the blue couch chair. My eyes focused on...What?...this guy's lying on my bed....he's snoring!

What is this!

My feet were glued to the floor. I'm standing in the middle of my room balancing my teacups and saucers and my toiletries bag.

I'm looking at this man in his khaki pants, black socks and black turtleneck curled up in the fetal position on my bed! Did I say something to give him the impression that I allow men to just come to my room and sleep on my bed!

What am I to do now, shake him and wake him up? Clang the teacups against the saucers when I put them on the shelf and allow him to wake up naturally? It's not that late. Just 9:30. He's sleeping pretty soundly. Maybe I'll just let him sleep. Surely, he will wake up soon...just a cat nap.

I deposited my cups and saucers quietly back on the rolling cart. I turned the lamp down low and sat in the blue couch chair that he was supposed to be sitting in. I didn't put on my night cap. I wanted to be presentable just in case he woke up ready to run some bases.

At around eleven p.m., I could no longer wait for him to wake up. I needed to be ready for my class tomorrow morning. I had to go to bed. I assessed the space available on the bed. There was enough for me.

I crawled in from the foot of the bed. I positioned myself next to him, but flush against the wall. I kept my pink house robe wrapped tightly around me.

Sometime in the middle of the night I woke up. I felt the bedsprings moving. I remembered. *I am in the bed with a man named Richard!*

The man sits up. I hear his socked feet cross the room toward the door. The door opens. He goes out and leaves the door ajar. The hallway lights paint half the wall above my head. I turn toward the open door. I hear feet going down the stairs. I hear the feet stop. All is quiet. Then I hear spraying water.

Water? There's no sink! Where's water…Is that piss? *I'm hearing piss!* I want to sit up. I want to yell out, *"Are you pissing on the stairs? Are you nuts?"*

I just lay there pretending to be asleep.

He comes tiptoeing back into the room through the open door.

I hear him retrieving his shoes from under the bed. I hear him lift his coat off the desk chair. *He's running away from the scene, away from that stinking piss. You bastard!*

He walks out of my room, clicking the door closed behind him. I scoot off the end of the bed, walk over and lock the door.

I brighten my room to better see the covers he slept on and the pillow his head rested on. What is this smeared all over my white pillowcase? I held the pillow up to the light. *It's hair dye!* Richard dyes his hair! Not only is he married, he's also a gray-haired old man who dyes his hair!

I changed the pillowcase and got under the blue blanket.

What's Bela going to think when she finds herself mopping piss off the back stairway!

8
A SHOW, A WEDDING, AN ALBATROSS

I began to attend and participate in some of Whittier Hall's activities organized by the Residential Services Department. On Friday nights in the lobby, there were mingles and get-togethers. Most of the residents of Whittier attended.

Cami was there sashaying around and basking in the attention she was getting from the guys, especially from the doctoral student, Ted. The two of them were sometimes seen together walking around campus. The South Carolina couple was always there standing together looking for a "Northerner" to join them.

During the holiday party, I dressed in my reds and greens, sang Christmas carols, and sipped on spiked holiday punch. In March, I joined in a sing-along to celebrate our return from spring break.

Even when there was nothing planned by Residential Services, Layla and I were always in the assembly hall making some kind of music. She was on the piano, and I was singing. Sometimes a friend of Layla's stopped by with a guitar. We spent many afternoons just jamming in the assembly hall.

In April, Sarah, the Director of Housing, sent me a note asking me to drop by her office. *What does she want? I am not moving out of my room!* It is because of her that I ended up rooming with a "working girl" at the YWCA!

I stopped by her office before my evening class. She is sitting behind a brown desk surrounded by assorted piles of papers. She is a slim, frizzy haired brunette with lots of split ends. A beret attempts to hold her frizz away from her face.

I try not to be defensive when I ask her, "You want to see me?"

"Oh, yes," she said, smiling, standing, and directing me to a chair.

"Marge, I am so excited about this. You have such a beautiful voice. I hear you singing all the time. I would love to hear more."

"Thank you." I said. "That's very nice of you."

She sits and begins looking through a pile on her desk.

"I want to ask you if you will do a show in next year's Residence Hall's Activities Program."

She stops shuffling papers and looks at me for a response.

I look back at her.

"Can you repeat that? I'm not sure what you mean."

"Sure. We have Residential Activities and Programs that we sponsor throughout the school year, and I would like for you to do one of our activities, to sing."

"You want me to sing here?"

"Yes! You would be the first resident to have an entire evening to yourself. I think you would be great."

"I sing, but you want me to do a whole evening? A show? Just me? By myself? I'm not sure I can do that. I don't know how this would work. The songs..."

I'm stuttering and spreading my arms and raising my shoulders.

Sarah leans forward, her elbows rest between the piles on her desk.

"You don't have to do anything. We do everything. We set up the room with a stage and lights. And we do the publicity, programs, and posters. All you have to do is tell us the songs you're going to sing. If you have musicians, you can bring them in. And you already know that you can use the piano and assembly room to rehearse. How does that sound?"

"That sounds great, but when would I do this? I don't have any musicians and I don't have enough songs. I'll have to think about it. Maybe I could."

I was talking too loud and too quickly. Sarah didn't seem to notice.

She pulled a calendar from a pile and flipped through the months.

"I'm doing the activity schedule for next year now, so you will have lots of time to prepare. I think a good time for your performance would be in..."

I lean forward trying to see what month she is fingering.

"Let's see...November, yeah...that will work. Does November work for you?"

"Yeah," I said. "I think that'll work. I'll just have to get some things figured out. I'll have to let you know for sure later."

I walked to class that night thinking, "Oh, my goodness, I don't know where to start. A one woman show! I know the words to a lot of songs. But I have no musicians, except maybe Layla. And I don't have anything to wear!

One thing I had to figure out was how to fit in Sylvia's wedding.

She called me with her news last month. She was at Fordham University working on a degree in public health.

"I'm getting married. His name is Arol and I want you to be my maid of honor. He is so great."

"Married!" I said. *She found a guy willing to wait until her wedding night to play baseball! I can't wait to meet this guy!*

"Also," she said. "I have a friend I want you to meet. He is a great guy...you'll love him! I gave him your number. Let me know what you think."

Her friend called me. His name was Travis. For the next two

weeks, we got to know each other over the phone. He had a very engaging and outgoing personality. I enjoyed our conversations, but I was getting suspicious. What kind of guy talks for two weeks on the phone without asking to meet in person? What's he hiding?

Travis finally invited me to his Brooklyn apartment for a home-cooked meal. I told Sylvia about our date just in case he tried something unsavory.

I took the train to his apartment. His apartment was small and well-appointed. He greeted me in that same engaging, upbeat manner that I had become accustomed to over the phone. He was medium height, dark skinned and had a slight accent. He was not enrolled in Columbia or Fordham.

He invited me to watch him prepare our dinner which included rice, green beans, and his specialty, stir fried beef. I like a man who is comfortable in the kitchen.

On the train back to Whittier, I knew Travis was not for me, but I decided to accept another invitation. He said he had a surprise for me.

He picked me up in front of Whittier on a Saturday afternoon. He was driving a small, red car. He had the top down.

I commented as he opened the door for me, "Wow, nice car! Is it new?"

"Yep," he said. "You ain't seen nothing yet!" He was giddy with anticipation.

Downtown near Herald Square, he managed to find and squeeze into a small parking spot.

"Wow!" I said. "That was impressive! Getting a parking spot in this area!"

He started smiling, excitedly.

"Watch this," he said.

He started pushing buttons on his car keys.

The car doors began to slowly lift out of their casements. I sat forward wide-eyed with my mouth agape. I was leaning away from my wayward door.

"What's happening?" I was looking from the rising doors to Travis's face. He was smiling big and maintaining his finger on that trigger button. He was like a twelve-year-old playing his first video game.

A small crowd began to gather. Everyone was laughing and pointing as the car was slowly spreading its wings like an albatross. Travis was laughing and looking around at the wings and at the curious faces of the crowd. He was enjoying the attention. I was not. *I don't like 'loud'!*

"See," he said. "I told you I had a surprise for you! Isn't this something!"

Yes, this is something. Where can I hide? Where can I go to escape from this spectacle!

When the doors reached their zenith, I did just that. I stepped out and folded into the crowd of onlookers while Travis remained in the limelight, grinning, pushing buttons and watching those wings fold back into doors.

I waited for him to find me embedded in the crowd of onlookers. He was beaming.

"Wasn't that great! This car has so many gems like..."

"I really just like opening the doors myself." I said.

When he called and had more surprises for me, I said, "Sorry, I can't. I have a big presentation to prepare for."

Keith called me. He was in New York for a conference.

"Want to see a show and go to dinner?" he asked.

He knew it was appropriate now to ask rather than proclaim. I was glad to hear from him because it had been a while.

"Sure," I said. "I'll meet you at Radio City Music Hall."

We admired the Rockettes and had an early steak dinner. My body tightened when he wrapped his arm around me in the theater and when he held my hand when walking around Times Square.

At dinner he talked about his medical practice and his plans to move out of the neighborhood. I told him about my studies and my upcoming 'One Woman Show'.

"You are really going to entertain an audience with songs for an hour…alone?" he asked. "This is astounding. I know you are a prodigious talent, but I never knew you were serious about singing on stage!" He was leaning back looking at me.

"Yes. When I came to New York, being able to sing in a small, intimate club was one of my dreams."

When we parted, we didn't make plans to meet again. We didn't have any new goals to share. Keith planned to move his practice out of the 'old' neighborhood, and I plan to use my show on Columbia's makeshift stage to jumpstart my singing career.

I met Arol at a house party. He was tall, dark, and a recent arrival from the Virgin Islands. He was all over Sylvia, holding her hands, kissing her face, and burying his face in her neck. Sylvia was smiling coyly and turning her body, pretending to resist his overtures. From the looks of them, that "wedding night" rule had propelled Arol toward an expedited wedding!

During Spring Break, I flew to Chicago, stood as her maid of honor, and wished them well. I left them and rushed back to New York. I had a show to get ready for. Sylvia forgot to ask me what I thought of Travis. The last time I heard from her, there was a baby crying in the background.

9

A SIMPLE REQUEST

The first year of the two-year counseling program was coming to an end. Some students were aware that we had met the one-year requirements for a master's degree. A petition went around requesting that the degree be awarded to us. I signed the petition. The administration relented and in May of 1971, we all received a Master of Arts Degree in Guidance and Counseling.

The second year Counseling Program for me was going to be very demanding. I had to complete two six-week practicums, find an adolescent willing to participate in two recorded counseling sessions, and present the counseling sessions to my fellow classmates for their 'suggestions and feedback.' I had to find time to sub occasionally to make some spending money, and, I had to find time to prepare for my show!

I was assigned in September to begin my Practicum in Group Counseling Techniques at Yonkers High School, a predominantly White school. My supervisor was Mr. Bennett, a Black counselor schooled in this technique.

When I entered Mr. Bennett's office, he rushed toward me in

his dark gray suit, yellow and light gray tie, white shirt, and black shiny shoes. He welcomed me with a warm smile and a long handshake. He had a young round face, a receding hairline and...*were his eyes wandering over my body or just my legs?*

This was a six-week practicum. I shadowed Mr. Bennett each day and witnessed his application of 'engaging warmth,' 'unconditional positive regard' and 'open ended' questioning technique. I took copious notes. I met with him to debrief and review. After a couple of weeks, I ran group sessions on my own.

I was nervous, but I was having fun learning. At my debriefing with Mr. Bennett, I was all smiles telling him how the kids were helping each other, and I was asking open ended questions like "How did you feel about that?" Mr. Bennett joined me in my excitement. He was smiling, nodding and added an occasional, "That was good."

One time after completing an analysis of my group session, Mr. Bennett said, "How about you coming to dinner with me after school so we can celebrate?"

My excited hands stopped talking in midair. I rested them on the front of his glass covered desk.

He leaned back in his high back burgundy desk chair. *I knew it...I knew he was going to try something. I am not going to get mixed up with this man...this married man!*

I had to be quick on my feet.

"No, I can't. I have class, and so many notes to transcribe. Thanks anyway."

Still smiling, I gathered my papers, stood up and headed for the door.

He stood up waving his right hand toward me and scurrying around his desk to reach me. He stood too close to me. He was half smiling and making eye contact. His voice was pleading; his arms were spread out in front of him.

"I'm only talking about dinner, an early dinner. You did a good job with the kids. I just want to take you to celebrate. What's wrong with that? I'll make sure you get back in time for your class."

I reached for the doorknob. As I was exiting, I said again, "I can't. I have a class."

During the final two weeks of my practicum with Mr. Bennett, we played hide and seek. I set up space in the conference room to meet with students. He dropped in on my sessions, requesting to speak to me in his office.

I needed a positive report on my activities under his tutelage, so I pulled my ankle length skirt down to cover my feet and smiled a lot as he wrote my final report. He read as he was writing words about me like "capable, warm and competent."

He folded his written words, stuck them into a manila envelope and pushed the envelope across the desk to me. I stood up, clutched the envelope in my left hand and extended my right hand across his desk.

He ignored my hand. He came to stand in front of me. He reached for my right hand. He was fondling my hand in both of his. His eyes were pleading.

"I'm going to ask you one last time to go to dinner with me, just to celebrate, to show my appreciation for your time here. I can't just let you go without a proper goodbye. That wouldn't be right!"

I gently wiggled my hand from his cradle. I smiled, flipped my swinging and bouncing hair and headed toward the door.

"Oh, the kids were great," I said. "They gave me a farewell card. And thank you so much for allowing me to work with you. I learned so much."

When I got off the train at my stop, I didn't go to my room and have a cup of tea with milk. I went to Sylvia's on 125th Street. I took home some collard greens, cornbread, and fried chicken. I wonder where Mr. Bennett was going to take me for dinner.

When I finished my dinner, I called Layla.

10
STAGE, LIGHTS, SING!

It is Thursday, November 4. The rehearsals are over. The stage is set. Students are filing into the assembly hall. They are spilling out through the open doors into the lobby, milling around, talking, laughing, and reading the mimeographed programs placed on each chair. I don't see any Black students.

Sarah's posters taped to walls and bulletin boards all around campus feature an Afro hairstyle surrounded with the words, "An Evening of Song With Marge...Doing it Her Way." She did a good job creating a nightclub atmosphere. Folding chairs fill every corner of the assembly hall. A small one-person stage is constructed with red, white, and silver streamers covering a movie screen backdrop. Tall green plants in clay pots are placed in front of the streamers.

Two spotlights hang from the ceiling. One is focused on the stage with a lone standing microphone. The other is focused on Layla and a friend of hers named Trey. They are seated on the right, off the stage. Layla is on the piano and her friend Trey is on the congos.

I am ready. My face is powdered and rouged, and my lips are

Ruby Red. My Afro is packed tight to encircle my face. From my closet, Layla and I agreed on my knee length sleeveless black dress with a hint of cleavage. My off-black pantyhose compliment my black slingbacks.

The evening unfolds as planned. At 9:15 p.m., the house lights dim. Layla and Trey take their places. The right side spotlight focuses on them. They play a two-minute music medley. During their applause, I take two deep breaths through my nose and blow the air out slowly through my mouth. I scramble up two side steps, walk through the red, white, and silver streamers and make my entrance onto the stage. I lift the hand mic from the stand. I am flooded with light. The applause is energizing. I am ready for my solo singing debut. I must deliver.

I introduce the evening with "Misty," followed by "Raindrops Keep Falling on my Head" and "Boy from Ipanema." I move on to "The Days of Wine and Roses" and "Watermelon Man."

I move from one song to the next, with no introduction. I pause only to soak up the applause. I conclude the program with a medley of Dionne Warwick's hits, "Trains and Boats and Planes," "A House is Not a Home," "Going Outta My Head," and "This Girl's in Love With You." The last song on the program is "What the World Needs Now is Love."

The audience is standing and applauding for more. I bow and bow and bask in my night. I wave a hand for them to include Layla and Trey. As the applause continues, I know I am meant to be on stage, a stage much bigger than this one.

11
TALKING LEGS

After my "Evening with Marge" show, I became a semi-celebrity. Lots of students, especially those in the counseling program, stayed back after the show to tell me how much they enjoyed my performance. Others congratulated me in passageways and hallways. Even Bill from the front desk started dropping by my room for tea. We had become quite friendly after my being housed in Whittier now for more than a year. He always laughed at himself commenting each time, "I'm sitting in a room with a beautiful woman sipping a cup of damn tea with milk and sugar. I never thought this would happen to me!"

One time, I was rushing through the underground tunnel from Whittier to the main building when I heard somebody calling my name. The voice was coming from someone in the mix of students coming towards me. I looked up to see Ted, the doctoral student who attends some of our counseling classes and who is known as the boyfriend of the "blonde bombshell," Cami. He is smiling and waving to me.

"Hi," he said.

He is wearing that same brown checkered sports jacket he

always wears when he attends our counseling classes. He is also wearing that big smile he wears when he is talking to the professors or those kids from the nearby towns. The only time he wears a serious face is when he is walking with Cami.

"Hello," I said, smiling and moving over to the wall and out of the way of student traffic.

"On your way to class?" he asked, joining me at the wall. Silly question, but I responded anyway.

"Yes, I have T-group tonight. I hate these group sessions. We're supposed to be learning about ourselves, but nobody has anything to say. We just look at each other. Anyway..." I keep smiling. He keeps grinning. He called my name, so I wait for him to speak.

"Oh, you were so good at your show. I didn't know you could sing. It was great! You were so professional. You should be singing on the big stage; you were that good."

He is spreading his arms and getting bright eyed. *This guy must have really enjoyed the evening.*

"Well, thank you very much. I'm glad you came and enjoyed the show."

I am easing past him to get to class when he adds, "I would like to hear you sing some more."

I am just passing him when he continues, grinning all the while, "And by the way, I just gotta say, you have the most beautiful legs I have ever seen!"

I hesitated. *What did this White boy just say?* My eyes widened.

I utter, "Oh, thank you." I looked at his smiling face and kept walking.

Should I be angry at this guy, or should I be flattered?

Most beautiful legs! What does he know about legs? Who is he to talk about my legs? He doesn't know me! He thinks he has the right to say something about my legs, because I'm Black! *What about your girlfriend Cami?* Do you tell her about her legs?

You White bastard!

12

DINNER STORIES

After that "beautiful legs" encounter with Ted, I seem to run into him almost every day now. We smile at each other and wave or pass each other and say "Hi."

Sometimes I run into him in the early morning when I am taking a shortcut through Morningside Park on my way to a substitute teaching job at PS 141. He is always wearing that same brown mosaic colored suit jacket with brown pants. I asked him one time where he was going.

"I'm the director of a daycare center, just down the street. I have to get there before the parents start dropping off their babies."

"Really," I said. "How did you get that job? You know how to take care of babies?"

I reached my turnoff, but I politely lingered long enough for him to explain that "I need the money" and "I don't do everything. It's a cooperative, so the mothers take turns helping out...it's fun..."

"Well, I gotta run. See you later." I turn right. He turns left.

We kept running into each other, me on my way to PS 141, he on his way to the daycare center. On these short walks I learned that he was using the population at the daycare center as part of his doctoral studies. I learned that he went to undergrad school at the University of Buffalo. He learned that I went to undergrad school at Southern Illinois University at Carbondale. He liked to talk, and I was a polite listener.

One time we were talking about the upcoming Thanksgiving holidays.

"It's so funny," I said. Whenever there is even a one-day break, this campus turns into a ghost town. Everybody leaves. You're lucky, I guess. Your parents live here. You going to see them and have some turkey?"

"Yeah, I'll probably just go there for dinner, and then come back." He was fiddling with his tan leather briefcase, trying to put the strap over his shoulder. "What about you? What are you doing?"

"I'm not sure yet, but I will *not* be having dinner with the nuns again. I'm probably banned forever from their nunnery." I started laughing.

He joined me with a clueless expression on his face. "Why? What happened?" he asked.

"I don't think it was that bad. But anyway, there was a sign on the bulletin board inviting students who couldn't go home to have dinner at the nunnery. I guess they do this every year. So, my friend Layla and I decided to go. There was another girl there too, but I didn't know her."

"The nuns were very nice, and the food was good, but I had never talked to a nun before, so I was sitting next to this young pretty nun in a gray habit with a white hat on her head and she was talking about her teaching and her work with the poor. I just listened to all that and finally I said to her, 'But you're so pretty. Why do you want to be a nun?'"

Everybody heard my question and everybody stopped talking for a minute or so. But the nun I was talking to just smiled and kept talking about the joy of doing God's work. Long story short, I'll be getting takeout from Sylvia's."

"That is funny," he said. "They probably get asked that question all the time." He was still adjusting that briefcase strap. "I'll just be at my parent's house for a little while, then I'm coming back. If you're around, there's some historic places around here like Grant's Tomb and Riverside Park, if you'd like to go. You ever been there?"

"No, never have. Yeah, I'd like to see those places."

"I'll call you and let you know if I can get back. My parents live on Long Island in Queens so depending on the traffic..."

"Oh, I knew some people who lived in Queens. Anyway, don't worry," I said. "There's no need to rush back." I did a little flick of my right hand. "We can go on Friday, if that works better."

When we parted, I wondered if Ted had assumed that all three of us students having dinner with the nuns were Black or if it mattered to him. He didn't comment on my getting takeout from Sylvia's. He's probably never heard of the place, and it was just down the street from his daycare center! He just seems oblivious to anything having to do with Black folks, even though he's a New Yorker!

13
THE HISTORY LESSON

At about one p.m. on Thanksgiving Day my phone rang. It was Ted.

"Hi. I just want to let you know that I won't be getting back until late this evening. Lots of aunts and cousins here."

"That's fine," I said, thinking that we had already decided to sightsee on Friday. "Have fun."

"It's very noisy here. You wanna meet tomorrow in the lobby at ten o'clock?"

"Yes, ten is good. See you then."

"Ok," he said. "Bye."

It was cold at ten o'clock in the morning in New York City on Friday. We were both bundled up in short jackets, scarves, and sock hats. We walked right from the front of Whittier and turned right to 120th Street. We crossed Broadway and made our way to Riverside Drive. I was in unfamiliar territory now. I was reduced to a follower.

Ted was very excited about our outing. As we headed to Grant's Tomb, he was pointing and stopping and talking about coming to the city as a kid with his parents to see Grant's Tomb.

"There it is, up there. It's such a great site. I don't know why more people don't visit. People just don't know Grant. The man was president of the country during the Civil War. Did you read this box? Wow! That is something. His wife is buried here, too."

"Do you know why he's buried here, and not at Arlington Cemetery?"

"No, I don't," I said. Ted couldn't wait to answer his own question.

"It's because he wanted to be buried with his wife. She couldn't be buried at Arlington. He chose this place for both of them. Isn't that something? The man was a drunkard, but he is right up there with Roosevelt and Lincoln."

I feigned interest. I tried to match his level of enthusiasm. That was difficult. He must have forgotten that my undergraduate degree is in American and European history. I didn't remind him.

"This is fun," Ted said. "There are so many places like this around New York. You ever heard of the Cloisters?"

"No," I said. "What is that?"

"It's like a museum. Beautiful art...it's in Washington Heights. We should go sometime."

A few weeks later, we went.

Ted began dropping by my room. He had doctoral news, family news and new places to show me. He always refused a cup of tea with milk and sugar.

14
TURNING THE PAGE

I should have known some Catholic protocols since my best friend in Whittier Hall, and in the counseling program that first year was a White guy named Jim. He was a priest, but he said he was in the process of leaving the priesthood.

One time, when we were having tea with milk and sugar in the cafeteria, he said,

"I found myself liking women and thinking about them all the time. I was feeling guilty. It was interfering with my work. So I made the difficult decision to leave the priesthood after almost nine years."

"Wow," I said. "That's a long time. That's a big change."

Every time we had tea together, Jim sat there looking forlorn and baffled because he was having little to no success finding compatible relationships with women on campus. I listened. But even though he claims he has been away from the priesthood for almost two years, he still dressed like a priest. He is bald and could lose a few pounds, but every day he still wears a black suit or black suit pants with a white shirt.

So, I said, "Jim, I'm gonna be frank with you. If you want one of these university women to notice you, you need to make yourself sexy and desirable. Give your black suits and white shirts to the Salvation Army and buy some new clothes!"

"It shouldn't be about clothes," he said, adamantly. "It should be about common interests and what's in my—"

I interrupted him. "Jim, you got to get a woman to notice you first. Buy some multi-colored sweaters and wear them with jeans and slacks." I lowered my voice to a coarse whisper and leaned into him.

"We women can tell a lot about a man by what he wears under his Timberland jacket. We take a second look when we see he's wearing a manly, multi-colored brown sweater!"

When the weather was suitable on some weekends, Jim and I took in sights around New York City, especially if they were conveniently located near a train stop. Jim knew how to get around the city and he had a way of finding out about everything that was free.

One evening after class, he came banging on my door.

"We gotta go. I can't contain myself. I love this man. I have been wanting to see him...and now he's here!"

He was waving his arms around and slamming the back of his right hand against his forehead. I'm trying to imagine who this "must see and must hear" person is. All the people I know like that are dead.

He was hyperventilating, so I said, "Who are you talking about? What's so great about—"

"It's Alex Haley! He's going to be telling his story, *Roots*...live! His book is unbelievable. We have to go...now." He was breathing deeply and pacing. "We want to get a seat...I hope we can get in."

As we were running from the subway and finally entered the church, I was embarrassed that I had never heard of Alex Haley, let alone read his book.

For forty minutes, this Black man stood in front of a standing room only multi-generational, multi-racial crowd and wove a heart wrenching, yet triumphant story of his family's history and their passage to America. It was an emotional and historic journey for me.

Jim did not return to Columbia for the second year of the counseling program. I miss my friend. I hope he bought a multi-colored brown sweater and met his match.

15

FRIDAY NIGHTS

One day I was walking the two blocks back to Whittier looking forward to the pleasure of devouring my loaded cold cut sandwich on brown bread along with a cup of hot tea. My mind was running full speed through my to do list: another practicum, find a student to record for a feedback session, find a...

"Hey, you better watch where you're going. You can get run over."

I looked down to ensure that my feet were on the sidewalk. I know this Amsterdam sidewalk like the back of my hand. I kept walking, holding my brown paper bag at my side.

"Wait a minute." I heard a car door open and close. That voice spoke to me again. "You go to school here?"

I stopped and turned. My heart skipped a beat. There was a Black man wearing a plaid short sleeved shirt, blue pants and brown sandals, leaning on the passenger door of a mustard-colored yellow car. He was smiling at me.

"Yeah," I said cautiously, not wanting to give away too much.

"I haven't seen you around." His mouth was speaking, but his eyes were undressing me. *I'm glad I was wearing my brown slacks so he couldn't see my legs. He's probably just like the rest...*

"I haven't been hiding, just working hard." That was my lame response. I wanted to get to the point...*are you eligible?*

He was opening the trunk of that mustard yellow car. *Who buys a car that color? So loud. I don't like loud!*

He joined me on the sidewalk holding a blue suitcase. He smelled of Old Spice.

"I'm Troy."

He was smiling big as he extended his right hand towards me.

"I'm Marge," I said, smiling back as I switched my brown paper bag to my left hand. Our hands embraced. His was soft and boney. *Must be a city boy.*

After I met Troy, I smiled more. I took more time picking at and framing my Afro around my face. I spent more time in front of the mirror pasting on makeup to cover present and past acne flare-ups.

I walked tall with confidence when Troy and I walked together to class. I learned that he was getting a master's degree in gerontology. He was adamant about "all the jobs everywhere working with old people" and "all the friends who already have jobs."

Troy made it clear that he was at Columbia not to socialize, but to learn everything he could about the field of gerontology. When he suggested that we limit our getting together to Friday nights only, I agreed. I was not going to grovel and beg for more of his time. I was soon to be twenty-five years old, but I was not desperate!

For our first Friday night date, I met him in his dorm room on the second floor. My Afro was oiled, shiny and packed down tight. I was wearing my peach, cinched waist long-sleeved dress and my multicolored London sandals.

I knocked on his door. When Troy yelled out, "Come on in," I lowered my expectations for the evening.

I let myself into his tiny dorm room and remained standing at the door. We were not alone. There were two men and a woman lounging on his bed. One of the guys I had seen around campus. All were sipping drinks and peering at me.

The female in her thirties was in jeans, the men, including Troy, were in shorts.

I'm overdressed!

Troy rose from his desk chair and greeted me with a peck on the cheek.

"Hey, Baby, come on in. This is Marge, everybody."

I could see approval in everybody's eyes. Lifting their glasses, I heard, "Welcome" and "Nice to meet you."

"Where you been hiding this girl, Man?"

Troy had a smile on his face like he was a proud father. The hand not holding his glass was leading me to a chair that was just right of the one he was sitting on. W*here did he get this extra chair?*

"What do you want to drink?"

Troy was asking me a question in front of his friends that he already knew the answer to. He knew that if a Singapore Sling was not available, my drink was a soft drink. He was at his table bar avoiding looking at me while the six ears and eyes of his friends were focused on my order. Their faces were poised to determine my character by the drink I ordered.

"I'll have whatever soft drink you have," I said, smiling and looking into Troy's disappointed eyes. There was a rattling of ice from the empty glasses of his friends.

"You a real teetotaler, huh," said the guy I had seen before.

"Yeah, I like tea. Troy can't make the drink that I like, so a 7 Up will be fine."

I took the can and a glass from Troy and busied myself with opening and pouring. For the remainder of the evening, I was mostly ignored.

The conversation between Troy and his friends was lively and disjointed. Glasses were clinking, and phrases like "All these White kids are crazy, protesting that War" and "This world is messed up" were seconded with bed slamming and 'high fives.' Twice, Troy remembered that I was there and turned to ask me, "Don't you have anything to say?" I had nothing to say.

When Troy and the guests had agreed to disagree and the liquor bottles were empty and Troy was nodding between spurts of wisdom, his friends headed for the door. I was left alone with his fumbling desire to be amorous. I had dressed for a quiet evening with him. I wanted to talk about the future as we were both leaving Columbia in four months. I pushed his fumbling hands and body away from me and went to my room. I had a cup of tea alone and went to bed.

When we were walking to class the following week, I whispered in his ear, "you might not want to invite your friends on Friday."

I noticed his no-tooth grin as I escaped to class.

There are no friends this Friday night. It is just the two of us. I didn't push him away. I dressed in "virginity-ending" attire. I chose a button-down green blouse and a zipper front brown skirt. Underneath was my black padded bra with matching bikini underwear. Brown slip-ons were on my feet.

I accepted a glass of white wine spiked with 7 Up. The lights were low, but I could see Troy's droopy eyes. He must have started to get into the mood without me.

I kicked off my slip-ons and sauntered over to his bed. I sat on the edge and did a one-handed scoot to the back wall. I crossed my legs, sipped my white wine, and waited. Troy was at the bar topping off his second or third glass of white wine. I watched him make his way over to the bed. He joined me on the back wall.

When I first met Troy, my acne was still flaring up, mostly on the right side of my face. I went with this new 'right side flare up' information to the University Health Unit to get some recommendations for coverage. The doctor on duty was a White man with a serious face and a foreign accent. *Just my luck to get a foreigner who knows nothing about Blacks and especially nothing about Black skin.*

I tolerated his closeness to my face. *He had not splashed on any aftershave. I like Aramis these days.*

He looked at my skin from all angles, turning my face from side to side, but saying nothing. He sat at his desk and started to write. He handed me the paper he had written on and stood to leave the room. With his hand on the doorknob, he stopped long enough to say, "I'm prescribing birth control pills for you. You just follow…"

"Birth control pills!" I interrupted him.

These White doctors think Black girls think only about sex. I was offended. He didn't know anything about me!

"I don't want…I don't need birth control pills. I want...something for my face, not...!"

The stoic-faced doctor with the foreign accent interrupted me.

"I wrote you a prescription for low dose birth control pills. For your kind of acne, these pills should affect the amount of estrogen and mitigate and improve breakouts. The pills do control pregnancy as well. We are focusing on your acne."

I left the doctor's office still skeptical about his intentions and about what birth control pills had to do with my face. I decided that I would tell no one about the pills. The first thing everybody would think is that "she is free of diaphragms and condoms and ready for sex anytime. She's on the pill!"

That foreigner was right. My face got better. And here I am, lounging on my boyfriend's bed, hoping to make use of those birth control pills.

At first, we were both holding drinks so there was just first and second base action. But when Troy took my glass and his in one hand, and placed them on the side table, all kinds of thoughts were running through my head. *It's about to happen…and I'm protected!*

He was moving fast towards third base. *Oh my goodness, he's experienced!*

My button-down blouse, my zipper-front skirt and my bikini underwear were all in play. My bra was hanging on by one strap. Fourth base was in sight!

My boyfriends before, like Sid and Bruno, had opportunities, but they couldn't make it around the bases. Troy is not interested in preserving my purity like Sid. He is not suffering from a father problem like Bruno. Troy is playing this game with passionate jubilation hoping for a climatic finish. The bases are loaded. A home run is on Troy's bat. He is swinging. The excitement is rising to a crescendo until we both felt the excitement dwindling into apologies of "Sorry, too much wine."

I was quick to sum up the evening with "That's Ok...it happens."

He should be proud to know that he got closer to making it around the bases than all the others!

Friday nights became game nights. Even if Troy had his friends gather in his room to drink and talk, attempts to play the game always followed their departure. After a while, I wanted to get out of his dorm room.

"Troy," I suggested, "This Friday night, let's take a walk down Broadway and go to a movie. Can we do that?"

"Yeah, I'll come pick you up, around six-thirty?"

He failed to show up.

The first couple of times he stood me up, I showed some annoyance, but accepted his excuses, "I had to meet some people in my group to work on our presentation" or "Some friends came down from Buffalo, I had to go hang out with them."

After being stood up three times, my understanding morphed into anger.

The next time he didn't show up and keep his word, I was not going to let him off with another lame excuse.

I swung open the door. He greeted me with a smile.

"How you doing, Baby?"

My arms were crossed, I was not smiling, and I did not respond to his attempted embrace.

"Troy, if something comes up all you have to do is let me know in advance! It's not fair for you to treat me like I don't matter and have me all dressed up to go out and you don't show up."

He stands at the closed door, shaking his head. My arms are waving over my head one moment and spread out in front of me the next. "Why do you do that? Answer me! Why do you do that?"

My mouth hangs open. My arms are spread wide, begging for an answer. I needed to hear him say it will not happen again. Instead, he said, "Well, obviously, you are upset and mad. I'll see you tomorrow when you feel better."

He turns, opens the door, and leaves me standing there, utterly confounded.

16
BREAKING GLASS

About a month before the end of the school year, Troy said, "I'm going to take you to my favorite place." I was skeptical since he had never taken me anywhere before, and especially not on a Saturday!

I decided to be cautiously excited. I didn't ask him where we were going. It might jinx the outing. I wanted him to know that I appreciated his sharing his favorite place with me.

For the evening, I chose my versatile blue button-down dress with red trimming down the front. I accessorized it with red stud earrings and a black clutch purse to match my low-heel black flats. While I was waiting for Troy to arrive, I busied myself before the mirror, checking my Afro for loose strands and pushing them back into place. When I heard the knock on my door, I exhaled. I opened the door to his smiling face. I was relieved that he was dressed in his pressed plaid shirt and brown slacks. His sandaled feet were a letdown, but nothing could quell my excitement tonight.

We took off in his mustard-colored Corvette and headed down Broadway, past familiar streets and shops. I had never been in his car before. I sat back and watched him confidently maneuvering the busy streets of New York City. We left the bright lights and headed into a neighborhood of row houses with steps up to brown painted doors. Troy brought the car to a stop.

Looking out the car window, I saw mostly Black and Spanish men. Some had their heads under the hoods of cars. Others were sitting on the sidewalk on folding chairs observing the gaiety of the streets. Coke cans and beer bottles were scattered about the sidewalk along with cigarette butts and Milky Way candy wrappers.

This must be an intermediary stop before we move on to his favorite place. He must be picking up something here. I can't imagine what!

Troy came around and opened my door. Before I stepped from the car, I asked cautiously, "Is this the place?" *Please tell me it's not!*

"Yeah, just watch your step."

I directed my low-heel black flats to a litter-free spot on the sidewalk. I tightened my clutch purse into my chest.

With a light hand on my back, Troy guided me around the corner through the cigarette butts, candy wrappers, and Chinese food cartons. At one of the canopied doorways, he said, "Here it is."

We entered a dark room with a squeaky plank floor and five red wooden vinyl covered stools placed under a long wooden bar. There were three or four tables across from the bar area. A few people with drinks in hand were sitting at the tables and speaking in quiet voices.

Shit! I'm very overdressed. My faded pants would have been perfect!

I followed Troy to the bar and sat next to him on a high vinyl topped wooden stool. He and the bartender exchanged greetings. They started chatting and laughing about something they found funny. A spritzer appeared before me. Troy ordered a chardonnay for himself. I was sipping my spritzer, while Troy was in conversation with the bartender about sports. I heard "St. Louis Cardinals."

I could have joined in the conversation. I could talk about my favorite sportsman, Bob Gibson and about how much I love watching him pitch. I chose to remain quiet. I just sipped, listened, and watched. I was looking at Troy and trying to figure out how his favorite place could be this dingy, rundown, hole-in-the-wall bar! *Why would he bring me here!*

The few people at the tables behind us suddenly started moving about and engaging in some kind of verbal altercation. I turn around to see what the loud talking and shuffling of chairs and tables is about. Troy said something to the bartender. To me, he said, "Let's go."

I slid off my stool as Troy was paying the tab. I was standing behind him, looking around, and straightening my dress. A woman in a loose beige shirt, dark pants and a tangled Afro emerged next to me from one of the tables. She leaned toward me and in a hoarse, quiet voice said, "Give me my purse."

With a look of incredulity on my face, I said to her, "I don't have your purse!" I turned back to face the bar and Troy.

She was at my back, insisting, "I want my purse!"

I hunched and tightened my shoulders around my purse repeating over my shoulder, "I don't have your purse!"

I kept turning my body away from her. Troy was moving toward the door. I moved behind him. The woman was following me, repeating loudly now, "That's my purse. Give me my purse!"

There was a hush among the few people still sitting. I was looking toward them for help.

The woman grabbed at my arm. I was expecting Troy's bartender pal to intervene. I expected him to yell to the woman, "Stop harassing my customer." But he said nothing. He was walking from the bar to tables and continuing to serve drinks seemingly oblivious to the attempted robbery taking place right in front of him!

I looked around for Troy. *Where is he? Why hasn't he come to my rescue?*

I managed to get through the open door. I see Troy standing, waiting, and witnessing the woman grabbing and reaching at me. I turned my body from side to side and moved away from the woman.

"Stop it, lady. This is not your purse!" I clutched my purse closer to my chest with my right hand. I pushed at her with my left.

The men in folding chairs leaned forward. The young men under raised hoods came up for air.

Troy yelled to me again, "Let's go!"

I tried to follow, but the woman spread her arms and posted her body to block my path like she was a guard in a basketball game. I turned my back to her and put my head down, still shielding my purse to my chest.

Breaking glass? *Who's breaking glass?* I hear silence.

The woman turns her head and looks over her shoulder. I turn my head and look in the same direction as the woman.

Troy? Troy is crouched in a fencer's stance, holding the jagged, glistening spikes of a broken brown beer bottle.

"Come over here, Marge," he commands. I straighten up quickly, still clutching my purse to my chest. I scrambled toward Troy. I watch the woman turn quickly to face Troy. She throws her hands up over her head like she is under arrest. Troy lowers his arm and holds the pointed spikes close to the woman's chest. Troy is in charge!

"Don't you take another step," he orders, directing her to the side with the spikes of the beer bottle.

"Ok, Ok," the woman said.

With her hands still raised, she shuffles to the side. Troy slowly releases his spike pointing arm and stands up out of his fencing crouch. He grabs my left hand and drags me backward with him. He releases my left hand and holds on to the spiked bottle with both hands. His eyes dance from side to side like he is expecting a surprise attack from a bystander. We make our way backwards toward his yellow car. Our feet trample cigarette butts and candy wrappers. Our feet scatter Coke cans and brown beer bottles. We round the corner past the men perched on folding chairs and leaning into open hoods.

We get into Troy's Corvette. With the car started and in drive, he throws the jagged bottle out the window into the gutter alongside broken bottles, candy wrappers and Chinese food cartons.

I focused my eyes straight ahead. Troy focused his eyes on the road. We drove home to Whittier Hall in silence.

17
WEST TO EAST

My second practicum was at the Manpower Training Center located in Lower Manhattan. The program was created to train unskilled women for employment. The women were paid monthly based on their attendance.

The counselor's job, according to my supervisor, Mrs. Dobbins, was to help these women resolve personal, social, or academic issues that impacted their ability to attend classes and complete their skill development program. If a woman was absent, a face-to-face meeting with the counselor was required to determine if the absence was "excused" or "unexcused." An unexcused absence meant a docked paycheck.

Mrs. Dobbins' no-nonsense, tough on absences approach was well-known among the women in the training program. The other two Black women counselors seemed to be more understanding and lenient in their approach to attendance issues.

I liked Mrs. Dobbins. She must have liked me, and how I handled assigned tasks. When my internship was ending, she offered me a full-time counseling job. I accepted with a smile, a hug, and "Thank You."

Having a job lined up after graduation freed my mind so I could focus on other important things like Troy and finding a place to live.

The Manpower Training Center was in a building that used to be a high school. On the lower floors, teachers taught a wide range of classes from typing and shorthand to how to fill out a job application to what to wear for a job interview.

I learned about what went on downstairs from Janet, who was a teacher in the Getting a Job department. Her job was to help the women dress and apply makeup appropriately.

I met Janet by chance one day in the teacher's lunchroom. She was a recent hire like me. She was tall, slim, and light-skinned with short, permed brown hair. She looked out of place in her little downstairs cubbyhole. She was surrounded by pallets of makeup on white shelves with assorted suits and dresses hanging on portable clothing racks behind her desk. Her walls were covered with pictures of work attire cut out from magazines. Three months before ending up at this Center, she had been a United Airline stewardess, "flying the friendly skies."

"It's been hard finding my footing after nine years in the air," she said. "My boyfriend keeps telling me to take my time and get used to being on the ground. I'm trying."

During most of our lunch break conversations, Janet talked constantly about her dissatisfaction with her job. "This job is just temporary. I don't make enough to pay the rent! Can you believe that?"

I suggested, "So why don't you move to some place cheaper?"

She threw her head back and stared at me. "Where's it cheaper? I don't want to move. My boyfriend lives nearby and it's...anyway, I've lived there during the whole time I was flying. I would land at LaGuardia, go to my little one-bedroom apartment, and go to bed. The doorman is always there, and I feel safe where I live. It's on the East Side, too."

I put on my counseling hat and said, "It sounds like you really like living in your East Side apartment."

All I knew about the East Side was that no direct train stopped there, and no poor or Black people lived there. I also knew that looking down at the sidewalk was a necessity to avoid stepping in dog shit!

I got the feeling that with all her "lack of money" talk, Janet was trying to figure out if I was roommate material. She needed help paying the rent. I knew it was coming. One day she asked, "How would you like to be my roommate? Like I said, it's a one-bedroom with a couch bed in the living room. The building has a doorman named Craig, so it's really safe. The rent and the electric bill…we can split those right down the middle." Her words to me were without enthusiasm.

My response to her words was equally apathetic. "I need to think about it."

I was desperate for a place to live. She was desperate for a roommate to share the $350 a month rent. I had three housing choices. I could look for an apartment of my own, go back to my life and home in University City, or move into Janet's one bedroom apartment and sleep on a couch bed in the living room.

The next day, I called Janet and asked for her East Side address.

In an effort to move the two-year Guidance and Counseling Program at Teachers College from pilot status to a regularly scheduled offering, our professors asked us for written evaluations on every aspect of the program. To ensure positive responses, last minute arrangements were made for us to utilize the services of the job placement center. I already had a job, but I was curious about the employment status of others, especially the Maasai woman, Grace.

After our last class together, I approached her.

"So, Grace, what are you going to be doing next year?"

She was all smiles as she squeaked, "Oh, I have accepted a position as a Dean. You didn't know? It's at a girl's college, upstate. You probably never heard of it since you are not from New York. I'm sooo excited."

No, I didn't know. And, yes, I'm not surprised. I'm sure the professors helped you get that job.

"That's great," I said, cupping my face in both hands and trying to sound like I was happy for her.

"What about you?" she asked. "You going back to—where is it—Illinois?" She creased her brow, pretending to be interested in my future.

I ignored her Illinois question. It was my turn to be all smiles. "Oh, I'm so lucky...my internship supervisor offered me a job...a counseling job, so I'm really happy about that."

"Well, good for you," she said. Her voice sounded like she was stroking her favorite pet. I wasn't angry at her. I was angry at our professors for picking winners and losers. I cooled off a great deal after I completed my program evaluation form.

18

DREAM CHASING

After graduation, everybody in Whittier Hall disappeared immediately.

I opened the door to my room the last week of school expecting to see a few of the usual groggy-eyed dormmates heading for the bathrooms wearing thongs and granny gowns. But this day, I was met with silence. I wandered into the hallways looking into rooms through open doors, seeing only walls without posters, cleared desks and bare mattresses.

When did everybody leave?

I know when Troy left. He was among the first to leave. He said his friend in Cleveland had a job waiting for him. With a master's degree in gerontology, he could "walk in and get a job just like that!"

Standing on the curb last week, his goodbye to me was a peck on the cheek and an enthusiastic, "I'll call you."

He turned and waved as he sped off down Amsterdam toward Harlem in his mustard-colored Corvette. I went back to my room, pulled my two green suitcases from under my bed, and turned on

Casey Kasem. I made myself a cup of tea with milk and sugar and leaned back in my blue couch chair. I was not in a hurry to pack. I was not in a hurry to move. Whittier Hall, Room 7-C had been my home for the past two years.

The night before I was to vacate my room, I was on the floor selecting which mugs and saucers to tuck among my packed clothes. I heard a knock on my door. Probably the security desk making sure I got the "notice to vacate." I took my time getting to the door.

"Ted!"

"What are you doing here? I thought everybody was gone!"

"No, not yet…I'm on my way out."

He is holding a thick black jacket under his right arm. An overstuffed backpack is attached to his back. A green duffel bag hangs from his left shoulder.

"Come in." I said.

"Ok," he said, "I can't stay long. I just came to say bye. I'm leaving for Europe tonight. I'm taking a motorcycle trip across Europe and...maybe across North Africa, too. I just have to see how it goes."

He dropped his backpack and duffel bag at the door.

"Oh, my goodness. Are you going by yourself?"

We are standing in the middle of my room. I'm wearing my long pink terry cloth housecoat with an attached belt tied around my waist. Ted is in jeans and a collared blue sports shirt.

"Yeah...I've been wanting to take a motorcycle across Europe for a long time…it's been a dream. So now I'm doing it!"

"I am *sooo* impressed." I was spreading my fingers on my cheeks.

"Well, I just wanted to say bye...and see you before I left…so…"

He stepped toward me. He was still holding on to that thick black jacket. I leaned in, protruding my left cheek for a peck. He put the arm not holding the black jacket around my waist and planted a wet kiss on my cheek.

I was pulling my cheek back from that wet cheek kiss, but I was being held in place. Ted's arm not holding the black jacket was pressing me against his body. His lips were on mine.

What are you doing?

I wanted to resist. I wanted to ask, *Am I a stand-in for Cami?*

I didn't say anything. I wanted to see what his plans were.

He tossed his jacket somewhere behind him. Both his hands were now free to roam. I felt my robe belt loosen.

Why did I have all these bright lights on? Would it break the mood if I asked him to wait until I lower the lights? Too late.

He was working his way toward second base...then third...*Is he planning on rounding third base? Does he think I'm going to just sit back and let him head for a homerun? No way. You're not going to hit a homerun and leave me...*

He doesn't seem to be in a hurry for that homerun. *This White boy still has his blue collared shirt tucked into his jeans!* We found ourselves on the floor rolling around among my teacups and saucers. I was impressed by the care and enthusiastic admiration he bestowed upon my body. I appreciated his attention to detail. I appreciated his realization that if he was to make his flight, he needed to end this pleasure. He rose abruptly, helped me to my feet and grabbed his black jacket off the floor.

"I've gotta run," he said. "I'm late...see ya."

He headed out the door with his green duffel bag and black jacket hanging over one shoulder and his overstuffed backpack hanging over the other. I was left standing at the door, watching him hurrying down the hallway toward his dream of motorcycling across Europe.

I felt the urgency of the moment. This is 1972, the last year of my five-year plan, created with my friends over Singapore Slings at Jimmy's back in Carbondale. I have dreams, too. If I am to have a night club singing career, I better get started. I pulled out my burgundy spiral SIU notebook. I turned to my five-year plan.

Become a night club singer' was already written there. With my black Bic pen, I added the word "Now"!

Before I turned in my room key at the desk, I scoured campus bulletin boards tearing off strips with names of people offering voice, dance, or acting lessons. I tucked the white, yellow, and green strips into a white envelope. I placed the envelope in my "Important Papers" cardboard box alongside my Master of Arts Degree in Conseling, my Master of Education Degree, and my burgundy spiral notebook containing my five-year plan. The "Important Papers" cardboard box also contained my counseling books, my radio, my sheet music, and my cassette tapes.

The next morning, I was standing on the curb waiting for a yellow cab to take me and all my packed belongings to New York's East Side. I was on my way to my new home, a one-bedroom apartment with a doorman and a couch bed in the living room.

Those strips of paper I collected from Columbia's bulletin boards lead me to a singing coach. He was a retired musician and singer named Mr. Wiley. Every Tuesday after work, I caught the #1 train up to Harlem, to Sugar Hill to meet him in his high ceiling, garish living room. He sat spread out over the stool of his baby grand piano.

"Your voice is sexy…and the delivery is unique," he said. "But you need to broaden your repertoire. Let's try adding different songs. Let's try 'Maybe This Time,' and 'Walking my Baby Back Home.' There are plenty of jobs out there…you just got to be ready!"

I'm paying you to get me ready!

His fat arms were swinging from side to side, and he was levitating his broad body off the piano stool.

"You got the singing part down, but you gotta move. Get your hips involved. Dance, act, perform…you gotta put on a show!"

I enrolled in Berghof Drama Workshops. We met on Wednesday evenings. The class focused on improvisations. One of the scenes I played was about having an itch in my private area during a job interview. I don't like improvisations.

I also signed up for jazz dance at Carnegie Hall on Saturday mornings and in the afternoon, I did volunteer stage work with the Off-Center Children's Theater group. I was pursuing my dream.

19
SWEET FIND

By the time I moved in with Janet, she had left the Manpower Center. She got a new job in the beauty department at *New Fashion* magazine. When we were both at the Manpower Center, we could commiserate about the "incompetence of the administration" and debunk the recurring excuses our students presented for not attending classes. Now I just listened to her talk about her "wonderful" new job.

"We went on a photo shoot today...the models were incredibly beautiful. Of course, I did their makeup."

"I stopped by Bergdorf's and picked up just what I needed for my job, a five-piece ensemble. Look at this."

She spread out on my couch bed five pieces of clothing, a blue jacket, a blue skirt, blue slacks, a blue vest, and a white blouse. Her new wardrobe looked like what a stewardess would wear.

"See," she said. "I can mix and match...my vest and pants, skirt and white blouse..."

When she stepped out of her room in one of her outfits, I kept thinking she's going to ask me, "Coffee or tea?"

This one-bedroom apartment belongs to Janet...and rightly so.

I came to the apartment with nothing except my clothes, a few tea mugs, and my box of important papers. The dishes, sheets, towels...everything is hers. She has the right to take a leisurely bath every morning before she goes to work. I just have to wait my turn. It still puzzles me that she can't just take a quick shower like other working people!

One good thing about her baths though is the lingering fragrance that floods the whole apartment. I try to identify that fragrance. Is it jasmine or mango? Whatever it is, it clings to her stewardess blues and hangs in the air long after she has left for work.

One time when it was my turn to use the bathroom, I decided to poke around on her shelf to see what fragrance she was using. I wanted some fancy ideas I could use for myself in my own apartment someday.

Her white bath shelf is hooked over the front side of the tub. I bend down next to her shelf. I push aside sponges, two metal nail files, and a half-empty bottle of red nail polish. *That fragrance couldn't be buried...she just took a bath thirty minutes ago!*

I have to get to work. I unzip my cosmetic bag, retrieve my bar of white Dial soap and shower. As I am drying myself, I notice a bar of soap in the far corner of the tub. I bend to retrieve the bar and give it the smell test. My nostrils are overwhelmed with Janet's fragrance...from a common bar of soap?

I turn the bar over in my hand. I move it close and use my pointer finger to trace the worn lettering. *I have to put a name to this bar!*

"Z E S...ZEST! It's Zest!" I control a scream.

I say aloud. "Janet's fancy fragrance comes from a bar of Zest!"

That is so disappointing.

~

Janet and I are able to co-exist in this one-room apartment because she has a boyfriend. His name is Jay. I never met him, but he is a godsend. He takes in Janet from Friday morning to Sunday night. Yes, she is at Jay's apartment every weekend! I said to myself, "This roommate thing can actually work!"

I revel in my freedom. I don't get up at 6:30 in the morning and fold my bed into a couch. I don't look at photo shoots and listen to her self-esteem-building stories about her upbringing.

"My father is a college president."

"Me and my brother were always at the fancy dinners and parties at our house."

The apartment is mine until she returns on Sunday night. I just have Mondays through Thursdays after work in the apartment with Janet…for now.

20
THE SLEEPOVER

I had not heard from Troy since he graduated from Columbia and moved to Cleveland. He rushed there to accept one of the many job offers he was expected to receive. That was almost five months ago.

It was a Friday evening and Janet was at her boyfriend's apartment. I was in my pink two-piece pajamas sitting on my couch bed enjoying a bowl of large curd cottage cheese topped with two tablespoons of canned mixed fruit. The phone rang.

"Hello, Marge. How are you?"

I hesitated before I responded. "I'm fine…Troy?"

"Yeah…I been thinking about you…so I'm coming down to New York this Saturday. Is that all right?"

"Well, of course you can come to New York. Why not?"

"You know what I mean. I want to see you…spend time with you. Surely you gon let me do that."

I had to gather my thoughts so that my response would be clear and level-headed. I got up from my couch bed and put my fruit covered bowl of cottage cheese on the table.

"Troy," I said. "Yeah, I'd love to see you…and catch up."

"Marge, I can't wait to wrap my arms around you...it's been a long..."

His voice had lost its playfulness.

"I can stay at your apartment, right? We have to make up for lost time."

"You're welcome to stay the night at my apartment. I have a roommate, but she...no, it's fine, as long as you understand that I'm offering you a bed to sleep in...nothing more. I can't wait to hear about Cleveland!"

"Ok," he responded. "I'll see you around five or six tomorrow. Oh, what's your address?"

Troy arrived at my apartment between five and six. I was impressed that he kept his word. A nice change. All day at work, I was nervous...a man in my bed after five months and I'm being a prude!

When he entered my apartment, his hug was tight, his body was warm and his kiss on the cheek was light and gentle. He smelled of outdated Old Spice. *He hasn't caught on to the new fragrance, Aramis!* His Afro was tightly trimmed. His broad chest and slim hips, familiar.

We sat on my couch bed. I asked him about his work in Cleveland and about all the job opportunities there for Blacks. We caught up on people we knew back at Columbia. We laughed and remembered as we sipped tea with milk and sugar.

During a pause in our reminiscing, he said, "You are still something else."

He was smiling and giving me a once over with his eyes.

I responded with a smile, and a yawn.

"Ok, I'm tired," I said. "We're sitting on the bed. Why don't you use the bathroom first and I'll get the bed ready."

When Troy snuggled up against my backside, my mind was saying "No," but my body was saying 'Yes.' *Who would know? It's not like I'm a virgin. I'm on birth control pills and they're going to waste. Why not just...*

I felt a hand on my back. I felt another hand…I moved away from that hand and sat up.

"Troy, what are you doing?"

I reached over and turned on the lamp. He sat up covering his eyes with one hand.

"I told you already…you can sleep here, and that's all."

He was leaning into me on one elbow and mumbling.

"You can't be serious…I came all this way to see you and you gon treat me like this?"

"Yes, Troy, that's the way it is. Where have you been for the last five months?"

We parted the next morning the same way we parted back in June. I stood on the curb waiting for him to bring his mustard-colored Corvette to the front of the building. He placed his bag in the trunk, gave me a peck on the cheek, promising to call. He waved as he rounded the corner of Second Avenue, heading back to Cleveland.

21

THE CHOSEN ONE

As part of my job at Manpower, I listened to women crying through stories about "no money for transportation," "sick children" and "really bad headaches." Each was hoping their performance would lead to an excused absence and in turn, a full paycheck. Their stories intrigued me. I listened for hours, which meant I was keeping them from going to class. I could see Mrs. Dobbin's glaring eyes through the tiny window in my door as she crossed back and forth. When she hired a White woman named Cece to "embellish" our counseling staff, I got the message loud and clear: I was no longer the chosen one. Cece was replacing me.

I liked Cece. She was tall, frizzy haired, and wrapped herself in fringed, colorful shawls and low waist linen dresses. She was a privileged hippie.

One time we were having lunch in Cece's office. Mrs. Dobbins, with her darting eyes, was munching on a tuna sandwich on white bread. I was organizing my broken pieces of cheddar cheese onto saltine crackers. Cece was standing, opening a plastic container. I looked closer and saw the words Tupperware. The container was filled with chunked watermelon and cantaloupe. A ripe banana lay on her desk.

The conversation got around to the upcoming long weekend.

"Are you doing anything special this weekend, Cece?" Mrs. Dobbins asked.

"Oh, yeah," Cece said as she was tooth picking chunks of fruit from her blue covered Tupperware.

"My daughter and her boyfriend are coming down. Actually, my daughter arrives tomorrow, and her boyfriend arrives the next day."

"Wow!" I said. You must have a big house…where is everybody gonna sleep?"

Cece was still munching on a watermelon chunk.

"I've got enough room…it's a two-bedroom apartment. My husband and I are in one and my daughter and her boyfriend are in the other."

The office went quiet except for the sound of Cece's crunching and munching.

Mrs. Dobbins was fumbling with the wax paper on her tuna sandwich on white bread. I was staring at Cece, my mouth hanging open waiting for more sleeping together talk.

Cece threw up her hands. She was looking at me.

"You mean to tell me you have a problem with my daughter sleeping with her boyfriend? Come on…this is 1974!"

She was laughing out loud now and encasing her shaking head in her hands.

I felt her privilege coming through.

I defended myself.

"Hey, wait a minute. I didn't say there was anything wrong…I was just wondering…"

"What do you think these kids are doing back in Colorado? Where do you think they're sleeping? Believe me, they are sleeping together!"

Cece's arms and her body were reaching out towards me.

Mrs. Dobbins was looking at me with scolding eyes. How dare you ask such a question? But I could tell…she was intrigued by this spicy talk. She was a divorced sixty-something-year-old Black woman. Working is her life. She admired Cece. She liked the freshness that Cece brought to our stale lunchtime menu.

It soon became obvious that Mrs. Dobbins had soured on my Ivy League credentials. She was not happy that I was using class time to listen to women whose stories intrigued me. She seemed to relish Cece's privileged sassiness.

22
THE INTERVIEW

The New York Times classified section was my source for job hunting. I saw the following advertisement, "Counselor needed at Cooper Rehabilitation Center for Boys, Spanish preferred." I mailed in my cover letter and resume. Three days later I received a telephone call requesting an interview.

I arrived at the Rehabilitation Center's entry gate for my interview. Three or four large, muscular Black uniformed security guards manning the gate saw me and began rushing about, smiling and jostling with each other. A tall, muscular Black man in a dark blue blazer stepped out of the fray and unlocked the gate.

"Hello, you must be Ms. Edwards." He ran a finger down a clip board as he spoke.

"I'm Jim Bradley." The gold-colored name tag pinned to his lapel said Mr. Bradley, Head of Security.

"Yes, I'm Margaret Edwards. I'm here for an interview."

"Ok," he said. "You will be meeting in the conference room."

Keys started jangling among the security guards and en mass they rushed to open the series of locked doors to get me into the conference room. Mr. Bradley spoke and silenced the jangling keys.

"Benoy, please show Ms. Edwards to the conference room."

Benoy's keys started jangling. I turned and gave a big smile to the guards not selected. Their faces broke into big grins as they retreated back to their posts.

In the conference room, I was met by an older White man named Sam, who introduced himself as the Director of Counseling, and a younger White man named Aaron who introduced himself as the Assistant Director. They spent the hour telling me about the facility and the clients.

Sam spoke first.

"This Center houses adolescent boys ranging in age from ten to fifteen years old. The boys are placed in this facility because they have been involved in non-violent incidents with the law such as stealing from neighborhood homes, possessing marijuana and one kid for commandeering a city bus and picking up passengers—without a license."

That brought a chuckle from the two of them and an "Oh, my" from me. I smiled and brought a manicured right hand to my right cheek.

Then it was Aaron's turn.

"This facility keeps the boys locked up until interventions by the Counselor and the Group Leader determine that a boy has made sufficient use of offered resources to receive a home pass. Also, after a meeting with the administration and the Director, he can be approved for release to his home. A great deal of emphasis is put on student readiness for release in an effort to prevent recidivism. That's the job of the Counselor on each floor. We have three Counselors now and we are looking to hire one more."

I listened quietly as Sam and Aaron took turns explaining the program. They were both sitting across from me with their round bodies stuffed under a long polished brown table.

I was wearing my peach long-sleeved dress with a flared skirt that accentuated my waistline. My hair was flipped and my makeup was applied for maximum coverage. I could hear the security guards still jostling, jangling keys, and loitering outside the open door of the conference room.

The three floor counselors dropped by during my interview with Sam and Aaron. The first to show up was Jerry, a noisy White, older man in pressed jeans, platform shoes and a frizzy Jheri curl. He was laughing big and reaching high to high-five the guards and pulling himself up tall in his tight jeans. He was trying hard to appear well-adjusted.

Rushing in behind Jerry was a tall, thin young White woman named Rita. She was in brown slacks with her scalp exposed through her stringy brown hair. Her eyes were puffy, and her arms clutched stuffed manila folders to her chest. She exuded nervous anxiety. Jerry sneaked knowing glances at her. Something was obviously going on between the two of them.

Another young male named Bill showed up. He was about my height. He was dressed in a blue blazer. He was smiling and expressing, "I love this job. I always wanted a government job."

Looking at him with his blue Bic pen sticking out of the pocket protector in his blue plaid shirt, I believed him.

A tour of the center was the final step in the interview process. Mr. Bradley, in his blue sports jacket and slicked-back wavy hair, joined Aaron for my tour.

He pointed out the administrative offices on the first floor, the classrooms and food service on floors two and three, and the boys' housing on floors four to seven. He knew without hesitation which piece of metal hanging from his belt opened the locked doors on each floor.

When I stepped off the elevator into the hallway of the fourth floor, I expressed my surprise that it was so quiet. A security guard and a team leader were at their station, the hallways were empty of boys.

Mr. Bradley guided me past the first room of boys who were

lounging on their beds wearing their institution-issued uniforms of blue pants and gray shirts. Another group was sitting on beds and chairs playing cards.

When I walked into view, both groups looked up, threw down their cards, jumped off their beds and rushed to the doorways and into the hallway. There was whistling and giggling. I heard "woo-whee's" and…"she look good." Some had questions. "Mr. Bradley, she gon be our counselor…is she?"

The commotion brought boys from every room out into the hallway.

I was smiling and trying to move away from all those hands that were getting close enough to touch me.

Aaron was using "counselor speak" and trying to position his round body and outstretched chubby arms in front of me.

"You all go back to your rooms…you know better. This is not the way to behave."

Mr. Bradley surrounded me with his tall, fit body and his imposing long, strong arms. He spoke loudly and clearly to the boys.

"Go back to your rooms…now! Or face a lockdown...Ok, clear the hallway."

The team leader and the security guard joined in corralling the boys and ushering them back to their rooms. I took a deep breath. My presence almost caused a riot! I was glad to be escorted back to the tamer environment downstairs.

From my count, every professional I had met so far was White. Every non- professional was Black or Hispanic. With a clientele of over 300 Black and Hispanic adolescent boys, with a sprinkling of White and Chinese, the lack of diversity among the professional staff was evident. I was a Black, non-Spanish speaking female with counseling credentials from Columbia University. I was hired. Sam's last words to me were, "You just have to take Spanish classes."

I left the interview, took the train to the Berlitz Language

Center, and signed up for private Spanish lessons after work on Mondays and Thursdays. All my weekdays after work were now booked.

After two years at the Manpower Training Center, I became a counselor at Cooper Rehabilitation Center for Adolescent Boys.

23
THE COVER-UP

I had been on the job for two weeks when Aaron told me during lunch that he needed to speak to me. We met in his office on the second floor.

"So how do you like working with the boys, all thirty of them?" he asked, chuckling. He was trying to be light and engaging as I sat in front of his desk. He remained standing. He was wringing his hands, cracking his knuckles, and belching.

Aaron was for me a real government employee. He had been moved into an administrative position, but his visible responsibilities were unclear. He was overweight, always took the elevator between floors and never worked through lunch. I liked him, but he was Sam's gofer.

"Oh, I've worked with adolescent boys before...I like this age group." I was still wondering what Sam had told him to speak to me about.

"What do you think of the boys? I mean how do you like, uh...how they respond to you?"

He was pumping his arms and scratching his head trying to get me to understand what he was getting at. I am not understanding, so I asked straight out, "What are you trying to say, Aaron? Is there a problem?"

He leaned on his desk trying unsuccessfully to conceal a belch in his throat. "No, no…Oh, oh no!"

He was waving his hands trying to erase that question.

"No problem…we just think that…I mean, the way you dress. Like some of the guards…and these boys have been locked up in here for a long time…and I know they are young, but some of them have not seen a female…they get crazy when…you know…"

I laughed out loud.

"Ok, I get it. You want me to dress more modestly...like Rita… pants or long skirts."

He kept trying to clarify.

"It's nothing against you…it's just…I mean wearing a dress. I know you can see all the guys around here get crazy…seeing your…uh…legs and stuff."

"Sure," I said. "I can cover my legs."

It wasn't just because of the boys that I needed to dress more modestly. I needed to protect myself from perverts on the #1 train platform!

One time I was standing on the platform waiting for the train. I was standing near a large schedule display case wearing my blue dress with the red seam down the front. My mind was on my after-work jazz dance class and the dance steps we were practicing. "Lift and bend…quick hand."

"Ahhhh…" I screamed. *My butt cheeks!* Somebody grabbed my butt cheeks!

I swung around. Who did that? Who grabbed my butt cheeks! I was poised to punch the culprit. How dare you!

My adrenaline was pumping. *Where are you? You coward!*

My tearing eyes searched for the one guy who dared to give me eye contact. Nobody was there! Everybody was there! Young men and old men were standing, waiting, and scurrying by. Didn't anyone notice my butt violation?

The next day, I wore my brown pants. The temperature in the fourth-floor hallway, and on the #1 train platform dropped precipitously.

24
LONG OVERDUE

"Please return the book Humanistic Psychology by Carl Rogers. Due date: June 27, 1972."

— Teachers College Library, Columbia University

The note appeared in my mailbox in late October, almost six months after I had graduated!

I found the book in my unpacked "Important Papers" cardboard box. It was stuck between my diplomas, my certification papers, and my cassette tapes. The book was old and obviously not in demand. Yet I had to find the time between Spanish lessons, dance lessons, acting and singing lessons to take the train back to the library to return the book. I decided that the best drop-off day for me would be after work on Friday.

There was a chill in the air. I walked briskly from the train in my knee length striped black and white coat over black pants. I entered Russell Hall from Amsterdam Avenue and climbed the stairs to the library on the second floor.

At the information desk, I took the book from my tote bag and deposited it on the book return counter. The young woman reached for the book, checked the name, and ran her finger along the frayed binding. She glanced at me as if the fraying was my fault.

My arms were folded across my chest while she flipped through the index card box.

"Here it is," she said. "This book is long overdue…but we're not going to charge you. You're an alumnus!" She was smiling broadly in her attempt to be affable. I smiled back showing no teeth.

"Thank you," I said, and headed hurriedly to the exit and down the stairs, wrapping my coat more snugly around my neck.

"Marge...Marge."

I turned around and looked up to where the voice was coming from. I recognized Ted.

"Marge, how are you?" He was standing at the top of the stairs. His voice sounded winded. I had not seen him since he left me standing in my dorm door as he rushed off for his motorcycle trip across Europe.

"Oh, hi, Ted. I'm fine. I was just returning an overdue book…a counseling book. What are you doing here? Studying?"

Ted was still standing at the top of the stairs.

"No, I'm working here…for now…still doing my research for my doctorate. I have to do something to make a little money. I used to work at the daycare center. I had to quit. Well, I don't mean to keep you…just wanted to say 'hi.'"

"Well, I'm glad you did…it's nice to see you." I was turning to move further down the stairs.

"Yeah, so, uh, maybe we can have a drink sometime…" He was shifting and running a hand through the front of his hair.

"Oh...yeah, we can do that," I said, forcing a smile.

"So, I'll call you…I can write down your number." He was

digging hurriedly in his jean pockets, one at a time. He pulled out a pen from his left pocket. "I don't have paper...that's Ok, I'll write it on my hand."

With my number on his hand, we said, "See you," and I continued down the stairs. I took two trains to get back to my apartment on the East Side.

25
MANAGING UPTOWN

My job was routine now. The boys who, one at a time, walked tall into my office, sat tall, smiled, and checked on my well-being were there for one reason. They were there to convince me of their readiness to be given a pass home for the weekend. Rarely was I convinced.

I spent my lunch time in the conference room eating carrots and strawberry yogurt and watching my fellow counselors Jerry and Rita attempt to cover up their blooming romance. Seeing them sneak out the front door separately just to meet up later in the parking lot was the stimulus for conversation between me and Terry, the security guard on my floor.

One day, Terry asked me, "What's in that big bag you're always toting around with you all the time? Everybody keeps asking 'What's in that bag?'"

"Well, you can tell everybody that it's my stuff for my classes. I love music, so after work, I go to singing and acting classes."

He put a grin on his face.

"What...you don't believe me?" I asked.

"No, nah, I can tell you ain't gonna stay in this job...you look like you want something else."

"Yeah, I love the performing arts. One day, I want to sing in nightclubs. So, after work, I go to classes."

On and off during the day, we stand at his station talking and munching on Nacho Cheese Doritos when the boys are in school.

Sometimes we talk about my night club singing career. One time Terry said, "You know what you need...you need a good manager. You should let me be your manager."

"You...my manager!" I said, looking around to make sure no boys were in earshot.

In a hushed voice I asked him, "What do you know about managing?" I was waving him off and giggling.

He was not laughing. He had on his "guard" face.

"I may not know much about music, and especially about singing, but I know people. I know clubs in Harlem, and I know how to get you in front of the right people."

I stopped giggling. I liked what I was hearing. Here was a square jawed, big Black man in a blue security guard uniform engaging in no-nonsense talk about my singing career. I liked that.

"Well," I said. "How would this work? We both work here. We can't be sneaking around like Jerry and Rita."

"We don't have to sneak around. Working here and your singing career are two different things. What we do outside work is strictly our business. When I have something lined up, I give you a call...and off we go."

Nobody 'manages' without some kind of strings attached.

I said, "That's all very nice, but why do you want to 'manage' me? What's in it for you? I have no money to pay..." He cut me off.

"I'm not looking for money...I like your drive and I wanna see you make it. Now, when you get to be a big-name singer...then we can talk about money!" He paused and jabbed his pointer finger in the air above his head.

I smiled at the sound of that.

So, Terry became my manager. He called me on Friday nights if he had an engagement lined up.

"There's an open mic night at a club on 155th Street. I'll pick you up at nine o'clock."

Singing in Harlem was hard for me. I had never sung in front of Black clubgoers before. I was a big hit singing for those rich White kids at Columbia, but the one time I stood in front of Black people singing "Mr. Bojangles" or "Ain't Misbehavin'," nobody noticed me, and nobody clapped. I blamed that on my repertoire.

So, I got a new voice teacher named Billy who was hired to get me stage ready with songs that would appeal to any discriminating audience. He added, "A Kiss to Build On" and "I Wish I Knew How it Feels to be Free."

26

TALK, DRINK, LISTEN

I still held out hope that Troy had learned a lesson. If he wanted a relationship with me which included allowing him to ravage me in bed, he needed to be more reliable and attentive.

So, when my phone rang at eight p.m. on a Thursday night, I assumed it was him calling to apologize.

I wanted him to think I had moved on with my life. He needed to hear the voice of a busy, breathless, and hurried woman. I didn't want him to hear the sound of longing. I took a few deep breaths, then I picked up the phone.

"Hello," I said, breathing fast expelling air from my mouth. I was ready for his lies.

"Hi, Marge. This is Ted."

There was a beat before I could speak. I had to adjust my voice and my attitude. I had to sound joyful.

"Oh, hi, Ted," I managed to say.

"Did I interrupt something? You sound busy." *Good acting, Marge.*

"No, no…just sitting here listening to music." I lied.

"Oh, good." he said. "I was just wondering if you would like to go for a drink somewhere tomorrow, not long, just to a place in your neighborhood."

"Yeah, that would be great. Uh, I'm just on the corner of 72nd· The doorman will ring me."

"Ok, I'll meet you in the lobby at around seven. Is that Ok?"

"Yeah, fine…see you tomorrow."

On the train home from work, I thought a lot about this "drink." That's exactly what we will have. If he thinks I'm going to let him finish the game he started on the floor of my apartment right before he left for his motorcycle trip to Europe, that is not going to happen. He will not step one foot beyond the downstairs lobby!

I took a Zest shower and slipped my green hooded jacket over my brown turtleneck and brown slacks. It was cold outside. When Craig called that my guest had arrived, I took the elevator down to find Ted and Craig standing outside on the curb. They were in conversation about Ted's motorcycle parked out front. Ted was wearing his black motorcycle jacket over a black turtleneck and black slacks. As I approached the door, Craig rushed to open it for me, explaining as we made our way to join Ted near the curb.

"We were just talking about his 650 British Triumph…lots of power."

Ted smiled at seeing me.

"Hi." He gave me a peck on my left cheek. *He wouldn't dare wrestle me to the sidewalk and...*

He extended a hand toward Craig.

"Marge, did you know that Craig here used to own one of these?"

Craig was smiling and fondling the handle of the motorcycle.

"Maybe you would like to take it for a spin around the block sometime?" Ted asked.

"No, no. I'm too old for that." Craig was scuffling backwards, chuckling, and fluttering his hands, dismissing the idea.

I was just standing there listening to two White guys laughing and talking motorcycles.

Ted and I walked to a restaurant bar three blocks from my apartment. The place catered to the younger, East Side crowd. We sat at a corner table for two. Ted ordered drinks, a Rusty Nail for him, a Singapore Sling for me.

Then he talked. I listened.

"I can't wait to finish my doctorate. My friend Carl is helping me analyze the data. I'm working in the library to make some money. I'll probably need to ask for a loan from Dad. I'm now a teaching fellow, so I have graduate housing on campus."

All the while, I was picking at the fruit stick that came with my drink. I ate the cherry first, then the chunk of pineapple. I sipped from my glass and when Ted took a breath, I threw in an "oh" or "ah" or "that's good."

Ted ordered another drink and while waiting, queried about me. "Oh, I'm fine…still working. I think you knew about the Manpower job I had. I left that and I'm now working at a place for adolescent boys. Still doing my singing classes…it's fun."

When our drink glasses were empty, we walked back to my building. Craig was there to greet our return with a smile and an open door. Ted walked me to the elevator.

"This was fun. If you are free maybe next weekend, we can do something, if you want."

"Of course," I said. "That would be good."

27
GOING, GOING, GONE!

It was a Thursday evening in November just after I had cleaned my dishes after a dinner of baked beans and two hot dogs. Janet came to the living room table with her weekend bag and a tennis shoe in each hand. I had never seen her pack for her weekend sleepover. I was always out learning Spanish and she was always gone by the time I got home. She seemed to be running late today for some reason.

She stuffed the shoes in her bag and struggled with the zipper to get it closed. I was sitting on my couch bed watching her struggle. Her bag was zipped. She closed her long-manicured fingers around the two straps and turned to face me.

"I want to let you know that I've decided not to renew my lease."

I think I heard her say something about the lease.

I shifted my body to the edge of the couch, leaned forward and asked, "What did you say?"

She pushed out an audible sigh, shifted her blue overnight bag to both hands and hung it in front of her knees. She emphasized her intentions, one word at a time. "I'm letting you know that I am not renewing the lease on this apartment."

I sat there, leaning forward with my hands folded on my lap.

"So, what does that mean?" I asked.

"It means that if you want the apartment you have to sign a new lease."

She was moving toward the front door with her blue overnight bag. She deposited it near the door.

I stood up now. I followed her to the door trying to understand this lease business.

I asked her, "Can't you just keep your name on the lease? I don't..."

She interrupted me.

"I've already given notice. You need to let them know if you want the apartment. I'm moving in with my boyfriend."

I was befuddled. *I'm not ready to sign a lease! I can't afford to pay the rent with my salary! But on the other hand...she will no longer be living here!*

"Wow," I said.

I was in a daze. I was staring at her but not hearing most of what she was saying. Her arms and her mouth were moving, and I heard words like..." leaving everything...my bed, the couch... moving in with Jay."

She left the apartment for the last time leaving behind the scent of Zest.

Three months after Janet left the apartment, I was still reveling in living alone. I had a bedroom, my own kitchen, and my own Zest. I was very busy dancing, singing, acting, and becoming a Spanish speaker.

Ted had kept his word and called almost every weekend proposing that we go out. One time he came over on a Saturday afternoon.

"I want to take you for a spin around the block on my motorcycle."

I was appalled at the idea.

"I can't get on that thing...it's too big and loud…I've never been on a motorcycle before. These streets are too crowded…it's dangerous around here."

And I was appalled at the idea for reasons I did not share. *That motorcycle is so loud. A Black woman sitting behind a White guy with her legs open wide and her arms around his waist holding on for dear life. What would these East Side White folks make of that scene? Doesn't he have any scruples about this scenario I just painted?*

Ted continued to encourage me.

"Ah, come on…it's loud because it's a British Triumph 650cc… it took me across Europe. Surely, you'll be safe just going around the block!"

Craig was standing at his post near the door, smiling.

"Here, put on the helmet." Ted handed me a red and white helmet.

I took it, wondering how I'm going to maintain my hair flip with this hard hat crushing down on my curls. I gingerly put on the helmet.

I took a deep breath, walked to the right side of the bike, grabbed onto Ted's black thick waterproof jacket, and threw my left brown pant leg over the seat behind him. He revved up the engine and we took off.

I was immediately smacked in my face by the cold wind. I hid my face behind his back. We were on level pavement, then we bumped through a pothole. We whizzed past slow vehicles and leaned into turns. He was slowing down. I raised my head and peeked around Ted's back. He brought that monster cycle to a stop. We were back in front of my building, and I was still alive and smiling! Ted debarked and gave me a helping hand. He was smiling and removing his black gloves.

"Now was that so bad?"

"No," I said. "It was just so cold." I shivered to emphasize the point…" It was Ok. I'm just not a motorcycle person."

I slipped that helmet off my curls and reached up to finger them back in place. My hair had to be in order. We had another Rusty Nail and Singapore Sling night planned.

28
AKI

Having my own apartment was a dream come true. I loved coming home and finding no one there. I loved sleeping in a bed in a bedroom. I loved creating peanut butter sandwiches and leaving the jar on the counter. I loved going to the bathroom and leaving the door open. I also loved my singing, dancing, and acting classes.

I had a choice. I could give up my dream of becoming a nightclub singer because I had no money for lessons, or I could get a roommate to help pay the bills.

I tacked my "Looking for a Roommate" note on two reliable bulletin boards at Columbia. I got a call two days later.

"Hello, you still looking for roommate?"

"Yes, I am."

"I want to rent."

This person sounds foreign.

"Are you a student?" I asked.

There was a pause. Maybe I spoke too fast. I asked again, speaking slowly this time.

"Are you a student...at Columbia?"

"Not now...before," she said. "I come tomorrow."

Her name was Aki. She arrived wearing bell bottom jeans, a striped long-sleeved shirt under a rawhide vest and sandals on her feet. Her long black hair was tied in the back with a red bandana. I didn't want to judge her by her appearance. I just needed basic information like, "What did you study, and where are you living now and have you had a roommate before?"

I was not clear what her answers were because I was not sure she understood the questions. All I learned was that her parents were in Japan, that she used to be a student, and that she would bring her things on Saturday morning. She understood that I needed one month of security and that her part of the rent would be $160 a month, plus half of the utilities. I pointed out that her bed was the pullout couch we were sitting on.

The whole time I was talking to her about the apartment, she sat quietly looking around like she was casing the joint. I showed her the closet space for her stuff and the location of kitchen utensils. I loaned her bedding and showed her how to make the couch bed.

I braced myself for Saturday morning when I would lose my freedom.

Aki arrived early with one large brown suitcase and two stuffed green duffel bags. She set about filling her assigned spaces with books, packages of noodles, and a few clothes. I tried to make conversation.

"So do you go back to Japan to visit?"

She answered, "Not for long time."

"Do you have brothers and sisters?"

"Only one sister."

She seemed reluctant to talk. *Probably a foreign thing*.

I left her to unpack.

I continued my weekly routine of going to work and going to classes. I expected Aki to also establish her own routines. I began to wonder what her routines were since every day when I came home, she was sitting on the couch watching television. As soon as I said, "Hello," she turned the TV off, folded her arms across her chest, scowled and shifted her back to me. *A foreign thing?*

Each evening, when I went into the kitchen to make myself some dinner, usually rice, beans or a salami sandwich, Aki followed me. She started reaching for pots to make her rice or tempura or soup. I opened the silverware drawer, she yanked open the top cabinet door. I dodged being hit in the head. I tried to wash my dirty plate, she vigorously stirred her noodles. The two of us in that tiny space meant reaching over each other and risking being banged in the head by cabinet doors!

One time I said, "Aki, you don't have to wait until I come home to make your food. This kitchen is too small for two people." She turned her head and body away from me saying nothing.

Every day, when I enter the kitchen, she gets up from the couch and joins me. She grabs, bangs, hoards, turns, pushes, and sucks her teeth. I escape to the dining room table with my loaf of white Wonder bread and my jar of creamy peanut butter.

I made it a habit to get up early, shower and savor my quiet time alone before Aki rose from the couch bed. In these early morning moments by myself, I felt the apartment was mine again. The bathroom was my sanctuary. I closed my eyes in the shower and caressed my body with the suds of Zest. I took a deep breath and wallowed in the sweet fragrance. I opened my eyes and reached for lotion in my bathtub bin and...*what is this?*

There is a white, miniscule paper roll up...or is it rolled cloth pieces laying on the inside of my bin? I pick it up, unroll the layers, and examine the texture. It seems to be a roll of thin paper...like papier mâché. *Another one of those foreign things?*

As I get out of the shower, my eyes scan the corners of the wash bowl and the bathtub. There's another one and...another! What are these things?

I walk to the kitchen. I peer into the corners of the kitchen counter. There's one in the corner...and there's one in the other corner! I open the silverware drawer. There's one! And in the refrigerator? There's one...two...three! My heart starts racing.

What is going on with this woman? Slipping little pieces of rolled-up paper all over my apartment! *This is not a foreign thing, this is crazy!*

At work, I tried to get more insight into Aki's behavior. I brought the situation up with Aaron since he had experience working with persons with aberrant behavior. After listening to my distressing story of finding tiny rolled-up paper hidden in the bathroom and kitchen corners, he burst into bending at the waist laughter.

"She sounds really, really weird to me. Who puts little rolled-up papers all around an apartment? You should go around and pick them all up and see what happens!"

"Thanks, Aaron." I was too scared to do that. But I had been warned.

The day after I interviewed Aki, I got a call from her landlady who said to me,

"Aki may not be the roommate you are looking for. She has some strange behavior."

I dismissed her warning. She was just a White woman uncomfortable around foreigners. I thanked her for the call.

When I got home that evening, I brought a rolled-up paper from the kitchen and held it in my extended hand towards Aki.

"Aki, I see these little rolled up things all over the apartment, what are these things?"

She didn't answer. She jumped up from the couch, grabbed the rollup from my hand and rushed into the kitchen. I followed her.

"These are mine," she yelled. She was frantically looking for the spot where I had removed the sample. "They belong to me." she proclaimed.

"Aki," I said in a stern voice. "I need to know what these things are. I don't want these things in my apartment!"

I followed her around. She was turning her back to me and

wildly scampering from the bathroom to the kitchen. Her hands were skillfully rolling and re-rolling the paper strips. Her eyes were attentive; her body was hunched. I was stymied.

I slept with my bedroom door locked that night.

One evening when I returned home from work, Craig greeted me with his usual,

"Good evening, Miss. I hope you had a good day."

I walked to my mailbox and retrieved my mail. He usually pushes the elevator button and bids me good night.

On this day, he seemed to be stalking me, following me from the door to my mailbox. He didn't push the elevator button.

Instead, he spoke in a shy, obsequious manner.

"Miss, I need to speak to you about something."

I moved with him away from the elevator door.

"Sure, what's going on?" I was examining my mail for bills.

"Well," he said. "It's not my place, but it's about your roommate."

I looked up from my mail and focused on his words.

"She's not good. She acts really strange…she won't let me open the door for her...she won't even say 'Good morning.' She acts real mean…maybe you should get another roommate."

"Oh, thanks, Craig." I smiled through clenched teeth.

"I didn't think she ever left the apartment."

"Oh yes, ma'am. She goes out…after you leave. She's out all day…until about four o'clock."

So, she does go out during the day! She's not a dependent recluse! And she has the nerve to disrespect Craig! I shouldn't have been so quick to let her move into my apartment. Right now, I have to find a way to get her out.

I have to play this right and not be too hasty. I have a lot to consider. She pays her rent on time…and in cash! Timing is key.

Almost every Sunday, Ted and I meet for brunch under the hanging plants in the garden at Greenways Restaurant on the East Side. It is my favorite breakfast place. I always order a well-done two egg omelet with bacon and cheese and sprigs of watercress, and a fruit cup on the side.

For the last couple of Sundays, my joyful brunch outings have been marred by my Aki dilemma. Ted tries to change the subject by talking about the hands he is sculpting in the art class he is taking. One time he brought a hand with the pointer finger pointing up and another time with a finger pointing to the right. I never understood why he was so fascinated by hands.

"I have a plan, Ted," I said, getting back to my obsession with Aki. "I am just going to tell her to leave…next Friday. What do you think?" I was munching on green grapes.

"Sounds good to me," he said. "Good luck. "

My drink on most Sundays was always black tea with milk and sugar.

"Ted," I said. "Today, I want a mimosa!"

When I entered the apartment after work on Friday, Aki switched off the television. I went to the bathroom and washed my hands, being careful not to touch the little rolled-up paper placed near the base of the washbowl. I walked to the kitchen. She joined me. She grabbed the one good saucepan, added water from the sink, slammed the pan on the stove and reached over my head to get a bowl from the cabinet.

I left the kitchen. I took a seat at the head of the dining room table with my loaf of Wonder bread and jar of creamy peanut butter. Aki came to the table and sat at the other end of the table with her left side facing me. She ate her noodles from a bowl on her lap. Not a word was passed between us. For the past three months, this was my experience with Aki.

Tonight was different. I spoke. I spoke with conviction. The words that she heard were definitive.

"Aki," I said. "I'm moving."

She stopped chewing and turned to look at me. Her eyes were wide. Her face was streaked with strands of hair that had escaped from her bun. I couldn't tell if she was surprised or frightened. She was holding a soup spoon. I moved my peanut butter spreading knife closer to my plate.

She placed her half eaten bowl of noodles onto the table.

"Why you need to move?" she asked. "This place Ok."

I kept my nerve. I continued my straight talk.

"It's not Ok for me, Aki."

I let that sink in.

"My lease is coming due in three weeks, and I don't plan to renew it. This apartment is too expensive. So, you need to find another place to live."

I stood up, gathered my loaf of white Wonder bread and jar of peanut butter, and headed for the kitchen. I expected her to hiss and turn her back to me. I expected her to follow me into the kitchen.

Instead, she turned her seated body toward the kitchen. Her face took on an animation that I had not seen before.

"I know a place," she said. "In Brooklyn."

She stood smiling to herself.

"Not much money and…very big. We can get place together. My friend can show us."

I spoke once again, slowly this time.

"Aki, I want a place of my own…in Manhattan. You need to find a place to live in the next three weeks.

Locking my door when I went to bed was now a habit.

29

CASH FLOW, STREET WALKERS, AND OTHER SEXY WORDS

I was alone again. The monthly $360 rent was mine to pay. I cut back on my activities that cost money.

I gave notice to Phil, my third singing teacher. I stopped attending jazz dance classes at Carnegie Hall, and I stopped drama classes at Berghof Drama Workshop.

I stopped taking Spanish lessons. No one at work noticed or seemed to care since I was never asked about the classes or asked to speak a word of Spanish. I spent money only on train fare to get to work and to get to the Off-Center Children's Theater group to volunteer.

I finally gave Craig permission to skip the phone call and allow Ted free access to my apartment. Ted was by now working on analyzing his dissertation data. Most of his visits to my apartment centered around his sitting at the dining table surrounded by piles of rubber banned notecards, all labeled and numbered. His hands were moving labeled and numbered notecards from one pile to another. His face and body expressed bewilderment.

One time he brought his friend and fellow doctoral student, Carl, to help him make sense of his data. I knew Carl as one of the most astute students in the doctoral program. But he had a drinking problem. One day he was the responsible father of two and the smart, articulate doctorate student. A few days later his family would be notified that he was found slumped over a table in a bar on the Lower West Side.

Today in my apartment, he is sober. His appearance defies that conclusion. The white fringe around the back of his head is scraggly as is his white beard. He hunches his long thin body over my dining room table peering at numbers and lines on sheets of white chart paper.

Together, he and Ted count the number of mothers here, count the number of babies there and record the words of the mothers. Ted moves notecards from one pile to another and scribbles numbers on sheets of chart paper now attached to my living room wall.

Anxiety is easing. A sense of lucidity permeates the air. I keep the potato chips coming.

As Ted was getting closer to finishing his dissertation, he had more time to spend at my apartment on weekends. Each time he came, he brought me a gift. He came with flowers or candy or jewelry. One time he brought me the "Moods" album by Neil Diamond. He knew how much I loved the song "Play Me."

One cold Friday night near the end of November, we decided to bundle up and take a walk down Second Avenue just to get out of the house. I had a scratchy throat so I gargled with salt water before we left. By the time we returned to the apartment, my throat required a cup of hot tea and a couple more gargles before I went to bed.

I tried to sleep. I tried to refrain from swallowing. My throat was pulsating and burning. I breathed through my mouth to get the air to cool my burning throat. At about one o'clock in the morning, the pain was unbearable.

"Ted," I whispered. He was fast asleep. I managed to shake him awake.

"What's the matter…you all right?" he asked, squinting, and sitting up on one elbow.

My throat pain would not allow me to speak. I pointed at my throat. All I could mumble was, "Doctor."

"Ok, let's go to Lenox Hill Hospital emergency room. It's just a few blocks away."

We bundled up, walked the three blocks to the emergency room and waited to be seen. A young White doctor invited me into a small office and waved me to a chair.

"How can I help you?" he asked.

My throat was burning so badly, I began to tear up. All I could do was point to my throat and whisper, "Hurts."

The young man spoke for me. "You have a sore throat. Let me take a look." He took a flat tongue depressor from a glass flask on the desk.

"Open up."

He pushed down my tongue and looked around. He walked to the garbage can, pushed the lid open with his foot and dropped in the used tongue depressor. He returned to stand over me.

"Well, you do have some inflammation…Are you always out walking this late?"

I looked at him with questioning eyes. I wanted to ask him to explain his question. I wanted to ask him if he was assuming that I was a whore or some kind of street walker. I wanted to call him a puny little White bastard. I wanted to slap him across his face.

I refrained from slapping him across his face. I couldn't ask him anything. I couldn't tell him anything.

My throat pain wouldn't allow it. All I could do was wipe away the tears of pain running down my face.

He handed me a pack of four menthol throat lozenges.

"Just suck on these…you should feel better."

He sent me on my way with lozenges that caused my throat to burn and throb even more. I was not able to talk, but I could think.

I thought about how regardless of my presenting ailment, the

White doctors treating me always found the cause or the cure to be somehow related to sex. *What is it with these White doctors?*

Even as a bumpy faced thirteen-year-old seeking help with my acne, the White doctor encouraged me to get a boyfriend (and have sex) and "that would help."

When I was yelping through a pelvic exam in the health unit at SIU, the White doctor stopped probing long enough to admonish me, "I know you have had sex before!"

At Columbia's health unit still seeking acne treatment, the White doctor gave me birth control pills. The pills did help, but was he thinking that I was having sex or too much sex? And now, this puny assed young White doctor sees sex as the cause of my sore throat!

The next morning, Ted and I took an early train to St. Luke's Hospital on the West Side hoping to get a doctor who would avoid connecting my sore throat to sex. A White doctor attended to me. He examined my throat, diagnosed my sore throat as strep throat, and prescribed medicine.

A week later, a bill from Lenox Hill Hospital arrived in my mailbox. It said, "Pay $95 immediately for emergency services."

I tore the bill in half and flung it into a trash can on the corner of 2nd Avenue and 72nd Street.

30

WHERE AM I?

"Hello Ted…Ted! I think I found an apartment…but I'm not sure."

I'm standing in a phone booth yelling into a pay phone looking around trying to figure out where I am.

"Where are you?" Ted yells.

"I'm on the west side…somewhere…I'm looking for the name of the street."

I leaned my head out of the booth as much as I could and looked on the street corner for a name or a number.

"All I see is 85th Street…and the apartment has a backyard…it seems really nice."

"Marge, is it anywhere near Central Park? If it's near Central Park…you should grab it…that is a great place to…"

"Let me ask the real estate guy…hold on…"

I let the phone dangle on its wire and ran over to the realtor.

"Excuse me, sir, are we near a Park?"

The realtor frowned.

"Well, we are not near a park unless you mean Central Park West, which is the main street right up there." He was pointing. I didn't wait for more information. I rushed back to the dangling pay phone.

"Ted, he said there is no park...just a street called Central Park West."

Ted started yelling excitedly now.

"An apartment near Central Park West...with a backyard! Take it. Grab it now!"

I hooked the phone back on its holder, rushed up to the realtor and said, "I'll take it!"

Book IV

"Love is like wildflowers;
it's often found in the
most unlikely places."

Ralph Waldo Emerson

1
WELCOME!

The day I moved into my West Side apartment, I was robbed.

A large brown shag rug covered the middle space of my new living room. My brown fold-out couch was pushed into place under the one barred window. My brown table with four wooden chairs were in place next to the kitchenette counter. I put my brown coffee table in front of my brown fold-out couch. That large living room space had a lot of brown stuff. I like brown.

My single twin bed was squeezed against one side of the small bedroom that was attached to the back of the front living space.

Ted said he needed a cold drink. He left to buy one from the restaurant on the corner.

I heard a knock on the door.

I rushed to answer. *Ted forgot something.*

It was not Ted. There standing before me was a young Black man. He had an unkept large Afro and was wearing a wrinkled long-sleeved blue shirt open at the top. His black chest hairs were exposed. He was wearing a big, friendly smile.

"Oh, hi," he said. "You just moved in, right? I live upstairs and wanted to just stop by and say 'Hi' and 'Welcome'!"

"Well, thank you." I said, smiling right back at him. *Wow, people here are so friendly...so different from the people in my building on the East Side.*

"Yeah, I just moved in today."

We were standing in my open doorway. My neighbor was fidgeting, scratching his arm with one hand, and blinking his eyes. *This guy is acting weird...but people on the West Side are like that, I guess.*

"What's your name?" I asked, keeping the conversation friendly and light.

"Oh, my name is Jerry…your place seems really nice."

He was bending and weaving his head and looking past me into my apartment.

"Would you like to come in?" I asked.

"I would love to."

He pushed past me 'oohing' and 'aahing' as he walked past my end tables, bookshelves, and television. He extended his hand to touch each piece as he moved into my small bedroom attached to the back of the living room. He was hurrying. His right hand continued to glide over furniture tops as he moved through looking and admiring how great everything was arranged.

I was following him with words like, "Yeah, I like that table", "It is a nice piece", "thank you", and finally, "it was nice meeting you."

I closed the door behind him. I leaned my back against the door.

What just happened? That guy probably saw Ted leave and came to my apartment. What for?

I retraced his path through my apartment. I went past the entryway closet, noted the end table his hand had glided over. I walked into the bedroom and looked at the small bedside table where I kept my watch and earrings. *My watch is missing!* I went to the kitchen counter. *My ring is missing! I've been robbed!*

I leaned on the kitchen counter. I couldn't breathe. How stupid! Who invites a robber into their apartment and gives him a tour?

What do I say to Ted?

Five minutes after "Jerry" escaped with his bounty, Ted returned.

2
ACTION!

I continued as a volunteer for the Off-Center Children's Theater. Every Saturday during the season, I joined the cast at South Street Pier to organize performances for children and their families. There was no music or singing involved, but I was committed to learning all aspects of show business. I helped secure scene backdrops with sandbags. I was also sometimes in charge of getting the right props in the hands of the right actors.

One time as I was fastening the hatch on the prop box, Andy, the Off-Center Theater director approached me. He was clutching a load of costumes under one arm and pieces of straggly papers in the hand not securing the costumes.

"Hi, Marge." He was breathless.

"I don't know if you're interested...but I got a call from a buddy of mine. He's looking for someone to be in a movie…or some kind of show he's making. I told him about you…so if you are interested, you need to go see him…here take the paper on top."

He moved the hand with the straggly papers toward me. I reached for the paper on top. I saw a name and address scribbled.

He was still talking as he was moving away. I was moving with him. I had questions.

"What kind of movie is it?" I had heard about women getting...

"I don't know...just show up on Monday and see if you wanna do it."

On Monday morning, I called Aaron and gave him a "not feeling well" story. I spent the next thirty minutes trying on clothes. I didn't know what I was dressing for. Should I put on a dress to show my legs or put on slacks to show confidence and nonchalance?

I took my cue from the Children's Theater actors. A pair of brown pants and a striped shirt had to do. I clipped my flipped hair up in the back but let a curly string hang bouncing in front of each of my ears. I applied face powder for blemish coverage.

When I arrived at the address listed on the paper, I approached a woman at the desk.

"Hi, I'm Marge Edwards. I was told to come to see, uh...Brandon." I read from the scrap of paper. "Meyers?"

The woman pointed behind her.

"Go in there."

I walked in the direction she pointed. A placid-faced, middle-aged White man with salt-and-pepper hair and a noticeable paunch was talking and waving a clipboard around. He was addressing an audience of one older woman and a few other younger people. Everybody was White. When I entered the room, he addressed me like I was somebody he was expecting.

"You sent by Andy?" he asked. His audience turned towards me.

"Yes."

I had trouble finding my voice. I tried again.

"Yes...Andy told me to come."

He was looking at me. He eyed me up and down. They all were looking me up and down. I felt like a specimen. *What kind of movie am I being scrutinized for?*

To the older woman standing to his left, he instructed, "Get rid of the twirls."

"This way," the woman said.

I followed her to a tent with open palettes of makeup, lipsticks, combs, and brushes scattered over the counters. Tall mirrors covered one side. The woman didn't ask me to sit. She found two hair pins and attached my two curly strings of hair to the curly pile in the back of my head.

I followed her to another, bigger tent. We walked past bottled water, a percolating coffee pot, and boxed donuts organized on a brown paper-covered table. We walked past men and women seated in folding chairs. Some were standing in groups munching on glazed donuts and sipping coffee from Styrofoam cups. I could tell they were actors. They ignored me. I was the only Black face in this space, and I was completely ignored! I liked that.

We reached a clothes rack where I was instructed to select my size. I asserted myself at this point.

"Excuse me, but can you tell me about this movie? I'm not sure what my role is."

The older woman stopped going through the racks and looked at me askance.

"Nobody told you?"

She was sucking her teeth and shaking her head.

"This is not a movie, Honey. This is a training video...for nurses and hospital staff. You're one of the nurses."

So that's it! Andy's buddy just needed a Black face in his video. That's why I'm here. I'm not special. My Black face is supposed to represent all Black hospital workers.

I was satisfied with my role. I selected my uniform, including a cap, white stockings, and white shoes. I treated myself to a donut. They didn't have tea bags, so I took another donut. I took a seat among my fellow actors. I was feeling good. I smiled at a woman a couple of seats from me. She mistook my smile to mean I wanted to make conversation. She leaned over to me.

"You an extra, too?"

I screwed up my face because I didn't know what she meant.

"I'm not sure...the lady told me that I'm a nurse."

"Oh, that means you're a primary. You got a title. You probably got some lines, too. I'm just a person who walks around...to fill space, I guess. That's why I'm called an extra."

"Do you do a lot of extra jobs like this?" I asked. I wanted to find out if being an extra could be something I could do.

"Not a lot. Only when I run out of something steady."

The older woman was standing at the snack table now yelling instructions at us.

"We're loading up now to go on location to Jersey. Have your wardrobe, your props...whatever you were assigned. Let's go."

Location was way out in the country, no houses or people in sight. I saw just open fields, patches of trees and farmland.

We all gathered in another tent much like the one back in New York. There were lots of other people already there when we arrived. We were told to get dressed and report back to the tented seating area. When we returned, Brandon was waiting up front with his clipboard.

"Ok, we're going to do one hospital scene at a time. You will be called when it's your scene. We intend to be efficient, but we will get the result we are after. So, relax, enjoy the snacks, and we'll see you later."

Later for me was early afternoon around one o'clock. Until then, I spent the morning trying to keep my cap from falling off and tugging at my sagging pantyhose. I walked to look out of the two plastic covered windows at blurred trees and wooden structures in the distance. I stood around the brown paper-covered table and feasted on ham and cheese, egg salad, and cucumber and tomato sandwiches. I drank two 7 Ups and ate two oreo cookies. I sat in a brown folding chair in the middle of the room and waited.

An hour later, I heard my name called. I followed the routine of those called before me. I boarded a bus and was told we were off to the hospital set. We were ushered into a set of a long hospital corridor with beds, IV poles, and a nurse's station. I was one of six nurses all dressed in our whites. Two orderlies were in green. Three other extras were in street clothes. A male patient occupied each of the two beds in the corridor.

Brandon was in charge.

"Ok, listen up. We are going to do three takes…two to practice and the last one will be the final take. We are here to make a video to demonstrate how to evacuate patients from a hospital or nursing home if there is a fire. Like I said, we will be doing three takes…two without the fire and finally we stage the evacuation with a fire and smoke and all the rest of it."

"Ok, nurses over here."

That's me! I joined him along with five other women in white. He directed me to stand on the right side of the first patient's bed and two other nurses on the left side. He left us standing there. He went behind us to bed number two and placed the other nurses on the right and left side of the patient's bed.

He stood back against the wall looking from side to side at his placements. I felt his eyes on me. He walked over to me.

"Marge, is it?" I nodded. He stepped in front of me as he continued.

"Nurses, your job is to urgently and efficiently roll these beds down the corridor and at the same time tend to your patient. Orderlies, you are managing the equipment, pushing and clearing the corridor of obstacles. Questions? Let's run it."

I'm not an actor...these other people have been 'extras' in films, I need this guy to show me what he wants me to do.

"Action!"

The beds started rolling. The orderlies and the other nurses were pushing but they were doing other things, too, like holding the IV and talking to the patient. I heard "You're going to be fine", "We're almost there", and "Just relax." *Brandon didn't say anything about speaking parts!* My job was to put my head down, push that bed and roll my patient down that corridor.

"Cut!"

He said to his staff, "Ok, guys, back everything up…"

To the actors he said, "Not too bad. Nurses...Nurses…I need to see you attend to the patients…a word…a touch. Leave the pushing to the orderlies…"

I know he's talking to me...the Black nurse he just picked up off the street! How am I supposed to know anything about nurses and hospitals and...

"Action!"

I straightened my back. I decided to become a nurse. I took my hands off the bedside rails. My eyes and hands moved up to adjust the IV drip. I was walking quickly alongside the bed. I reached for the patient's hand with my left hand. I was facing the camera, as I whispered to my patient, "We're gonna get you out of here."

"Cut! Much, much better. We're ready to shoot with the fire."

I could see that the fire had been set. Firemen and firetrucks were milling about off the set. Crackling sounds and sirens could be heard. Brandon was using hand signals to communicate with his people who were scurrying about like cats.

"Action!"

Smoke began to billow onto the set. I heard coughing. A raging fire was encroaching on us. My adrenaline was racing. I had to save my patient, but I had to do it calmly. With exaggerated hand movements, I adjusted the flow of the IV. I held the patient's right hand with my left hand. My right hand gently stroked his forehead. I leaned in toward his right ear keeping my face toward the camera. I whispered," Don't worry…you're going to be fine."

"Cut! We got it everybody…Great Job!"

People were smiling and clapping and "Woo-hooing" all over the set. I was clapping, too. Brandon was still directing us.

"Buses back to the office will be leaving in ten minutes. Make sure to take with you everything you brought to the set. When you are ready to leave, you can pick up your check at the front desk. Thank you, everybody. Great job!"

Brandon's assistant handed me my paycheck.

"Thank you," was all she said.

I moved out of the line and looked at the amount printed on the check. It read "Five Hundred Dollars." I caught my breath. I wiped my eyes and looked again. Five hundred dollars. *This is somebody else's check.*

I looked up. I looked around. I checked the name. "Margaret Edwards" was written there. I looked at the faces of other actors. Were there wide-eyed surprises on their faces? I listened for "so much money" chatter. I heard nothing. They were smiling, chatting, and exiting the building. Maybe they are just acting happy.

I tucked my five-hundred-dollar check in the side pocket of my black clutch purse, grinned big, and took the #1 train home to 85th Street.

3
THE AUDITION

I knew what I had to do. I had to keep making big money. And getting into show business was the way to do it.

I saw an announcement in the local newspaper that a former actress was recruiting people for a play reading group. There was no fee, and the meetings were a few blocks from my apartment. I called and joined.

The group was the brainchild of a thirty-something young White woman named Beth. She explained she was "taking a hiatus from acting until suitable adult parts for a small-stature female become more available."

Every two weeks she allowed eight or nine would-be actors like me into her apartment. All were White, except me.

We sat at her kitchen table drinking Cokes, eating cheese and crackers, and reading scripts. From the vastness of her apartment, and her occasional name-dropping, she could afford to be a thespian dropout. She gave us free advice like, "Be prepared...just in case an agent spots you having tea in a coffee shop."

I ran out the next weekend, got headshots and created an acting resume.

A few weeks later, I saw an announcement in *The New York Times* that the National Black Theater was holding auditions for new members. I didn't know anything about the group, but I called, scheduled an audition, and mailed in my headshot and resume. All I was lacking for the audition was a monologue.

I searched in monologue books. I was looking for words and a character that would showcase my range of emotions. I settled on the words of a middle-aged, Southern Black woman speaking of her ups and downs in life. In the beginning, the character is sitting, smiling, and speaking of happy times. As she recalls more harsh and hurtful experiences, her anger and hurt become more evident.

I practiced the monologue on my own, but I needed some professional input. I told Beth of my audition. She invited me to come by for private sessions with her. She guided me through "sitting tired" and through "angry smiles and tears." She was impressed that I could cry on demand.

The mission statement of the National Black Theater was to help enhance Black culture. I was ready to be part of a group that focused on Black culture.

Waiting with me outside the audition room was a young couple sporting Afros and holding manila envelopes. The young man was wearing a dashiki and bell bottoms and the girl was wearing a long African dress. They were laying familiar hands on each other, smiling, and talking quietly.

The long-patterned skirt that I was wearing fit the attire of my monologue character. I could hear a loud, passionate voice coming out of the audition room. *I wonder what that monologue is about?*

When they called the young man in the dashiki, he and the girl disentangled and parted with extended hands and a touch of their fingers. I needed to hear his audition. Maybe he will have soft words without all that passionate yelling and screaming. A minute after the door closed behind him, he followed the same pattern as the person before him. His voice was loud, forceful, and determined. *Oh, shit!*

When it was my turn, I entered the room holding my black purse in my right hand and a box of Kleenex in my left hand. The audition letter said nothing about props. I sat on the straight-backed wooden chair, let the skirt of my flowered A-line dress hang between my open knees and the box.

For the next two minutes, I was a middle-aged Black woman sitting wide legged, smiling, and laughing and crying and reaching for Kleenex after Kleenex to wipe away tears of hurt and sorrow.

When I left the audition room, I walked into the lobby full of auditioners milling around and waiting for their turn. I lingered long enough to hear more shouting and yelling and loud speech emanating through the walls of the audition room.

A week later, I received a letter.

"Thank you for your interest in NBT. All auditions were worthy, but the number of new members is limited. You were not selected at this time. We welcome your continued interest and support of NBT."

For the NBT, I guess I wasn't Black enough.

4

ANSWERING THE CALL

A hundred head shots with my resume attached to the back sat in a box on my kitchen counter ready to be distributed.

When my manager was not taking me to a club in Harlem, Ted accompanied me to nightclubs around town that advertised themselves as places that catered to walk ons. We took the subway to places like Catch a Rising Star and Never on Sunday. I never arrived early enough to get my name on the performer list. All I could do was leave a few headshots in the collection basket. Weekend after weekend, we went to places where agents were supposed to be embedded in the audience. They never revealed themselves, at least never to me.

I decided to stop waiting to be discovered. If I was going to make it in the nightclub arena, I had to have an act that I could take to a club. I needed a pianist. I put an ad in the local paper to test the market.

"Female singer seeking piano accompanist. Call Marge..."

I got calls from male pianists whose first question was, "How much are you paying?"

I explained that I had no money to pay. I was in need of a partner and that the money would come from the clubs that hired us.

Three White male musicians wanted to meet with me. Ted agreed to accompany me to the interviews.

I met each one in turn in a booth at Tom's Restaurant, a block from my house. Ted and I sat across from each interviewee. I invited each to order a soft drink. Ted was cradling cup after cup of black coffee. I sipped on cups of tea with milk and lots of sugar.

The first guy was a guitar player with tattooed arms and dirty hair. We all agreed that a guitar player would not be a good fit…at least not him.

The second guy was also a guitar player. He had too many ideas about nightclub singers and the kind of music that sells. According to him, my light jazz style was not what people want to hear these days. I didn't like that guy.

The third guy showed up saying, "What a great idea! I would love to be your partner!" His name was Larry. He was tall and lanky with a mop of curly brown hair. His hair, his hands and his body were in constant motion when he spoke.

"I'd love to be a part of creating a show…or act…or whatever you want to call it…it's so exciting!"

I was skeptical. He was too perfect…he was just what I wanted. He had ideas for songs and more importantly, he said he had contacts at local clubs! He even unpacked his portable piano right on the table in Tom's Restaurant and ran through a few chords. I liked him. Ted liked him.

The very next evening, we met at my apartment and started creating our nightclub act. We selected songs from my repertoire, and he suggested new ones. He created and played possible transition music between songs. Each evening we met, our two-hour session was full of laughs, enthusiastic support, and a single-minded, creative focus. The following Tuesday we planned to begin work on the songs to include in our on the road program.

On Monday night around 7:30 pm, the phone rang. I had just finished my favorite dinner of two thin ribeye steaks with steamed broccoli and white rice. My phone never rang this late on a weeknight.

"Hello? Hello?" I listened for a sound. I heard nothing. I hung up.

Again, my phone rang.

"Hello?"

I heard breathing on the other end of the line.

"Hello?" The breathing was getting heavier, louder, and faster. "Hello? Who is this?...Hello?"

I should have hung up the phone. I should have, but I wanted to know who had my number.

The heavy breathing was making it difficult for me to hear my own voice.

I screamed, "Who is this? Hello? Larry? Is this you?"

The heavy breathing stopped.

I continued to scream. "Larry!...Larry...! Hello? Larry...Is this you? Answer me!"

I hear a soft whisper through the phone.

"I'm sorry...I'm sorry...I shouldn't have called you...was just thinking about you and I just..."

I cut him off. "What? Larry...you are calling me...with this weird stuff...on the phone? I can't believe this!" I was screaming and stuttering trying to find the words that would help me understand what was happening...what would be lost. "What is your problem? Why would you do this? You just ruined everything!"

I had to stop this pleading for an explanation. I had to stop his efforts to provide one.

"I won't do it again, I promise. I'm working on all the songs we practiced..."

I cut him off again, definitively.

"Forget it, Larry. It's over! We can't do anything together

anymore…it's over! Don't call me again…and don't come to my house ever again. Any music you have of mine…just keep it!"

I slammed the phone down. I was shaking. There goes hope… there goes the lights. And there goes Larry's flying fingers on the piano.

I could have been on stage in glittering gowns mesmerizing my audience with songs like "Misty" and "You Can Have Him." The audience would applaud…they would be on their feet begging for more. Larry and I would bow and bow with our hands over our hearts as we exited the stage!

I went to bed. I woke up Tuesday morning, grabbed my black Bic pen lying next to my To-Do List and drew a line through the words *Music Rehearsal 7:00 p.m.*

5
KATE AND SETH

Ted's first job after he finished his doctorate was as an intern at the Children's Psychiatric Center in New York. His supervisor was a woman in her late thirties named Kate. He described her as "very smart " and "classy." She had a boyfriend who was a special education teacher in the school at the Center. He was in his late twenties. Ted became friends with the two of them and especially with Seth.

I first met Kate and Seth at a holiday dinner at Kate's apartment. Ted had suggested that I bring his favorite dish, and my specialty, a broccoli cheese casserole, with a breadcrumb topping.

When we arrived, the table was set for four with wine glasses, Upstate Pottery plates and rolled cloth napkins. Kate brought out her lightly sautéed Parmesan chicken, crisp stalks of asparagus and a mixed green salad splashed with her own special dressing. She arranged each of her dishes center stage.

My broccoli casserole is a vegetable, so I placed it stage left next to her asparagus stalks. She gave me a no teeth smile. Was that smile telling me that my casserole was plebeian and out of place on her table? I guess so since no one dared dip into my casserole. Ted didn't partake of his favorite dish either!

I watched Kate. From what I could see, she seems to have adopted blueblood tastes and tendencies, from her Citroen to her three-bedroom apartment, to her poodle named Riley. She wears blueblood well.

She is tall and thin. Her blonde hair is bobbed just below her ears. She is dressed in ankle-length white jeans and a cleavage showing, button-down orange shirt with the sleeves rolled up to her elbows. She is scurrying about getting ice, opening wine bottles, fiddling with cups and saucers.

I asked, "Can I help?"

"No, no!" she responded. "You just sit and enjoy yourself."

So, I sat and smiled. I stood and smiled. The three of them talked shop. All the while Kate was giving Seth back rubs and thigh rubs. It was obvious that her intentions were to get him into her marriage bed, and quick. Time was running out.

I knew what was going on in her clever mind. If an unlikely pairing like Ted and me can make a go of it, why can't an unlikely pairing like her and Seth do the same?

She saw Ted, and me as conduits toward her end. That was ok with me. Almost every weekend, we would go to her property up state, or we would have dinner at her apartment. I was enjoying hanging out with a faux blueblood. I just didn't contribute any more of my special dishes.

6
DEEP-SEA BLUES

One time during one of our dinners, Kate said, "We must go deep sea fishing for Blues off Montauk!"

The two New York males agreed.

"Yeah, let's do it."

I don't want to go deep sea fishing! I don't like water! I don't like the smell of fish and I don't touch fish. What is this 'deep sea fishing' stuff?

I had questions, but I didn't ask them.

We took off for the three-hour drive to Montauk. Kate handled her Citroen with confidence and skill. Ted and I were sitting in the back seat so there was time for him to show me on a map where we were going. Montauk was at the tip of Long Island and after that tip, there was water...the deep sea!

We connected with our Captain, an overweight, sunburned White man wearing faded whites and a Yankee baseball cap. He showed us around the main deck and the lower deck.

"You want to be on the main deck if you are prone to seasickness," he said. "That can happen if you're not used to waves."

I was not used to the waves. I had never been on a boat this big!

I got all life jacketed up and we set off.

Every time we hit a wave, Kate laughed and threw one arm up allowing the wind to flutter through her hair.

"Wooo, that was a big one…another one is right behind that one…"

She and Seth were holding onto rods and steading themselves with their legs spread wide.

My legs were spread apart also, but I was not holding on to a rod. I was holding on to the side of the boat to keep from getting thrown overboard. I watched the Captain to see if his eyes were wide as he was navigating the ocean and to see if his fat hands were fighting to keep the boat upright. His eyes were not on the sea, he was walking toward Kate! Who's piloting this boat?

Ted was trying to steady his feet and yelling to me, "Come on… Get a rod…put on the bait…like this. Grab the rod like this."

I ignored him. I was trying to survive!

My head was reeling, my legs were weak. My stomach could not take the rocking and rolling and dipping and swelling. I spent the hour heaving my breakfast over the sides of the boat. I did what the Captain did not recommend. I went to the lower deck and laid down on the bench seat. It was smoother there. I had no more breakfast to give.

The two hours on that boat fishing for bluefish in the ocean was different from anything I had experienced before. I was seasick the whole time. I didn't cast a rod, I didn't put on bait, and I didn't touch a fish. But somebody did because Ted and I took home in our red cooler a cleaned bluefish. The next day, we stuffed that blue with lemon slices and garlic, rubbed it well with olive oil and threw it on my backyard grill.

I said to Ted, "This fish is delicious. I would like to go back to Montauk and give ocean fishing another try."

About three weeks later, Ted and I went back to Montauk. This time the sea was so rough the Captain himself decided to return to the shore. No Blues this time. That was disappointing.

7

SOMETHING SCENIC, SOMETHING INDELIBLE

After almost a year at the Children's Center, Ted got promoted to a full-time psychologist position. With an increase in salary, he started again talking about buying land "with scenic views."

Almost every weekend, he would call me to talk about "a fantastic piece of land" in the Catskills or the Adirondacks in upstate New York. He would always add, "But it's too expensive."

I was too busy searching for stage lights to keep track of his wanderings up and down the East Coast. He was on the lookout for reasonably priced land with rolling hills and open green pastures surrounded by mixed wooded areas. He even started searching in other states like Vermont and New Hampshire hoping to find something that he could afford on a first-year psychologist salary.

One weekend, he invited me to go with him to see a property in the Green Mountains of New Hampshire.

"It has a beautiful house with stables, surrounded by rolling hills," he said.

I had not been on a road trip outside New York state, so I said, "Ok."

I didn't know what to expect, but I knew the trip would be a seven- or eight-hour drive. So, I packed peanut butter sandwiches, baloney sandwiches, bananas, and grapes. My red and white cooler was full of ice, 7 Ups, and bottles of water. Ted threw in his two-person sleeping bag, just in case.

We got on the road in his blue Toyota at about five o'clock Saturday morning. At about ten, Ted was yawning every five minutes. He decided to stop and rest. We passed through some tall trees and underbrush and saw what looked like a logging road. He pulled off the highway onto the road and buried the Toyota from highway view.

"You think we should be parking on somebody's land like this?" I asked. I had seen no Black people anywhere since we left New York City. I was not comfortable sleeping with a White guy on fold down seats in a blue Toyota parked on some White man's logging road! I suggested an alternative resting spot.

"Maybe we can park at a McDonald's...they must be somewhere in these small towns."

"Oh, we'll be fine here," he said. "I just need to rest for a half hour or so."

I didn't tell him that we were traveling through White country and headed to even Whiter country in and around New Hampshire. I had done my research.

Ted wrapped himself in the sleeping bag and fell asleep sprawled out on the fold down back seat. I stayed awake. I ate a baloney sandwich, looked out the windows and listened for intruders. I ate half a banana and drank a half glass of water while I waited and watched. What if some redneck pulls up in a mud splattered pickup truck and looks in our window? He would call the cops!

"Der's a White fella sprawled out in the backseat of a beat-up old car settin heah in do woods on my propertee."

"Hit's a old blue car...I thank he's dead...and the worse part is...der's dis nigra gal in der too. She's eatin a sanwich...hit looks like a...let me see, yep hit's penut butta and jelly...looks like grape jelly...'

Ted woke up a half hour later. I gave him a peanut butter and grape jelly sandwich. He washed it down with a bottle of Coke.

We found our way to the property and met up with the Realtor. The property and setting was as beautiful as advertised. It had a white clapboard house with manicured, white stables out back. The entirety of the property was surrounded by rolling hills. We walked the hills and down into valleys. There were yellow reeds of grass and sunflowers everywhere.

A woman and a little girl in a flared skirt were traipsing through the tall grasses on the hills above us. I couldn't see their faces, but I knew they were White. I could hear the woman calling out,

"Alexandra...Alexandra..."

The wind collected "Alexandra" from her hilltop and echoed it down to the valley where we stood and on to the next hilltop we reached.

"Alexandra..." Ted and I stood and listened. The sound of "Alexandra" bouncing off hills and dells was mesmerizingly peaceful.

Ted bought no land on this trip. But the name "Alexandra" left an indelible mark in my memory.

8

FIFTY ACRES AND A GARDEN

"Hello."

"Marge, I just bought some land." Ted was yelling into the phone from somewhere. I know he was not in New York City.

"Oh, wow...That's great. Where is it?"

"It's in New York...upstate near Syracuse. It's beautiful...you gotta see it. It's got lots of open pastures and a logging road where they used to cut down trees. And there's a windmill and a big waterfall..."

I stopped listening after I heard Syracuse. I let out a sign of relief at the strong possibility that there would be Black people still in that area. I was remembering from my sorority days at SIU that the Black Greek fraternity Alpha Phi Alpha started on the campus at Syracuse University.

"...the Jones family used to own all the land around here and they still live here...and they are so nice...they want you to come."

And a few weeks later, I went.

The land he bought was not in Syracuse. It was in a very small town about forty miles south of Syracuse. It was in Eaton, a small town of clapboard houses, red barns, pastures, cows, narrow tarred roads, and antique billboards.

Ted had paved the way for me with the Joneses. The ninety-year-old Grandfather Jones, his daughter Sarah, her husband, Bill and their two small sons could not have been more welcoming. I forgave them for name dropping the teaser that "We have exchanged visits with our good friends from church in New York City." Their good friends happen to be Black.

With the Joneses, it was family style dinners. It was educational walks through the wooded areas to learn the history of the old brick wall, the logging roads, the newly discovered second waterfall and the windmill.

They introduced us to the Wingates across the road. He was a Colgate professor and his wife was a homemaker. Both had grown up in the area and once married, they had been hoping to expand their acreage by acquiring the fifty acres Ted just bought. For now, they were "weekend farmers" and "happy to have y'all in the neighborhood."

We met the Taylors, a young mixed couple, a White man, and Black woman. They had two young children, a four-year-old boy, and a one-year-old girl. They were not farmers.

Their house was held together with tarps and tar paper, plywood, and planks. Jeb was bearded and dressed in overalls in need of a wash. The wife, Dot, was herself mixed and had grown up in a Black community in a nearby town. For a fee, Jeb had always pastured his twelve cows on the grassy hillside of now Ted's land. To keep the grass down, Ted allowed him to continue to pasture his cows on the grassy hillside, but for free.

With his fifty acres of land, Ted had plans to use a small portion to make a garden on the hillside just under some of the tall trees near the road. Because I was a farm girl, I was designated the gardener. The Joneses smiled at our intention to grow tomatoes, lettuce, a few stalks of corn and maybe watermelons. They made their hoes and rakes available to us.

On one of our gardening trips to the land, we were raking, digging, planting, and watering when a neighborhood boy biked his way over to us. He seemed to be about fourteen years old.

"What y'all doin?" he yelled from the road. He dropped his bike and walked over to us.

He was in overalls with no shirt underneath. His hair was cropped short.

Ted stopped digging.

"Hi, we're making a garden. We're planting tomatoes, and corn, and maybe watermelons...we're gonna see what happens. What's your name?"

"I'm Billy...ain't no crops gon grow up here...ain't nothin up here but sand and rocks..."

"Anyway, I'm Ted and this is my girlfriend, Marge."

The kid named Billy looked at me and chuckled. He kept chuckling, throwing up his arms and turning around with gawking eyes.

"Your girlfriend! You gotta be kiddin!"

He was looking from Ted to me with his mouth agape.

Both Ted and I stopped gardening. I was leaning on my hoe watching the kid.

"You gon marry her?" he asked, looking at Ted with wide-eyed anticipation, and gesturing with his body and his right hand in my direction.

Ted didn't respond. He straightened his back.

Billy was still looking from Ted to me waiting for a reply.

"I don't believe..." He started backing away toward his bike. He was mumbling and shaking his head. He mounted his bike, looked in our direction, laughed out loud and wheeled on down the dirt road.

I wasn't sure which he found more unbelievable, our making a garden in rocky, sandy soil or a White guy having a Black girlfriend.

9

EMBRACING BLACK

I had no friends in New York. Sylvia was back in Chicago with her husband and babies and Layla went back to Atlanta after Juilliard didn't work out. All the people I knew were Ted's friends. They were either from his neighborhood in Elmont, his colleges in Buffalo and Columbia, or his jobs in New York City. When I moved to the West Side I was determined to meet and become friends with some Black people.

I like living in my neighborhood. I can walk out my door and be one of the people hurrying by to go to Tom's restaurant on the corner or to a grocery boutique or to catch the train around the corner. My neighborhood has all kinds of people doing all kinds of things and they are friendly and open to conversation.

When I moved to 85th Street, I called Uncle Pete to give him my new address.

"Why you move to a place like that?" he said. "There ain't nothin but hoes and prostitutes over there. They be walking the streets around there all night."

He was a taxi driver, so he should know.

I defended my neighborhood.

"I don't know anything about what you're talking about," I lied.

I had seen ladies who live in the big house at the end of the block. It looked like a house of ill repute.

One time I was walking by the house in the early morning and a Black lady in a fur coat, tall, spiked heels and a bobbed wig was exiting a taxi. She acknowledged me with a big "Hi, how are you?" as she made her way up the steps. Seeing her in fur on a spring day confirmed what Uncle Pete seemed to know.

I saw her again one day on the street behind my apartment. I was in my backyard picking up cigarette butts and beer cans. The guys who live on the third floor of my building played their loud music that amplified throughout that corner of the neighborhood. They had a habit of flicking their trash,especially their cigarette butts out their open window and into my yard.

"Hi," she said, peering through the slats of the high wooden fence surrounding my building. "You cleaning up those guy's mess...they are such slobs. My name is Fifi. What's yours?"

I walked to the fence. She was scantily clad in a green spaghetti strap top and a short black skirt, but no fur coat and no spiked heels. The same bobbed wig framed her face. She was wearing too much powder and lipstick, but she was very pretty when she smiled.

"Nice to meet you," I said. "I'm Marge."

I didn't know what else to say to a prostitute, so I just smiled at her and said, "Do you know those guys?"

She didn't answer. I guess that was the wrong question. She just rolled her eyes. I didn't know if eye-rolling meant she knew them or not, so I just waited for her to continue speaking.

"I like this street...I'd like to live here someday. It's so clean and quiet." She was looking up and down the street. She was no longer smiling.

"So, uh, why don't you look for a place…maybe there's something…"

I was trying to find the right words to use when talking to a prostitute.

"I'm looking for a new job," she offered. "I don't like my job. I have to wear heels for hours...and...look at my feet."

I was peering through the slats as she slipped one foot out of a black satin slipper. She held up her foot so I could get a better look.

"Look at what those heels did to my foot...look at that," she demanded.

I saw the mass of smashed and contorted toes she was displaying. I offered some encouraging words as any good counselor would do.

"Surely you can have that looked at by a doctor and I'm sure..." She cut me off.

"No, they can't rebuild my toes...I need to stop the damage...I need a new job. So that's what I'm working on now. She was smiling again now as she pushed her foot back into her black satin slippers.

"Gotta go," she said, throwing up her hands as she continued down the street.

We waved to each other around the neighborhood over the next few weeks. Then she was gone. Maybe she got a new job and moved away.

I should have said "No." I could have said, "I'm busy." But I accepted his invitation.

His name is Samuel. He is the one Black guy who lives in my apartment building. I ran into him often in the foyer. He was always dressed in a flannel, striped shirt, and blue pants. His shoes were metal toed like the ones Daddy used to wear. In his hands were goggles and a hardhat. Samuel didn't look like a university man.

When he knocks on my door for our date, I see a handsome man in gray slacks, a white shirt, and loafers. His short, cropped Afro is shining. He is smiling shyly. *Umm, not bad.*

I am myself, the same young woman he always meets in the foyer. I have the same friendly smile and the perfectly flipped hair.

I sense his breathing rhythm quicken when he sees me in my peach dress that exposes my legs. Pants were my usual attire when we met in the foyer.

On our walk to a nearby restaurant, he is fidgeting with his hands, taking them in and out of his pockets. But he has good manners. He walks nearest to the curb, and he is quick to open the restaurant door.

Sitting at a dinner table with a man with dirt under his nails is new for me. My usual conversation starter is, "What are you studying or what do you do for a living?"

I can't talk about majors and studying and graduate school with Samuel. I have to sanitize the conversation. I ask a lot of questions because there is silence coming from his side of the table.

"How long have you lived in the apartment building?"

"Where did you live before?"

"Where are you from?"

From one- or two-word answers, I move to questions requiring a response of at least a phrase.

"What do you usually make for dinner when you come home from work?"

"What do you usually do for the holidays?"

"What do you like most about New York?"

By the time we said, "Good night" in the foyer of our building, all my questions had been answered.

A Black woman moved into the apartment next door to mine! I ran into her in the foyer. We exchanged "Hellos."

She is dark skinned, a little taller than me and a bit older than me. She has a short, trimmed Afro that frames her flawless face. She is wearing slacks.

One day as we were both searching through our bags for our keys, she had more to say besides "Hello."

"You know we speak to each other all the time," she said, with a no-teeth smile, "We should at least know each other's name…I'm Vonn."

"Yes…you're right…I'm Marge."

I was delighted by her overture. I wanted to keep the conversation going.

"Isn't that the New York way? People live next door to each other for years and never even speak? I'm not from New York…I think that is just crazy."

"Yep," she said. "That's New York."

We found our keys and opened our doors.

"Well, nice meeting you, Vonn…see you later."

I ran into Vonn again on Saturday morning as I was leaving the building and she was coming in.

"I've been thinking about you," she said. "How about stopping by this afternoon for a drink?"

"I'd love to," I said. "What time?"

"Oh anytime…I'll be home all afternoon."

"Ok, great. I'll see you around two o'clock."

Having a drink with a next-door neighbor requires no special preparation. So, when I got home from picking up some cheese and black olives from Zabar's, I knocked on Vonn's door. She opened the door, smiling and holding a glass in her left hand.

"Come on in," she said. "I started early."

She twirled her glass above her head.

Her living room is sparsely furnished with an orange sofa, a matching chair and a round, brown dining table. I sat in the orange chair.

"What do you want to drink?" she asked.

She is reading the labels on the bottles sitting on a small roll-away cart.

"I've got gin and tonic…vodka…aaaand…"

"Well," I said. "How about a soft drink…you got a 7 Up?"

"Soft drink?...I don't have those in my apartment…surely you drink something stronger than that."

She is still moving bottles around.

"How about some wine? I got some red here…Merlot. How about that?"

She is not going to give up on her desire for me to have something stronger than 7 Up.

I don't like the taste of red wine.

"Yes…I will have that…not too much."

I'm sitting in the orange chair taking small sips of Merlot from my fluted wine glass. Vonn is sitting on her orange sofa taking gulps of a light brown substance from a water glass.

I want to get this friendship going. I want to see what we have in common. I ask her questions about where she is from, how long she's lived in New York and what kind of work she does.

Her answers are short with no elaboration.

"I'm from Arkansas. I've lived in New York for five years and I'm in sales…Now I'm not going to ask you about your past…I'm interested in the present and the future."

She is again at her rollaway bar pouring more of that light brown liquid into her water glass.

She is eying me with a wry smile on her face. I decided to tell her about me anyway.

"I'm a counselor…that's my real job, but I really want to be a singer."

"You sing…where do you sing?" She moves to her sofa seat, interested.

"I don't sing anywhere yet…I'm taking lessons and working with a manager to get me...ready to perform on stage."

She stands and moves next to my sofa chair. I shift my body

away from where she is standing. I am beginning to sense something different about Vonn. She is still standing over me, sipping and smiling.

"You can sing for me," she said. She walks back to her orange couch and sits down. She pats the space next to her with the hand not holding her glass of brown liquid.

"Come over here and sing for me." Her voice is low, almost like a whisper. She is leaning against the back of the sofa with her legs spread apart like a young man on the prowl.

I stood up. I put my fluted glass on the rollaway cart. I walked toward the door.

"I better be going, Vonn. Thanks for the drink."

She didn't move from the couch. I heard her say, "You and I are different."

She did not look at me.

I let myself out.

10

ROBBED...AGAIN!

I walked into my building after work on a Thursday, looking forward to a dinner of rib steaks, a baked potato and broccoli. I had my keys out. I pushed the key toward the door and...my door is open! Who? What? How did my door get opened? Did I forget to lock it? Maybe Ted came over...and left it open?

"Ted?" I whispered loudly. No answer.

I looked around. Nothing looked disturbed in the foyer. Should I scream? Nobody would hear me...Vonn moved out a week ago.

My mind is running through possibilities and impossibilities. Maybe I should have had more locks! Maybe I shouldn't be in this neighborhood! Maybe...but I have a bolt and an iron sliding rod...

I was just standing outside my open door wondering what I should do. Should I go in? Maybe the robber is still in there... waiting.

I eased the door open wider. I didn't see or hear anything. I walked into the entry hallway, leaving the door wide open so I could make a quick exit if I had to. I looked around. From my vantage point in the entry, I saw nothing missing…Oh, my television is gone!

I should call the police! I should call Ted first! He probably knows what to do.

I made my way to the phone.

"Ted, I've been robbed."

"You've been what?"

"I've been robbed…my door is open…somebody got in and my television is gone!"

"Did you check to see if anything else is missing?"

"No…I'm not going to start looking in drawers and closets…I don't know how this happened!"

"New York apartments are always getting broken into…"

Why is he talking like nothing happened! Somebody came into my apartment and took some of my stuff...can't he see that I've been violated!

"Ted, Ted, are you coming over here? What am I supposed to do? I need to call the police. How do I do that?"

I waited outside for Ted. When he arrived, we went inside. My closet door was open. My black leather jacket was gone!

Ted called the police. Two officers arrived. I told them about my television and my black leather jacket. Both scribbled on notepads. They looked around.

"Small-time burglars look for easy access." one cop said. "Get a second lock on this door."

I spent the next three nights at Ted's apartment. We slept on a plank bed in the kitchen to be near the radiator. The hissing, sputtering, and banging of the radiators kept me awake. On the fourth night, I came back to my apartment. I had a chain lock installed.

11
TALKING FRESH

Sometimes on the weekends, I stay at Ted's apartment. But because I preferred not to spend time in my old University neighborhood, we spent most weekends at my place. It also helped that my air conditioner and radiator did not bang, strain and sputter throughout the night.

One weekend, as I always did, I tried out a new recipe. Most weren't new to me; they were new to Ted. When I stayed at his place, lunch and dinner was always hotdogs or hamburgers, with a can of something like baked beans, green beans, or a lettuce salad on the side. At my place, dinner was made from scratch. My notebook of saved recipes was well used.

One cool, Saturday morning, I opened my notebook to the section labeled Beef. I wanted something easy, all-inclusive. I settled on a short ribs recipe. The midtown grocery store had everything I needed: short ribs of beef, carrots, potatoes and onions.

Ted was always in the kitchen watching me cook. He watched me scrape the carrots, peel and quarter the potatoes and onions.

He watched me put the beef, the onions and water in a big pot, put on a lid and set the temperature on low. He always had questions.

"You're using fresh carrots?"

"How long do you cook the beef?"

"Why aren't you putting in the potatoes?

I was always baffled by his questions. I explained to him,

"I grew up watching my mother cut up pigs, chickens and sometimes a cow. And the vegetables we ate came from our garden. Every meal my mother made and every meal we ate was fresh.

"You mean you didn't eat canned food? Everything I ate as a kid came from a can or from the deli. I didn't know what fresh vegetables taste like...until I met you."

I didn't know whether to feel sorry for him or to just smile and throw the potatoes into the pot.

When the beef separated from the bones, and the vegetables were firm to a fork pierce, the short ribs were ready. I tasted them first.

'Wow," I said. "This turned out really good."

Ted concentrated on eating the fresh vegetables. Then he tasted the ribs. He had a second helping.

Next week, I'll introduce him to smothered chicken, fresh green beans and corn on the cob.

12
QUITTING TIME

It was a Thursday in March. I arrived home after my Spanish class, had my usual ribeye steaks and sat on my brown couch. I turned the TV channel to *All in the Family*.

The phone rang.

"Hello?... Oh, Hi Ted."

"You want to come over now?"

"Yeah, Ok. See you in a bit."

That's strange. He needs to see me in person...about what?

There is a knock on my door a few minutes later. I rush to open the door.

"Hi, Ted. Why so mysterious? Come in."

"No...this won't take long." he said with a determined look on his face.

He maintained his stance outside the door.

I looked at him with a smile and a roll of my eyes.

"What are you doing? You're acting weird. Come in!"

"I can't do this," he said.

"You can't do what?" I asked, stepping back from the closing door.

"This…this." He caught the door with his right hand before it slammed shut.

He was pointing from himself to me and back again to himself.

I frowned, stared at him, and exclaimed, "Ted, you need to speak English. What are you talking about…you can't do what?"

He straightened his back and looked me in the eyes.

"I'm not ready for this kind of relationship…it's too fast. I got a lot of things to do…and I'm just not ready for this…so I want to just call this off."

"Call it off! What's wrong with you? Where is this coming from, Ted? You're talking rubbish. After all this time, you are just going to stand here and say you want to call it off?"

I'm flummoxed. My thoughts are incoherent.

Why? What happened? Why today? Is this a joke? April Fools' Day?

"I just don't understand why–what you're saying, Ted! I'm confused! What happened?"

He was still planted outside the door with that unwavering look on his face. That look brought tears to my eyes.

I pushed the door open wider with my left foot.

His arms are outstretched, and his body is leaning forward as he makes his case.

"I'm just not ready. I'm getting too involved. The best thing is to stop…now. I have some things I want to do…and so do you… you don't need me in the way."

"Ted…I can't believe this is happening…what are you saying? Why are you doing this? You want us to stop seeing each other? You want to break up?"

"That's what I'm saying," he said.

My tears start flowing. I wipe my eyes on the sleeves of my pink terry cloth robe.

My nose is running. Snot is running down my chin. Ted does not attempt to console me, nor does he hand me a Kleenex. He stands tall outside my door unmoved by my anguish.

My foot is holding my door open wide. I am sniffling and

wiping. My mind is racing. How will I fill the vacuum? Who was I before Ted?

Why am I crying? He has to do what suits him!

I remove my foot from the open door. The door slams shut.

I lock the door, dry my tears, wipe my nose, wash my face, and go to bed.

All in the Family can wait until tomorrow.

On Friday night, my manager,Terry took me to a club somewhere in Harlem where he said, "The people will love your singing." I couldn't tell if the people loved my singing or not.

The people consisted of card playing old men and loud, frisky women, neither of whom noticed me when I walked in. I was dressed in one of my two nightclub outfits. One was a white, blousy, silk spaghetti strapped top and wide-legged black pants. The other outfit was a short, long-sleeved sack dress with large blue, gray, green, and yellow flowers on the front and back. On this trip to Harlem, I went with the black and white.

Most times, Terry left me at a crowded table with loud, cursing men and fast women while he went to the back. He said he could speak privately to his manager friend about booking me for a gig. His gig request never paid off. I could always get up and sing a song or two. This time, like all the other times, is what I did.

On Saturday and Sunday, even without Ted, I followed our usual routine. I went to Zabar's. I went to breakfast on the ground floor of our favorite boutique hotel on Broadway. I walked and window-shopped down Broadway. I went home and had leftover short ribs with vegetables. For dessert, I had cottage cheese topped with canned fruit cocktail.

At work on Monday, I followed up on a promise I had made with my teacher friend, Bob. He was an older White man who taught shop. He was a student of trans-actional analysis, and he wanted me to join him at a meeting. I joined him and repeated, "I'm Ok" along with all the others seated in a circle.

On Friday night, I allowed a male friend of mine from work to come over and hang out. We got a bite at Tom's. By the time we finished eating and talking, it was late. I told him to stay the night on my couch bed.

Early Sunday morning, the phone rang.

"Hello."

"Marge, where you been? I called you three times yesterday!"

It was Ted. He was rushing his words, breathing fast and talking too loudly. I could hear traffic in the background.

I took my time answering. I was not obliged to tell him where I was yesterday or any other day. I was not going to engage him in conversation.

"What do you want, Ted?"

"I want to talk to you...I just need to see you and...to talk about what I said last week. Can I come by in the next hour?"

I was in no mood to talk any more. He had said "I can't do it," and I accepted that. I was now into the moving on stage.

"No, I won't be here...I have to go out." I committed a lie of necessity.

"When will you be back?"

"Ted, I am in no mood to see you and I'm in no mood to talk to you." My voice was even. Stoic. "You made your position clear. There is nothing more to talk about."

"Please, let me come by, Marge. I need to talk. Will you be back by twelve? Maybe we can go somewhere and have a little lunch."

"I'm not hungry."

"Please Marge...can I come over?"

"Ted, what do you want? I'm busy and especially too busy to play games with you...I'll try to be back by twelve."

Ted still had a key to my apartment, but he knew not to use it. I allowed the doorbell to ring three times before I opened the door.

I made myself irresistible. I wanted him to take notice of what he had given up. Every strand of my flipped mane was in place with maximum right side face coverage. I dressed casually, but smart. I wore blue bell bottom jeans with a blue and white button-down long-sleeved shirt. The sleeves were folded up to my elbows.

Ted was standing there with his head down, looking like he was at confession. I stepped away. He let himself in.

I stood near the kitchen table with my head held high waiting for him to speak. He was still standing near the door looking from the door to my face like he was trying to decide whether to go or stay.

"So, I just wanted to come by to see how you're doing."

Are you serious? You expected me to crumble! You're the one who can't do this. The onus is on you!

"I'm fine, Ted. You don't need to check on me. I'm doing all the things I was doing before…Life goes on."

"Yeah. I know it does…Anyway, I was hoping we could just go to Tom's for a sandwich or something. I need to talk. I don't like what is happening."

We walked to Tom's in silence, sat in our usual booth, ordered the usual chicken salad and grilled cheese and ordered our usual 7 Up and Coke. The only thing different this time was the lack of laughter. I told no sneaky tales about Jerry and Rita. He told no stories about the dance between Kate and Seth.

I wanted to hear what he had to say. I sat there holding onto my glass of 7 Up with both hands and sipping through a white plastic straw. Ted was sitting across from me. He got the waitress's attention. He ordered a Coke with no ice. While he waited for his iceless Coke, I waited for him to break the silence between us.

"I just needed to see you. I made a big mistake. I was just scared. And…it had nothing to do with you…you know that. I was thinking that…I was getting ahead of myself."

Silence is all he got from me.

"I don't want to lose you…you're the best thing that's ever happened to me. I had a drink and talk with Seth. He couldn't understand what I did. Kate was really concerned. She and I talked a long time about you."

Our sandwiches arrived with lettuce and a tomato slice on the side. I took off the top slice of whole wheat bread, added the lettuce and tomato along with a little salt and pepper and carefully replaced the bread on top. I cut the sandwich in half and was raising a half to my mouth with both hands when Ted grabbed my right wrist. I closed my mouth and lowered my sandwich back onto my plate. I watched my tomato slice fall to the table. He let go of my wrist.

He had not touched his sandwich. He was holding his glass of Coke with no ice in one hand and speaking softly to me.

"I made a mistake…I'm sorry…I didn't mean to hurt you. We're good together…I'm not good without you. And I don't understand why you're acting like this…we broke up for only one week, Marge! Do you hear what I'm saying?"

I was looking into his pleading eyes. I know what he's saying. But *I am not happy that you lost your nerve...even if it was for just one day!*

"Yeah, Ted, I hear what you're saying. But I don't understand why you just found out last Thursday that 'you can't do this.'" I raised my fingers and air quoted the phrase. "I don't need this, Ted. I know there are other contingencies you have to deal with, but everybody has stuff to deal with. You don't get the right to walk away from me and expect me to roll over and allow you to come back into my life because you made a mistake. It doesn't work that way."

Ted was looking at me with pleading eyes.

"I never meant to hurt you. I was just scared. I had a miserable week without you. I care about you. I want us to get back together."

"I'm sorry," I said. "I need time to think about what I want to do. I'm not good at playing games."

"I know you're not." he said, nodding his head in agreement.

I had another concern.

"And Ted, you had the nerve to break up one day after you had just gobbled down a big plate of my vegetables and short ribs! How crazy is that?" I was gesticulating with a befuddled wide-eyed look on my face and waiting for his explanation.

He smiled first and then he started to laugh. He laughed so hard he was having difficulty speaking and I was having difficulty hearing. Somewhere in there, I heard, "I love you and your short ribs..what can I say...the best. . .any leftovers at home?"

13

NATURE CALLS, ANTIQUING AND BREAKFAST

White folks always want to sleep in tents under the stars. They call it camping. Ted went to Europe on a motorcycle for the whole summer just to sleep in a tent! The only camping I ever did was when my class at Columbia spent the weekend at a commune in upstate New York. All twenty of us slept in tents on the ground, tolerating mosquitoes and sore limbs. I didn't like tent living. I had to do it...it was part of the curriculum.

Now that Ted is back in America with all his camping gear, he wants to put it to good use. So, when he said, "Let's go camping at Lake George," I didn't make a fuss. I didn't want him to think Black folks don't know how to camp.

We folded down the back seats of his Toyota. We threw in the two person- sleeping bag, a blue two-person tent, a ground cloth, two red fold-up camping chairs, two umbrellas, a pair of boots for each of us, flashlights and a cooler full of 7 Ups, beer, and water. I brought along peanut butter and baloney sandwiches on Wonder Bread just in case our plan to grill hot dogs and hamburgers got rained out.

We arrived at the lake. I was sitting in the car admiring the water slapping gently against rocks on the bank.

"This is great, Ted…there's a great spot for our tent over there."

I stepped out of the car and was pointing to a clearing under a giant tree away from parked cars.

Ted looked at me.

"This is not the campsite. We have to cross Lake George to get to the campsite."

"What? Ted, you didn't tell me we had to go across a lake. I thought we were camping here."

"Oh, it's only a five-minute crossing. Come on, here's our boat. Help put the stuff in."

He was unloading the Toyota. He was not looking at those waves that were no longer gentle. They were rushing to the shore.

I was watching the waves as he was putting the tent, the chairs, and the cooler into a small boat with a motor in the rear. I did not hide my annoyance.

"Where am I supposed to sit in this thing, Ted? There's too much stuff in here."

I removed my hands from my hips and started pushing the bag of hot dogs, buns, and hamburger meat to the rear of the boat. I squeezed my behind onto the cleared space in the middle of the boat.

"Ted, I don't like this…look at those waves…look how the boat is rocking and we haven't even left yet!'"

I was waving my arms, pointing to the lake and waves rushing in. The boat was low in the water and rocking precariously.

"I need something to hold on to…!"

"Marge, stop being ridiculous…here, put on a life jacket…these are not waves…they're just white caps…now let's go before the winds pick up."

I sat wearing an orange life jacket over my green waterproof jacket with a hood. I covered my flipped hair with the hood. There was a cool breeze coming from the lake.

Ted revved up the motor and we sped off. *Shit! I forgot to ask Ted if he knows how to drive this thing!*

The boat was hitting white caps and bouncing up and down. Ted was turning toward me and saying something. I could see his mouth moving. His left hand and fingers were pointing left like we were on a field trip or something. I was not on a field trip. I refused to let my eyes follow his fingers. My eyes were searching for the shoreline.

When I set foot on the wet sand, I did so with unsteady legs.

We found our plot among the other campers, pitched the tent, fired up the grill for our hot dogs and burgers and sat in our red fold-up camping chairs. I sipped on a can of 7 Up. Tim guzzled down a can of Budweiser.

The smells of grilling meats permeated the air. The breeze was relaxing. I could hear muted voices coming from surrounding campers. I could see campers walking, playing, talking, and laughing.

I didn't see any Black folks camping at Lake George.

I got used to camping and sleeping in tents under the stars. When Ted wanted to camp on his new property upstate, I didn't object. He even decided to invite Gabe, one of his childhood friends. Gabe had finished college but was between jobs and between girlfriends.

On this trip he brought along his current girlfriend, Sandy. I had never met Gabe. He was long and tall with curly brown ringlets for hair. Sandy was a petite, fresh undergrad, with dark, straightened hair, manicured nails and an innie belly button. We left early Saturday morning and drove the six hours. Our two cars were packed with food, water, boots, mosquito repellant and toilet paper.

We drove our cars into the property along the logging road and parked near the waterfall where we set up our tents. After letting the Joneses know we were camping for the weekend, we went antiquing. We walked along the side of the road, stopping in shop after shop. We didn't buy anything.

After the reception I had gotten from young Billy a few months earlier, I expected to get a similar reaction from others as we traversed among local folks and tourists. I got looks, and some double takes. I could understand their confusion...were the four of us students associated with Colgate University? Or were the four of us couples?

In one shop, two little White kids ran crying to their mothers when they looked up and saw my Black face moving in their direction. I spotted an ethnic shelf in one shop. I bought a book by Ida Chubbs called *Little Pickaninnies.*

Gabe and Sandy didn't need instructions on how to live in nature without amenities. Gabe was first to take a waterfall shower. We all marked territory behind a tree or a bush when it came to answering the call of nature. To announce our presence or to check-in in the morning and at bedtime, Gabe determined that "A-O-A" should be the call. After three days of walking the land and two nights on the ground in sleeping bags, we packed up for the trip back to New York City.

We agreed to stop for breakfast at a restaurant we had seen on the way up. The signs plastered on the door and windows said, "The best breakfast in town." We walked in to give it a try.

The smell of coffee and bacon and pancakes was hanging in the air. The place was busy with red-faced men in overalls and John Deere hats, and overweight women in print dresses with sashes tied in the back. Waitresses were bustling from table to table carrying aluminum pots of coffee in each hand. Everybody was White, except me.

Three White people and one Black person stood in the doorway waiting to be seated. Seeing us waiting, the patrons hushed. The men in John Deere hats turned to stare with their hands in midair, clutching stained white coffee mugs. The women in print flowered dresses averted their eyes. Their hands nudged their John Deere hatted husbands to follow their nodding heads.

My Black face had upset the restaurant's equilibrium. Everybody and everything were off kilter. I had encountered this syndrome before. My response was always the same. I looked through and beyond those overalled men holding stained coffee cups in midair. I didn't see the hushed stares and the nudging from overweight women in print dresses.

I saw myself sipping a cup of hot tea with milk and sugar and eating two dry scrambled eggs with pork sausage and two buttermilk pancakes on the side.

When a waitress seated us, that's exactly what I had.

14
MONKEY BUSINESS

Sometimes Ted and I took a ride out of the City just to get away. One time, we went to the outskirts of Queens and got a room in a hotel. Lots of police cars were in the parking lot. I assumed a training meeting was going on.

Police in uniform and men in plain clothes were overheard telling police stories in the lobby. Later in the afternoon, kids and wives and the policemen from the lobby filled the swimming pool and the snack bar area. It soon became evident that there was no security meeting. Instead, we found ourselves a blemish on a getaway weekend for White New York City police officers and their families.

We took a dip in the pool. Ted dived in at the deep end. I stepped in at the shallow end. I was among screaming girls, roughhousing boys, and mediating mothers.

My presence stilled the waters.

Mothers assisted screaming children scrambling over the sides of the pool. Roughhousing boys added language to their splashing about as they exited the pool, "Hurry up...get out...there's a monkey in the pool! I can't swim with no monkey!"

Ted and I were alone in the pool. He did a few laps; I floated around, keeping my head above the water. I was in no hurry to exit the pool. Surely, with all these New York's finest around, what did a young Black woman like me have to worry about? I'm sure they told their wives and screaming kids that their job was to respect and protect all citizens.

New York City's finest sat poolside, listening, watching, and waiting. Their sons, daughters and wives sat with them scowling, wrapped in red, white, and blue towels.

The next day, we drove back to the City. New York City's White 'Finest' and their families now had the pool all to themselves.

15

NANTUCKET IN BLACK, WHITE, AND PINK

One weekend, Ted's dissertation buddy, Carl invited us to dinner at his Lower Manhattan apartment. He warned us, "You're not coming to the fancy housing you may be used to. I live in the real New York!"

I knew this was New York, but how was it possible for a family of four to live in a one-bedroom apartment? Carl's wife, Carol, was excited to show us how it's done.

"Everything folds into the walls during the day and unfolds in the evening," she said. "Phil and Sarah unfold this ladder to reach their bunk beds, and Carl and I sleep on this fold out-couch. It's tight, but it all works." She smiled, spreading her arms wide. I admired her.

We sat down at a fold-out dining table that was a slab of wood across the top of the bathtub. We feasted on chicken Marsala, rice, mixed vegetables, and homemade apple pie with ice cream. Carol lifted the tablecloth to get the ice cream from the ice bucket which was stored under the table in the bathtub. I was fascinated by their creative and minimalist lifestyle until the dinner conversation revealed that Carl and Carol own a house on Nantucket Island!

"You have a house on Nantucket?" I asked. I tried not to look around at my cramped surroundings. White folks with money always try to live like they are poor.

"Yes," Carol said. "We bought it a long time ago, when we were hippies." She smiled.

"Carl still goes there on holidays. The kids and I wait until the summer."

Carl was leveling the tabletop slab with folded cardboard pieces.

"Yeah, there's money to be made. I make leather sandals and sell them to tourists. It's a pretty good business. Ted's been up there."

"Yes, I have," said Ted. "It's beautiful...panoramic views...I love it up there. It was a great place to write my dissertation. I would sit in the bedroom upstairs and look out over water, grasses, narrow quiet roads. Just beautiful."

"Marge, why don't you come with Ted in the spring. You still coming, Ted?"

"Yes, I'm coming. I love it up there."

"Well, sure. I'd love to come."

Getting to Nantucket meant driving to Cape Cod, taking a ferry over to Nantucket, and getting a taxi to Carl's house on the outskirts of town. I was glad Ted had made this trip before and knew his way around.

I was mesmerized by the quiet lanes, and boats bouncing in the water a short distance from the house. We walked into town, roamed the narrow streets, peered at unique trinkets, and munched on shortbread cookies.

During the three days I was there walking, peering, and sampling, I didn't see one Black face on the streets. Based on my background in history, there should be Black people on this island. Massachusetts had slaves. Massachusetts was also the home of the abolitionist movement back in the 1800s. Some of the descendants of slaves must have remained in this part of Massachusetts.

But based on the stares, the double-takes, the nudges, the sneaky peeks, and question mark expressions, these locals and out-of-town tourists must have forgotten their history. I had not.

At night, we went to the harbor and watched the well-heeled light up their boats, turn on their music and frolic into the night. The men were dressed in blazers, khaki trousers, and sockless loafers. The women were tall, thin, and blond. They dressed in white. They were in slinky white, ruffled white, short white, long white, and flowing white.

When I got back to New York City, I looked everywhere for a white dress.

Ted and I liked Nantucket. We came back another time and rented a cabin on the beach. We made our way into town every morning and returned to the beach cabin in the late afternoon. I was not a beach person, and neither was Ted. He walked along the water's edge and occasionally took a swim. I walked along the water's edge in my bikini and spent most of the afternoon reading under an umbrella.

Dinner was usually leftovers from lunch. One night before we were to return to New York, we decided to treat ourselves to a lobster dinner. We planned to cook the lobsters ourselves.

We bought two one-pounders, each wrapped in separate brown paper bags. We also bought a small tub of coleslaw and two pieces of fresh yellow corn on the cob. Cooking lobster was new to us, so we walked through the process step by step.

My job was to fill the largest pot available with water and set it to boil on the stove. I was to keep the lid close by. When the water was boiling, and on the count of three, Ted was to open one bag, grab the lobster and throw it into the boiling water. I was to slam on the lid. We were to repeat the process for lobster number two. Ted was to do the counting. He selected the bag to open first.

"Ok, ready? One, two, three!" Ted grabbed the lobster from the bag, dropped it into the boiling water and I slammed on the lid. Success...we were all smiles.

Ted was counting again for lobster number two. I was hovering over the stove wearing burgundy potholder gloves ready to lift the lid for lobster number two.

"Ok, ready...One, two...three!" He opened the bag, reached in, grabbed, and pulled at the body of the lobster.

"It's not coming out!" he yelled. "It's holding onto the bag!"

He pulled on the bottom of the bag. He started shaking the lobster and the bag. The bag fell to the floor. He was holding the fighting lobster at arm's length, trying to get to the stove. He yelled to me, "Open the lid! Take the lid off."

I raised the lid with my hand wearing the burgundy potholder glove and saw that lobster number one was quiet and behaving.

Ted dropped lobster number two into the boiling water. I slammed on the lid, but it wouldn't seal. I pushed the lid with both hands.

Ted yelled, "He's getting out...he's getting out!"

The lobster's claws were struggling over the top of the pot. Ted added his hands on mine. We were both pushing the lid.

"I need a wooden spoon...over there!" Ted yelled.

I left the lid pushing to Ted. I ran to the tall vase where over-sized utensils like wooden spoons should be and foraged through salad forks, spatulas, carving knives, and two-pronged forks.

"I don't see any wooden spoons!"

"I need something...this thing is getting out!"

I grabbed the spatula and held it towards Ted. He couldn't take it. He was using both hands to hold the lid down to keep that lobster from crawling out. Another tense minute went by. The lobster finally relented and succumbed to the boiling water.

We both just stood there, looking at that boiling pot. I didn't like what had happened. *I can't eat a fighting lobster!*

I enjoyed the corn on the cob and the coleslaw. And I was obliged to eat the lobster meat that Ted extracted and put on my plate. I couldn't waste that lobster meat.

I just hoped I wasn't eating the meat of that fighting lobster!

16
PARTING GIFT

After two years at Cooper Rehabilitation Center, I lost my job. Warning signs were all round me. I knew something was afoot.

The security guards had their heads together talking with serious faces. The Counseling Director, Sam, was wringing his hands more than usual. Aaron was eating more and stifling more and more belches. The two of them were directing Jerry, Rita, Bill, and me to "schedule more appointments with kids," "keep detailed records," and "cut back on weekend passes."

Everybody seemed on edge. Rita's hair loss exposed more of her scalp. Her furtive glances toward Jerry made him stand taller in his brown platform shoes. Bill loved his government job and stayed late to complete paperwork almost every evening.

Aaron broke the news to me.

"Uh, you probably heard that the government…I mean, the New York City government is cutting back on programs like this one…they say…you know…they keep saying…there's just not enough money to keep places like this open…so…every department has to lay off people. And we have to...since you were hired…

the last counselor hired, you have to be the first. It's nothing against you…you've been great…it's just that…"

"When is my last day?" I asked. I didn't care to continue watching his belching and hand wringing.

"No rush…you should be finishing by…Friday." He turned to look at the calendar. "Payroll decides these things..."

"It's all right, Aaron. I'll be out by Friday."

I wanted time to bid farewell to a couple of people, especially one male teacher, Jordan, who was a kindred soul when it came to the arts. He loved to sculpt, and he had shared small pieces of his work with me. When he learned that I was leaving, he wanted to deliver to my apartment a larger work, if I had space for it.

I said, "Yes, I have space for something bigger."

I didn't know that Jordan would need a wheelbarrow, two friends, and the Super to get this larger work into my apartment. I couldn't see what I was getting. It was wrapped in newspaper and masking tape. I chose the corner near the window for the unveiling.

"Just wait till you see this." Jordan was carefully pulling one piece of tape off, then another.

"Jordan, just tear the paper off." I grabbed at the newspaper.

"Ok, Ok." Using both hands, he ripped the newspaper off. Revealed was a sculpted torso of a voluptuous woman. She had an ample bosom, a pinched in waist and a curvaceous butt.

I stepped back. I didn't know how to react. Is this a work of art or a piece of porn? Is it worthy of praise or scorn?

"Wow," I said. "I didn't expect this…this is really…"

"How long did it take you to do this?" I was moving around the voluptuous figure, looking closely at the curves and angles.

Jordan was smiling, polishing, and adjusting.

"It took me a long time…I have so many pieces I'm working on, so I thought you would like this one."

"Well, I'm just blown away. Thank you!" I was covering my mouth in awe, bending close, and laying a hand on Jordan's arm.

He left with a bounce in his step and an arm full of torn newspaper and masking tape.

Ted came over the next day. He noticed the new acquisition in the corner near the window. "Where did you get that piece of porn?"

17
COLLEGE BOUND

My job at Manpower lasted two years. So, leaving the job at Cooper Rehab after two years seemed to be the norm for me so far. I was optimistic about finding and moving on to a new job. Until then, I endured standing in line at the unemployment office.

The New York Times classified section had been the place where I found my job at Cooper. I went there again.

I found two counseling openings that were of interest to me. Both were State University of NY (SUNY) counseling positions.

One was SUNY at Oneonta, NY and the other was at SUNY at Old Westbury, NY. Oneonta's location in upstate New York was most likely a deterrent for me. I learned later that a male with overseas experience had been hired.

A call came from the Counseling Program Director at SUNY at Old Westbury. She wanted to set up an interview for Thursday. *Thursday! Where is Old Westbury?*

I had to think fast. She must not hear panic in my voice. When she said, "Is ten o'clock a good time for you?" I had to say, "Yes, ten o'clock is perfect. I'll see you Thursday."

Panic set in. I was running my hands up and down the phone cord. Where is Old Westbury?

"Ted...you have to help me. I have an interview for a counseling job!"

"You have an interview? Where?"

"It's at a university in Old Westbury."

I waited to be disappointed. I waited for him to say, "That's ridiculous," or "That's an awful place," or "That's so far away," or...

"That's on Long Island! That's right near here...it's a few towns over from where my parents live."

"Great, Ted...but that doesn't help me. How do I get out there? The interview is Thursday!"

I was talking loud, asking for his help!

His voice was calm.

"You take the train. It goes right there."

I didn't believe him.

"You mean I can take the #1 train to Long Island?"

"Marge, calm down. It is very easy. You take the Long Island Railroad, get off, and take a taxi to the University."

"That's not easy!"

Ted couldn't believe I was being interviewed for a counseling position at SUNY at Old Westbury.

"This is crazy," he kept repeating. "This is crazy...what are the chances of that?"

With his excitement, I had to get this job. I had one day to prepare. The trains, the stops, the taxi number. All were written down. My resume could speak for itself. The woman I spoke to on the phone sounded Black. So, first impressions were going to be very important.

My peach-colored dress with long sleeves, button-down front, and flared skirt was the perfect attire for this occasion. My legs were pantyhosed in off-black. Black patent leather shoes tied it all together. My hair was straightened, with the ends flipped and parted and pushed to the right side to ensure maximum coverage of facial flares.

I sat before three Black people, the female director and two male counselors. I saw their wide eyes, their sneaky stares at my legs, and their nods of approval. The color peach was a hit.

The Director, Laura, a middle-aged round woman with a frizzy Afro was stuffed into a blue pantsuit. Both the two males wore creased jeans and pressed short sleeved shirts.

One male, Malik, was small-framed and spoke with an accent. The other, Eddie, was tall, fidgety and spoke like he was from the streets. Looking at them, I was overdressed in my peach dress with a button-down front, long sleeves, and flared skirt.

I learned from Laura that I was interviewing for a counseling position in a special program created to help minority adult students succeed in college and graduate. Special programs counselors helped to set academic goals, schedule classes, help students access financial aid, employment opportunities and housing. She was proud that she had been one of the first graduates of the program.

"And look at me now," she said. "I am the program's first director!"

After two months of unemployment checks, I was offered the position of Special Programs Counselor.

18
ECONOMICS 101

When I lost my counseling job at Cooper Rehabilitation Center, I lost the money I needed to pay for everything related to my nightclub singing career. No more singing lessons, no more acting lessons, and no more ads for performance collaborators. I also lost my Manager and any possibility of making singing inroads into Harlem.

For two months, I was homebound. I did leave the apartment to people-watch up and down Broadway and Central Park West. I had time to think about the things that were important to me. Pursuing my singing was important and required money. I had to find a way to hold onto as much money as I could.

Around the same time that I got my counseling job at Old Westbury, my apartment lease on 85th Street came due. I had resided in my garden apartment for two years. My rent was holding steady at around two hundred and thirty-five dollars a month. I still got some satisfaction from the fact that I was saving about a hundred dollars a month since making the move from the East Side.

Ted, on the other hand, had been living in graduate housing at

Columbia since he was a doctoral teaching fellow in the counseling and psychology department. And after he completed his doctorate, he continued to reside in his Columbia apartment. I decided to talk to him about Columbia housing when we were eating Chinese takeout on his kitchen table in his cramped one-bedroom apartment. We were using chopsticks to pick through my favorite dish, shrimp egg foo young.

"Ted, you know my lease is coming due in a month or so."

"Has it been that long?" He was using his fingers to push rice onto his chopsticks.

"Yeah. I've lived there for two years. I want to find something cheaper."

I put my chopsticks on a napkin and placed them on the table to the left of my plate. I picked up my fork, jabbed a shrimp, and put it in my mouth. I chewed normally. I kept my eyes on my bowl of shrimp egg foo young.

I could feel Ted's wide-open eyes staring at me. I heard his chopsticks slide off his plate.

"What?" I could hear incredulity in his voice. He was leaning in towards me.

"You want something cheaper? Where are you going to find a beautiful garden apartment like yours for less than you are paying now? This is New York!"

I put my fork on my plate and looked him in the eyes.

"Ted, how much are you paying for this apartment?"

He straightened his back.

"I pay about $95 a month but look at this place. It's a one room dump. It's nothing like yours!"

He was waving his arms toward the walls and the floor with a sneering grin on his face.

In the middle of his waving arms, I asked, "So why don't you get a bigger and better place." He was regarding me.

I was not going to stop now.

"You could get a bigger place here...and...I could move in...and we could split the rent...and save money."

"You're saying we should move in together?"

He was using words I had not spoken.

"What are you saying? You want to move here...in an apartment here?"

I responded, "Well, those are your words. I'm just trying to save money."

Ted upgraded from his one-bedroom apartment on 121st Street to a two-bedroom apartment on 122nd Street. Two weeks later we moved in together. The rent was one hundred and twenty dollars a month.

Since moving in together, Ted and I spent more time at home and less time sightseeing and going out to restaurants, especially during the winter months. Saving money was one of the reasons we moved in together. I especially wanted to keep to that plan.

Ted was working two jobs and arriving home late some nights with a leftover McDonald's hamburger and french fries that became his dinner. Other times, I would make salads, with tuna, egg, or just lettuce.

Every weekend, before it got too cold, we got up early and walked to the public tennis courts. We loved tennis. We loved being the first ones on the courts. I would prepare the hot drinks, black tea with milk and sugar for me, black coffee with milk and sugar for Ted. I poured the hot liquids into our two green Thermoses. I put the Thermoses into a tote bag.

We bundled up in hooded sweatshirts and sweatpants, grabbed our tennis balls and racquets, and headed out the door. On the way to the courts, we stopped at the sandwich shop down the street from Whittier and ordered two sesame seed bagels piled high with cream cheese, and a copy of *The New York Times*. We crossed over Broadway to Riverside and took the steps down to the courts.

We always chose the same court, the one near the benches, and farthest away from the court entrances. The bench we liked faced away from the morning sun. We didn't want to be disturbed after tennis while we sat on our favorite bench, sipped our hot drinks, ate our bagels, and read sections of *The New York Times*.

19
THE DIAGNOSIS

I hadn't been behind the wheel of a car since I handed over the keys of my green hatchback to my brother Frank back in University City. That was almost five years ago! With my new counseling job on Long Island at SUNY at Old Westbury, Ted said I needed to buy a car.

I protested. I was happy to take the Long Island Railroad and a taxi to the college every morning and do the reverse every evening. Ted's argument was "That's too inconvenient and too expensive. You need to buy a car!"

This car buying business was new to me. My brother and my father had facilitated my buying the car in University City. I told Ted he would have to facilitate my buying this one in New York City.

Ted knew I didn't like driving. His diagnosis, "You have a driving phobia and you're directionally challenged."

I responded, "I already know what my problem is. Why do you think I don't want to get a car and drive twenty miles a day to and from some place on Long Island!"

Ted took out road maps and traced the route in red in order for me to visualize the highways and roadways that would get me to work and back. The problem was, I've never liked maps, never used them, and found nothing real about them.

I stood next to the kitchen table with my arms folded looking down at the map with red lines drawn all over it with a thin red marker.

"That's fine looking at a map, but it doesn't show me where to park on campus and especially it does not show me where to park once I get home."

I unfolded my arms. *I will win this argument.*

I waved my pointer finger at the map with red lines all over it. "And what about finding a space on the correct side of the street or getting towed? It's too much to think about."

"Marge, you're being ridiculous. You've driven before, you've traveled on planes, you've got a master's degree—a couple of them—and you can't drive twenty, twenty-five miles in a car? It's not rocket science. If you don't work in the city, you have to drive!"

On Saturday morning, we went to a car dealership and selected a car. My only requirement was that it be small, easy to park, and automatic. We found a new green Datsun. The following Monday was our day to bring it home.

Ted finished work at the Children's Center around four o'clock. He picked me up and we took Highway 495 during reverse rush hour traffic to the dealership. After papers were signed, credit plan approved, and keys handed over, I got behind the wheel.

I drove around the dealership lot to test the tension in the steering wheel and to locate the knobs for the lights, the windshield wipers, and the air conditioning. I pulled into parking spaces, turned the ignition off and started the car up again. The sun was going down.

Ted leaned into the window of my new car and looked at his watch. "We've gotta get on the road." He slapped the side of my door. "Now…all you have to do is stay right behind me."

I yelled to him from the driver's seat of my new car as he was walking away. "Just make sure you don't do any fast driving or change lanes or any of that stuff."

Ted drove his blue Toyota to my parked car. I followed him along a side road and held my breath as his left signal light came on. *Shit. Now I'm gonna have to move over into all that traffic.* I followed him as he merged into the traffic onto a highway with a sign that said Cross Island Parkway. We stayed in the right lane.

This is not so bad. Ted is leading, I'm following. I didn't have to think about where to go next. Driving on the parkway was something I could do.

I heard cars blowing their horns. I took a peek into the mirror above me...why are so many cars lined up so close to me...and passing me and blowing their horns at me? *What is their problem?*

Ted was signaling right. I followed his Toyota off the parkway onto the curb. I put the gear in park and watched Ted slam his door as he approached the driver's side of my car. I pushed the button and lowered my window halfway. He put his mouth up to the opening in the window.

He started yelling. I think he had to yell because the traffic was so loud.

"Marge, you can't drive this slow on this parkway. You're gonna cause an accident! Do you see all these cars trying to pass you and blowing their horns? The speed limit is fifty and you're going thirty!"

I couldn't see his hands, but I was sure he had clenched fists. I spoke through my half-opened window.

"Ted, I'm following you."

We made it back to 122nd Street. He found an open parking spot for me to get into, front first and on the correct alternate side of the street. He then drove off to find a parking spot of his own.

The next day we were on the parkway again, with me behind the wheel doing a practice run across the 59th Street Bridge to Old Westbury and back to 122nd Street and alternate side of the street parking.

20
WARNING SIGNS

The weekend before I started work at Old Westbury, I cut my hair.

The first words out of Laura's mouth when I walked into the office on the first day of work were, "Why did you cut your hair?" I got sad eyes, pushed out lips, and disappointed signs for the remainder of the day. I knew then that any independent move or decision I made was not going to be met with approval from her. Everything associated with this program belonged to her, including me and my hair. I concluded that what she said and what she wanted was to be the final word.

I listened to Laura's "understand and continue to support our students" speech. What I saw were adult students and their families living in University housing for years and students prolonging their stay even longer by taking one or two courses a semester. I witnessed Laura coming into the office late and leaving early. I saw her grooming Eddie to be her heir apparent. It became the Malik and Marge team vs. the Laura and Eddie team. After a month on the job, I knew that my pattern of being on a job for two years would be broken here.

Malik became a good, reliable friend. He was a refugee from Mozambique and was able to get a counseling degree and a job at Old Westbury. He was principled and fastidious.

We were about the same height and we both liked nice clothes and we wore them well. Malik's sewing skills were evident in everything he wore. He was what I called self-sufficient. Eddie and Laura called him other names when he appeared in jeans with a deeply pressed crease down the middle of each pant leg.

We didn't get a chance to talk much at work for fear of being accused of conspiring. A few times on weekends, Malik came into the city. We went to Tom's and over tea with milk and sugar and a tuna sandwich, we talked and laughed about work. We talked about how Laura needed leadership training and how Eddie seemed untrainable as a leader. We talked about how and why students were allowed to have their friends and relatives move into their university housing units. Malik would look at his watch and realized he had to run if he was going to get the six o'clock train back to Long Island.

The job had some collateral benefits and rewards. I confidently made that twenty-mile drive from my 122nd Street apartment, over the 59th Street Bridge through Long Island City and on to Old Westbury. I got home before most parking places were taken on the alternate side of the street. It allowed me to practice backing into small spaces. When that didn't work, I had time to drive around the block to find something bigger.

I met Betty, my first Black woman friend at Old Westbury. She was a university counselor. When I decided I wanted to conduct group counseling sessions for all Black students at Old Westbury, not just those in the Special Program, I contacted her. She agreed to co-lead the groups with me.

We both had an interest in helping all Black students with course selections, time management and work study opportunities. It was through these group sessions that Betty and I became friends.

She was a tall, big-boned woman with a short, cropped Afro. She was in her early thirties, single, born and raised in New York. She had a Pakistani boyfriend. She was having trouble with him.

"I don't understand him. He never wants to go out. We just stay in my apartment most of the time. What do you think is going on?"

I was in no position to give a Black woman advice on men. But it sounded to me like he wanted to keep her undercover. It sounded like he was up to something. I didn't say that, but I thought she would get the hint when I said to her, "You said he's Pakistani? What about his relatives or his friends?"

Frustration was visible on her face and in her stiff fingers as she framed each side of her face. Her long body hung passively in her orange desk chair with rolling wheels.

"He said he has no relatives here. I met one friend of his...but I tell Malik all the time 'I want to go out to a restaurant to eat or go to a movie,' but no. The only outing we have is to a Burger King or something...but we never get out of the car!"

When I talk about my relationship with Ted, her comments are mixed. "Girl, I wish I could find somebody like that. I'm really bothered by his hiding me! But I have to say, behind those closed doors, he is everything I want in a man!"

We would both laugh it off...until we got together again.

One day I got a phone call from Madeline Graham who introduced herself as the new Affirmative Action Coordinator. She said she wanted to speak to me confidentially.

Affirmative Action Coordinator! I agreed to meet her the next day, before my workday began.

When I arrived for the meeting, the secretary was sitting behind a big brown desk with her coffee cup in front of her. The word "SUNY" encircled the rim.

"I have an appointment to see Madeline Graham," I said, looking at the scrap of paper I had in my hand.

The secretary behind the big brown desk smiled and stood up.

"Great," she said. "Thanks for coming. I'm Madeline."

She extended a manicured hand. I took it.

I hoped she didn't see my eyes widen. I didn't expect the Affirmative Action Coordinator to be a tall, brown-haired White woman. But there on her desk was a gold- plated plaque with the words "Madeline Graham, Affirmative Action Coordinator."

"My secretary is out today."

She gathers papers and manila folders from the desk.

"Let's move into another room."

I followed her into a small meeting room with a brown table and four chairs. I sat in a cushioned chair across from her. She began to look through a folder.

"You're probably wondering why I asked to speak with you. Well, I have some questions about your work environment, and part of my job is to make sure all staff are complying with rules and protocols."

I was still not clear why she wanted to talk to me!

"I have not been here very long, so I don't know much about the staff," I offered.

"That's why I think your observations are fresher and clearer than the old timers," she said with a smile. "So let me ask you about Laura...does she come to work every day?"

Her Bic pen was poised to note my response.

I hesitated.

"As far as I know, she does."

"What do you mean by as far as you know? Don't you talk or gather at some point every day?"

She looked at one of the papers spread out on her side of the table.

"There's just four of you in that program."

I didn't say anything. She continued.

"What time does Laura come to work? When does she come in?"

I was not going to talk with this White woman about Laura or any other Black person.

I said, "She's usually in her office before I get there."

Madeline continued her note taking and her questioning. "What time does she usually leave the office?"

I think this woman is trying to get me to play an Uncle Tom! She wants me to be the snitch to get Laura in trouble or to even get her fired! I was not going to do that. Laura needed to take a course or two in leadership, but I want no part of this case.

"I'm sorry, Madeline, I have to get to my office." I stood up and pushed my chair under the table. "It was nice meeting you." I said with a smile and a little bow from my waist.

Madeline was quick to pick up on my reluctance to talk. She didn't pick up the part of my thinking that said, *A Black person should be the Affirmative Action officer.*

"Nothing is held against you for talking to me. You're protected when you're talking to me." She started gathering her papers and placing them on top of other papers in her manila folder. "I hope we can continue to talk over the next few weeks."

She followed me into the outer secretary's empty office.

"It's a very busy time now," I said as I stepped out of the office door.

I hope nobody Black sees me leaving this Affirmative Action Office.

21
CULTURE WARP

I liked getting to my office early. It gave me time to make myself a cup of tea with milk and sugar, lean back in my black swivel chair, and look over my schedule for the day.

I was looking over notes for my ten o'clock meeting with the job placement officer when my phone rang. I looked at the time. Nobody calls me at seven-thirty in the morning. It must be a wrong number.

I went back to my schedule and back to sipping my black tea with milk and sugar. The phone rang again. Who could be calling me this early?

I picked up the phone.

"Hello?"

"Hello...is this Margaret Edwards?"

It was a woman's voice.

"Yes, this is Margaret Edwards. Who is this?"

"This is Rose Baskins, Ted's mother."

"Oh."

That's all I could say at that moment. *Why is she calling me?*

"I was wondering if we can meet for lunch today. I'm going to be near the university around noon time. Is that possible?"

Lunch with me? Why is Ted's mother wanting to have lunch with me? Ted never said anything about...

"I think I can get away…at around twelve-thirty?"

"Twelve-thirty is fine. Do you know that restaurant...it's just on the corner from you…I don't know the name, but it's…"

"Oh, yes, I know the place. It's called Flaherty's."

"Good, I'll see you there at twelve-thirty."

Click. She hung up in the middle of my saying, "Ok…bye."

Lunch with Ted's mother! Why does she want to meet with me? Ted never mentioned anything about this...I've never talked…I'm not ready to meet his mother!

If I had known I would be lunching with Ted's mother, I would have prepared. I would have worn my peach dress. And I would have worn my hair down for more acne coverage on my right side.

But here I am in my burgundy dress with a fitted waist and a flared skirt preparing to meet the mother of my live-in boyfriend!

All during my meeting with the placement officer, I was distracted, not my usual decisive self.

I should have been less compliant. I should have postponed this lunch meeting. Instead, I applied strawberry lip gloss and wiped a red smudge off my front tooth with my pointer finger. I hung the strap of my briefcase purse over my right shoulder and drove to Flaherty's.

As I was getting out of my car to go into the restaurant, I realized, *I don't know what Ted's mother looks like. All I know is that she's White.*

When I walked in, my eyes landed on a White woman with salt and pepper hair sitting alone at a table for four. I looked at her, she looked up over her coffee cup at me and gave me a no-teeth smile. I was looking at Rose for the first time.

I smiled in kind and headed to her table. I didn't know what I expected her to do. She didn't stand, she didn't reach for my hand, and she didn't put down her blue coffee mug. Her fingers were multi-ringed.

"Hello," she said. "I'm glad you could make it. "It's hard sometimes in the middle of the day." She placed her blue mug on the table. "Would you like some coffee?"

I seated myself across from her and placed my briefcase purse on the empty chair to my right. I could feel her eyes on me. "No, actually, I'd like tea." I was eyeing her as well.

She's attractive...dark hair fringed with graying strands framing her pointy features. Ted has her features.

She was brightly dressed, like she just stepped out of the fashion section of *Woman's Day* magazine. Her shoulders were draped in a multicolored shawl of reds, greens, yellows and white.

"Good. What would you like to eat? Anything you'd like."

I ordered a tuna salad sandwich. She ordered the same.

I covered the mundane about me.

"I like my job."

"I'm from Illinois."

"My family is in Missouri."

Our sandwiches arrived with a plate of potato chips on the side.

She bit into a chip before she spoke.

"Yes, family is so important."

She was still chipping away on her chips.

"I understand that you and Ted have moved in together."

Bam! I got a tickle in my throat. I had a mouth full of tuna salad. I coughed. I wasn't ready to talk about living with Ted. But I admired her for that. I believe in straight talk.

I took a chewing moment before I spoke.

"Yes. We're sharing an apartment."

"Does your family know about your, uh, living arrangement?" She had given up on her chips. She was sipping coffee from her blue mug and peering at me over the top. She was waiting for my answer.

I placed my half-eaten tuna sandwich on my plate next to the pile of uneaten chips. I swiped my mouth with the white paper napkin.

"My family?" I asked. "Do you mean my parents and my sisters and brothers? No, they don't know. I've not mentioned it to them."

"You mean your family doesn't know that you are living with a person—someone who is different—culturally different than you are?" Her facial expression was one of incredulity. Her lips tightened and her hands tightened around her coffee cup.

"I don't talk to my family about my personal life…and they never ask. They're not paying my rent!" I smiled and spread my hands, displaying the absurdity of talking to my parents about who I live with.

"Well, some families do care. They value their culture...and their traditions. When a family member is doing something that's not part of the culture, something needs to be said."

I put my elbows on the table and teepeed my hands. I helped her clarify her thinking. "I think you're saying you object to Ted and me living together…because we are culturally different?"

She placed her coffee cup on the table. "Ted is Jewish. I'm sure he has talked to you about that?"

"No, not really. I don't see what being Jewish has to do with sharing an apartment."

"I just think moving in together is a step too far. Parents all over the world want what's best for their kids. I'm sure your parents want the best for you. It's parental instinct. These culturally different relationships are fraught with all kinds of problems and I think you and Ted need to recognize that."

"Actually," I said. "Ted and I have a great deal in common. We met at Columbia University, after all, and we have common interests. We like music, plays, and travel. We are good together."

Freed from her blue coffee mug, her hands started waving

around in front of her. She was looking away from me like she was searching for the correct words. I tried to help her.

"Have you talked to Ted about your 'cultural concerns?'" I asked.

She shook her head vigorously. "Nope…no, I have not…and that would not be a good idea."

"Well, I think you should." I said. "You shouldn't be talking to me about your cultural beliefs. Ted is the bearer of your culture. I'm not forcing Ted to violate his culture. He's free to do whatever he wants."

"In our culture—in our Jewish culture—it is not just what he wants. He has a family to consider. We are his family. We have the right to intervene when we see a family member going against the family's wishes."

I was shaking my head, but I spoke calmly.

"Rose, Ted is a grown man. I am a grown woman. We are both thirty years old! My parents would never tell me who to see. They never ask about my friends, and especially they never ask about my male friends. Ted and I…we enjoy each other's company…we are good together. I support him and he supports me. But if you feel you want to see an end to our relationship—because I'm Black and a non-Jew—you need to talk to him about that!"

"He is not the easiest person to talk to."

She tightens her lips and looks down at the table.

I look at my watch. I want to end this conversation with the ball in her court.

"Well, I don't know what to say, but it's not up to me. You need to speak to Ted and voice your objection to our living together. But frankly Rose, I don't think what Ted does at this point is anybody's business except his." I checked my watch. "Sorry, I really need to get back."

I stood up and grabbed my briefcase purse from the chair and slung it over my shoulder. "It was nice meeting you, Rose…and thanks for lunch."

I gave her a no-teeth smile and rushed toward the door. I left her sitting, sipping on coffee gone cold.

Two-and-a-half tuna salad sandwiches and a pile of chips were sitting on the table untouched. I wonder if it would be considered uncouth to request a doggy bag.

22
CALL WAITING

"Guess what happened to me today?"

It was a cold night in late January and Ted had come home from teaching psychology in the adult education program at LaGuardia Community College. We had been living together for about four months now and every evening, I had grown accustomed to hearing stories from at least one of his jobs. If it wasn't something crazy a kid did during his day job at the Children's Psychiatric Center, then it was a peak learning experience he witnessed by one of his students at LaGuardia.

I didn't venture a guess. I sat at the kitchen table with interlaced fingers under my chin waiting for him to tell me what happened at work. He seemed more animated tonight as he pulled his two strapped briefcases over his head. He tossed them on the table and straddled a chair across from me.

"I got the weirdest phone call. Some guy wanted to speak to me about a job in India and the crazy thing was...he offered me a job! It was crazy. I got a call. I was leaving one job..." Ted was grinning and waving his arms and hands dismissively.

"Ted, Ted, slow down. You talked to a guy in his hotel room, and he offered you a job…in India?"

"Yeah. He said he called the Counseling Psych Department at Columbia and Conley told him about me. He said he's the Director of the American School in India—yeah, New Delhi—that he was in the States recruiting."

I'm standing over Ted as he is shuffling through a notepad looking for confirmation of his story.

"Yeah...look here."

He points to words he had written on note paper.

"His name is Don. He is looking for a psychologist willing to go to India and he is going to call me next week, on Tuesday to see if I want the job."

I stare at the scribbles on his notepad. I am befuddled and confused. I ventured to paraphrase what I think I heard.

"You had an interview with…this Don in his hotel room…and he offered you a job in India…correct?"

"Yeah…that's what happened...it was..."

"Well, let's go!" I said.

"What are you talking about, 'Let's go'? Go where? This guy is probably just some crazy. Who knows? It was just weird, sitting in a hotel room…"

"He offered *you* a job, but what about me?" I asked.

"What about you? I didn't tell that guy anything about you. He probably won't call. You're getting all worked up over nothing. It was a crazy night. Anyway, if he calls next week, I'll tell him about you. I don't plan to go anywhere without you in any case."

Ted was sitting at the table holding his head in his hands. I was hoping Ted would get that phone call from Don on Tuesday.

During the next seven days, Ted refused to talk about the job offer to work in India. He said we needed to go about our lives, at least until next Tuesday night just in case the whole thing was a prank. Even though we didn't talk openly about the possibility of living and working in India, all I could think about was the possibility of living and working in India! This could be my United Nations!

Tuesday arrived like any other day. I had Raisin Bran with two percent milk for breakfast and drove to Old Westbury as usual. I met with two students about adding a course for next term. I checked in with Betty. She was smiling a lot and had a great weekend with Malik. Laura was not in. Eddie was sitting at Laura's desk holding papers in both hands and watching for any passersby to notice his elevated status. I noticed him and his paper shuffling. I went into Malik's office before I left for home.

As I was driving home, I made myself focus on things I had not noticed before.

Oh, there's a walking path along Long Island Highway...and people are out and bicycling, too. There's LaGuardia College where Ted works. I should go there sometime. The 59th Street Bridge is really old...it feels old...bumpity bump.

How's my gas...half full. I'll stop and fill up. I like getting gas when there are no lines...

It's Tuesday...so right side of the street parking...right here, easy, peasey...glad I don't have to back into a space...no worries, there are lots of open spaces. Ted never worries about parking...but I do.

There's probably no mail...I'll check anyway. Like I said...nothing.

At about four o' clock, I walked into the apartment. I headed straight to the phone on the kitchen wall. I took the phone off the hook, put it to my ear and listened for the dial tone. The phone is working. I wiped the mouthpiece and the earpiece with the palm of my right hand and placed the phone carefully back on the hook.

Ted came home at about five o'clock. We both were knowingly quiet. Ted decided that this would be a good time to organize the papers in his two briefcases. He dumped the contents of both onto the kitchen cabinet and commenced to make piles.

I needed a cup of tea with milk and sugar. I filled the hot pot with too much water. I knew it was too much because I could see that the water level was above the 'fill line.' I poured half the water out. When I did that, some water dripped down the sides of the pot. I went to the towel drawer, got a towel, walked back to the pot, wiped the sides of the pot to remove the watermarks. I saw water spots from past drips on the side of the pot, so I rubbed those stubborn stains out as well.

I plugged in the pot and stood there waiting as it hissed and spewed and boiled and finally turned itself off. I opened the tea canister, searched around, and found a packet of English Breakfast black tea. I opened the packet slowly and carefully to avoid puncturing the tea bag and spilling loose leaves into my cup. I placed the teabag in the cup making sure to hold on to the string with the paper tab. I filled the cup three-quarters full of the boiled water. I got the two percent carton of milk from the refrigerator, poured enough to fill the cup, and returned the milk to the refrigerator. I took a teaspoon from the silverware drawer, opened the sugar bowl, scooped out a teaspoonful of sugar and poured it into my cup. I stirred five times to dissolve the sugar. I lifted the tab attached to the tea bag string and dunked the teabag three, four, five times before I squeezed the excess water and residual tea flavor from the bag. I pushed the pedal on the garbage can. The phone rang. I froze. My right foot was on the pedal of the garbage can and I was holding a squeezed-out tea bag by the string in my right hand.

"Ted, the phone...the phone is ringing! Get the phone!"

I was shouting.

Ted dropped his papers, rushed to the phone, turned, and gave me a finger to the lips quiet sign. On the third ring, he lifted the phone.

I dropped the squeezed teabag in the open mouth of the garbage can and closed the lid softly. I lifted my cup of black tea with milk and sugar and took a seat at the kitchen table facing Ted.

"Hello."

"Yes...Yes, Don. I'm fine...how're you? That's great, I'm sure..."

Ted was smiling and gently fingering the telephone cord.

I rose from my chair with my cup of black tea with milk and sugar and positioned myself directly in front of him. With the hand not holding my cup of English Breakfast tea, I stabbed my pointer finger at my chest.

"Me…me," I mouthed silently.

I felt like I was at a protest rally. I needed both hands involved in this attention getting effort. I placed my cup of tea on the table and turned back to Ted.

He gave me a few backhand flip offs.

I splayed my arms and raised my shoulders and pantomimed, *"You haven't brought up my name...why not?"*

Wait...What's this...That's me! They're talking about me!

I brought my arms down and folded them together tightly across my chest. My eyes narrowed in on Ted's face looking for clues.

I focused on his words, his smile, and the ease of his delivery.

"Well, no. I haven't got cold feet...but there are other feet in my life."

"Social studies? Well, yes…she has a degree in history."

"You know, Don, there's one other thing…no, no…uh, her feet are not the same color as mine…"

Is his smile fading? Is that a frown? Upbeat to downbeat? His voice is still upbeat! He's smiling...and chuckling!

"Oh, she's very good…she's excellent. Yes...she 'll be delighted to speak to you."

"Tomorrow. Ok…that'll be great."

"Bye, now."

Ted is naturally pale. When he hung up the phone, his face was ashen. His speech was truncated.

"I'll be damned!"

"Unbelievable!"

"Social studies?"

"India!"

I grabbed his left arm as he was stumbling to a chair at the kitchen table.

"Ted, what did he say? Did you get the job?"

I'm standing over him with my hands waving in the air trying to get him to focus.

"Tomorrow he's calling…tomorrow…to interview you...to teach social studies! This is unbelievable…crazy!"

His elbows are resting on the table. His face is covered with both hands. "I'm blown away! What is going on! This can't be happening!"

He suddenly raises his head and looks at me like he just had an epiphany.

"You heard what I said. I said your feet are not the same color as mine…and did he care? No! He just said, 'I don't care what color her feet are, is she any good?' Did you hear that?"

"Yeah…so…uh…he's calling me tomorrow…for an interview?"

"That's what he said...maybe he was just saying that…I don't know about this guy. I'm tired. I don't know what to say…unbelievable!"

We didn't sleep that night.

I didn't stay awake because I was concerned about the interview. I stayed awake because I was concerned that Don wouldn't call. I had reason to be concerned. Ted had interjected the 'different color feet' issue into the process and that fact could be a spoiler. White folks say one thing to your face and do something else later. And what could we do? Did he give us his phone number? No! That's because he is probably a closet racist and was just pretending not to be. He's a coward!

But just in case he is not, I should get prepared.

At about 4:30 p.m. the next day, I hung around the kitchen near the phone, wiping the counter, discovering and scrubbing at dried food spots that I had previously missed.

At five p.m., the phone rang. I abandoned the spaghetti pot, turned, and stared at the phone. It was Ted's turn to yell.

"Answer the phone! Answer the phone! That's him!"

I ran to the phone, raised my right hand to lift the receiver and took two quick breaths. On the third ring, I lifted the phone.

"Hello, Margaret. This is Don. I told Ted I would call…how are you?"

"I'm doing well…"

"Great…so tell me about yourself."

I hate that question!

As I talked about myself, including my degrees, my teaching experiences, my travels, and my avocations, I kept it light, tight, and humorous. I convinced myself that it would be Don's loss if he didn't hire me…even if he is a coward.

I turned the table and began to interview him. I asked him what subjects and grade level I would teach. I asked him about class sizes and the nationalities of the student population. I asked him about the teaching styles of the faculty and their nationalities. Fifteen minutes later, Don offered me a social studies position at the American Embassy School in New Delhi, India.

"Tell Ted that both of you will be receiving letters of intent in the mail in a couple of weeks. Just sign them and get them back to us. Welcome aboard. Looking forward to working with you both."

I hung up the phone. I turned to face Ted. I jumped. I laughed. I screamed. "He offered me the job! He offered me the job!" I sat down at the kitchen table across from Ted with a "What the hell just happened?" look on my face!

We sat looking at each other. Ted looked gobsmacked.

"Where is India?" I asked.

Ted said, "I'm not sure. We should go to the library and look it up. Come on…it's still open."

Getting out of the apartment where the phone calls had taken place energized both of us, especially Ted. He had a task to complete. He was back in the library among the stacks, and we were looking for the atlas that was going to show us where India is located.

Ted led the way. He knew where the atlases were. He was back in the library where we had reconnected three years ago.

"Over here...the atlases are here."

He thumbed through a large book that was placed waist high on a wooden pedestal.

"India...here it is."

My eyes were following his finger. He seemed to know his geography.

"It's not near Europe...look, it's way over by China. You can't tell distances by looking at a map. To get to India from here,you have to go through Europe."

Ted moved his finger to the topographical key.

"There's a lot of brown in India...looks like we're going to a desert!"

I countered, "But what about New Delhi? That's where the school is."

Ted said, "Lots of brown around there, too."

We decided not to say anything to anyone about India. We would not know what to say anyway. We were waiting for letters of intent.

Until then, we went about our regular routines. We were both up and out the door on weekdays and headed for work by seven in the morning.

In my office, I smiled through the furtive glances and silent treatment from Laura and her Assistant Director, Eddie. I countered by leaving the office and meeting with students in the library or the cafeteria or in the parking lot. When the leadership left the office early as usual, Malik and I were free to talk.

23
STAY THE COURSE

The letters of intent arrived about two weeks later, just like Don said they would. There was one letter addressed to me and one addressed to Ted. By signing, we were agreeing separately to accept positions at the American School, me as a Social Studies teacher and Ted as the Psychologist/Counselor. Since we had received no information on salary, housing, or plane tickets, we continued our old routines and our pact of silence.

Ted was adamant that we say nothing. Almost every evening when he got home from work, I sat at the kitchen table enjoying a cup of black tea with milk and sugar and listening to him perform a rendition of "Why I Can't Leave My Jobs and Go to India." He had all the right stage business including the waving arms and wry smiles. I hoped his show would close soon.

"What are we doing? Why are we even thinking about going to India? We don't know what we're getting into. I've been through this before. I tried so many times when I was in grad school to get money to go overseas, to Ceylon, to work for the U.N., but they kept turning me down. But now, I like my job at the Psychiatric Center. I've been moving up. Kate hired me as an intern, then she promoted me to a psychologist position. And my teaching job at LaGuardia, my friend Jessie, she asked me to teach one class, and I moved up from being an instructor to an assistant professor. I bet in a year or so, I'll be an associate or even a full professor! That's what I've always wanted to be."

During Ted's monologue, I gave him eye contact, furrowed my brow, and nodded understandingly when appropriate. But all throughout these nightly performances, my thoughts were focused on leaving my job at Old Westbury and taking off to India!

24

THE "M" WORD

On Saturday, in early March, a thin envelope arrived from the American School. It was a cool spring morning. Ted and I had moved the kitchen table closer to the radiator trying to keep warm.

A thin white envelope from the school was unusual. We were used to getting thick manila envelopes with booklets and brochures. *Is this a bad news envelope?* I opened it. A folded one-page letter was enclosed.

I hesitated. A one pager at this point in the process is always a bad sign. Is it a rejection letter? *I can't bear that...not now!*

"What do you think the school is saying now?" I asked Ted, still holding the folded letter.

"It could be anything."

Ted got up from the table, taking his glass to the sink and turning on the water.

"You might as well open it and get it over with."

I closed my eyes, unfolded the letter, and willed my eyes open. I scanned the first sentence looking for rejection words like, "sorry" or "regret."

"What is this? Ted...What? Ted, listen to this! It says in bold that we must be married. Look at this! Must be *married*!!" I rose from the table knocking over my chair and thrusting the letter in Ted's face. "Look...read it!"

Ted read the letter out loud, one sentence at a time.

Dear Margaret Edwards and Theodore Baskins,

As per the American Embassy School Board of Governors, all new staff hired as a couple and residing together in the same school apartment, ***must be married.*** *This new policy stems from a shortage of housing when disputes arise between unmarried couples. Please forward as soon as possible a copy of your marriage license.*

When we receive your marriage license, we will proceed with the hiring process including forwarding contracts for your signature. Upon your arrival at the school, please submit to the Director's Office a certified copy of your Marriage Certificate.

We apologize for the short notice. We look forward to welcoming you to the American Embassy School.

Sincerely,
Don Winfred
Director

I was standing next to Ted, following his finger moving across the typed words on the letter. He lowered the letter with both hands to his waist. He turned to look at me. His face was contemplative.

"So, what are we going to do?" I asked. "It says we have to be married!"

"Yeah, that's what it says." Ted said.

I didn't know anything about how to get married. There were married people everywhere, but I never thought I would be one of them. All the Edwards sisters were married...except me. Even my younger sisters were married.

I moved in with Ted not because I wanted to get married. I wanted to save money. And after only five months of saving, I'm supposed to get married!

A few days after we got the "must be married letter," Ted asked me, "Should we look into getting a marriage license...just in case?"

"Yeah, I guess so. They need that pretty soon."

Ted started researching the marriage process. He was good at researching since he had just finished his doctorate a year and a half ago. He took charge.

We took a half day off work and went to the Marriage Bureau in the City Clerk's Office. I did what I was told to do.

"Fill out this paper."

"Show your driver's license."

"Sign on the dotted line."

"Raise your right hand."

"Write a check."

With our marriage license in hand, we stood embraced on the steps of City Hall until Ted said, "Let's go. That's done."

The next day, a copy of our marriage license was in the mail addressed to the American School of New Delhi.

We didn't talk about getting the marriage certificate.

25
COUNTDOWN

At the end of March, a thick manila envelope arrived. I knew it contained our contracts. I couldn't open the envelope because Ted and I had agreed that any correspondence from the school from now on was to be opened only when both of us were present.

I sat at the kitchen table looking at that thick manila envelope. When Ted walked in the door at 8:30 p.m., I grabbed that manila envelope, lifted the metal tabs, peeled the glued flap open and dragged out two packets of stapled pages.

The word "Contract" appeared at the top of each packet.

"We got them…they came," I was flipping through the packet with my name at the top.

Ted said, "We gotta get copies so we don't ruin the originals. I want to underline and circle things…let's go get copies."

We rushed down the block to the corner copy store and made our copies. Back home, we made rules for going through the contacts.

We would read from one copy together. We would not read

ahead or talk over each other. We would use my teacher contract to read since both contracts would be the same except for the salary and the number of workdays. We would take turns reading.

I read the section on Terms of Employment. Ted read the section on Work Year. We checked each other for understanding before we moved to the next topic. I read the Teacher Assignments, Rights, and Class Size sections.

We were both yawning and resting our heads on our hands. We had to get through the remaining pages to see what was expected of us.

At eleven o'clock, Ted said, "I'm tired. We've read enough. Let's just sign and go to bed. We can finish reading tomorrow."

We penned our names in the highlighted spaces on the two original contracts. We each folded our own and placed it in an addressed manila envelope. On my way to Old Westbury the next morning, I dropped the envelope at the post office.

It was already April 14 and according to our contracts, we needed to be at the school in India for orientation by Thursday, July 21. But Ted was still not ready to talk to anybody about our going to India.

"I like working with my kids. And I'm about to rent an office and start a private practice!"

I listened as I always did, and I appreciated his dilemma. *But I am going to India!*

Every letter we got from the American School was opened with caution. There was always the possibility that Don could change his mind about hiring us. So, when we opened a letter from the American School on April 20, and the first line read "Congratulations, and Welcome to the American School!" we knew we were India bound.

We started jumping around the kitchen table laughing, hugging, tearing, and shouting, "We're going to India...I can't believe it...We're going to India."

"Yeah," I said. "Now we can start telling people!"

When we stopped laughing, hugging, and exhaling, Ted said, "We still need to get the marriage certificate."

I was so relieved that Ted finally seemed to accept the fact that he could be a psychologist at the American School and pursue his professorship ambitions when he returned to the States. We no longer had to hide like two bandits behind locked doors hovering over secret documents at the kitchen table. I could now walk into Laura's office, look her in the eyes, smile and say, "I won't be returning next year, Bitch!...I'll be leaving in July to take a job in India!"

The next day, I told Malik and Betty. I made them promise not to tell anyone.

Ted relapsed occasionally and started reciting his "I'm moving up in my career" monologue. One Saturday morning, we were sitting at the kitchen table. *Casey Kasem's American Top 40* was on in the background.

"Ted," I said, loud enough to drown out his monologue. "What are we going to do about getting married? The school needs a wedding certificate."

"I know..."

"Well, if we are, I think we should have a wedding...or at least a big party. We could have all our friends and relatives come...it could be a send-off...if we go to India."

I rose to my feet, waving my arms, twirling, and dancing around the kitchen table. Ted was smiling and shaking his head while watching me from his seat at the head of the table.

"You want a wedding...now?" he asked. "How are we gonna have a wedding? We don't—we have no time."

"A wedding would be fun." I said, still twirling around the kitchen table. I grabbed Ted's hand and pulled him onto the floor. He began to feel the beat of Barry White's "You're the First, the Last, My Everything."

I was being swung around, pulled into his body, and flung out again. His hips were gyrating and grinding. His feet were rhythmic, and his arms were flipping up and down and side to side. He was alone with the music. I was watching him.

Wow! This White boy has some moves!

"Ted, are we going to have a wedding?"

We were standing at the kitchen table organizing documents.

"I don't know if we have time. We have to be in India by July 21. That gives us just about two months."

We were piling documents like passports, visa applications, vaccinations cards, and college transcripts on one side of the table. On the other side of the table, a calendar was open to the month of July. The 21st was circled in red marker.

"Well," I said, flipping the calendar between May, June, and July. "If we're going to have a wedding, it has to be sometime in June."

"Early June," Ted said, looking over my shoulder. "How about Saturday June…the eleventh…that'll work. I like it!"

"Me, too…June eleventh!"

I created a Wedding To Do List and assigned each major assignment on the list to either Ted, Marge, or Both. I made myself keeper of the To Do List. Ted said that was best.

The wedding venue we both wanted was Butler Hall's rooftop restaurant. The Hall was a block from our apartment and housed graduate students and faculty. Last year, we splurged there on a four-course meal of Greek salad, seafood crepes, spinach souffle, and strawberry shortcake. We were seated at a table by the window overlooking Morningside Park. Classical music was playing as waiters in white arranged utensils on white tablecloths. After dinner, we strolled through the glass doors onto the outdoor balcony to witness the dazzling lights of Upper Manhattan's skyline.

We inquired and learned that the restaurant was now the Terrace Penthouse Restaurant. The new owner, Mr. Girard was French, as was the menu.

"A wedding at the Terrace! Magnifique!" said Mr. Girard.

I understood enough French to know also that he wanted thirty dollars per head for each guest, and the 'vino' was extra.

I said "C'est bon,ça marche. Merci."

Ted signed on the dotted line.

When we got home, I crossed out Wedding Venue on the To Do List with a blue Bic ballpoint pen.

"Ted, are your parents coming to our wedding?"

I was sitting at the kitchen table making a list of the thirty people we were inviting.

"No," he said, definitively.

I was waiting for an explanation to follow. When none came, I said, "No? How do you know? Did you ask them?"

"They're not coming, and I am not going to ask them to come. There's a lot you don't know."

I didn't know everything, but I knew a lot. I never told Ted that his mother and I had met for lunch. I never told him that she had expressed cultural concerns about us living together. Now that we were going to get married, I can imagine the conversation between Ted and his parents.

"Can't you put aside your prejudices and give me your blessing by coming to my wedding?"

"No! What you are doing to this family is unacceptable! We will be the talk of the neighborhood. What you are doing...to our culture...to this family!"

"Ok!"I said. "No parents. We'll just invite friends and siblings."

I called my parents in University City to let them know that I was getting married and moving to India.

"Hello, Mama. How are you all doing?"

"Margaret! We ain't heard from you fer a long time. Where you been?"

"I haven't been anywhere, just very busy."

"Jean is heah, she jus got heah. She was asting 'bout you…I told her I ain't heard nothin."

"Oh, hello, Jean. How're things in California? Guess what? I'm getting married."

"You're getting married? Mama, Margaret's getting married! Oh, my goodness. Who are you marrying?"

"His name is Ted…and he's White."

"He White!"

I could hear mumbling and grumbling in the background.

"Who's that talking?" I finally asked. "What's the problem?"

Mama was back on the phone.

"Yo daddy just asting about what you said."

"Mama, put Daddy on the phone."

I know Daddy hates talking on the phone. I knew he was on because I could hear his breathing.

"Daddy, did Mama tell you what I said?"

"I heerd wat you said."

"So, what do you think?"

"I don't thank nothin…you wont to marry some peckerwood… dat's yo business...but I ain't changing fer nobody! I ain't gon be watchin what I say 'round no peckerwood. I'm gonna talk jes like I talk now and say what I say now. So don't thank I'm gonna change fer nobody. I don't care nothin 'bout wat color he is."

"And I agree with you. You don't need to change for anybody, and nobody expects you to. Anyway, I'm going to India."

Mama was back on the phone.

"You goin where?"

"I'm going to India. I got a job there."

"India? Ain't that where all dem po peeples live?What in the world you gon be doin over dere?"

"I'm going to be teaching at a school."

"She say she gon be teachin at a skool in India."

Jean is back on the phone.

"I'd like to be teaching in India. How can I get a job over there?"

With a black Bic ballpoint pen, I wrote out thirty wedding invitations.

Please share with us our wedding ceremony and celebration on

Saturday, June 11 at 7:00 p.m. at the Terrace Penthouse Restaurant.

– Marge & Ted
R.S.V.P by June 4

"Ted, we can't just have White folks at our wedding…we gotta have some Black people."

We started counting.

"My sisters, Kay, Joyce and my brother, Frank will be there."

"And my secretary, Jade, and we definitely gotta invite Jesse from LaGuardia...she and her husband."

"Well, her husband doesn't count," I said. "He's White."

"And what about my friend, Joe…and his wife…what's her name?"

"Vonnie."

"Yeah, Vonnie."

"Ok…this looks much better. Oh, yeah...and Betty and her Pakistani boyfriend, Malik. This is gonna be a real international wedding!"

Our first RSVP came from Kate. She offered to be my wedding emcee. I didn't know I needed such a person, but I told her, "Sure."

26
THE TAKEOVER

One day in early May, Ted came home with a green shopping bag swinging from his right hand. He passed up the kitchen table which was covered with paper, booklets, contracts, and lists and found me standing in the bedroom.

"Got something for you," he said, smiling big as he pushed the bag toward me.

"Here, open it. I just love it."

I took the bag reluctantly, wondering why he was spending unnecessary money on gifts for me! I looked at the writing on the bag: Cache. *Pretty good women's clothing store.*

I reached in and pulled out something soft wrapped and taped in white tissue paper. I laid the package on the bed and tore off the tissue paper. I could tell it was a piece of clothing of some sort. I could feel Ted's eyes on me. I decided to scream for joy regardless of the contents of the package.

I screamed for joy.

"Oh, it's a dress!" I gently shook out a long, high waisted, off-white sleeveless, rayon dress with a turtleneck collar and matching strings hanging from each side.

"I love it!" I lied.

Smile and say more nice stuff.

"Oh, nice neckline."

"Yeah," Ted said, smiling big and proud. "It's your wedding dress! I think it's just beautiful."

I looked at him thinking I must *really* channel lessons from my acting classes.

I smiled shyly and exclaimed loudly, "You bought my wedding dress!"

You're kidding me. You had the nerve to go out and select my wedding dress! What is happening here? This is going to require my best improv skills.

I held the dress up to my shoulders. The top part seemed to fit, but there was a pile of excess dress hiding my feet. I was moving toward the full body mirror that was attached to the back of the bedroom door when my foot got caught in the pile of extra dress. I fell forward holding on to the dress with my right hand and breaking my fall with my left hand by grabbing onto the bed. Like any student of drama, I regained my composure quickly and quipped, "A few tucks in the hemline here and…it'll be perfect." I was turning in front of the mirror and pulling the skirt from under my feet.

Ted had moved to the other side of the bed. He was emptying his pockets onto the bed. Keys, scraps of paper, and Bic pens. He was fingering through the scraps.

I threw the rayon dress onto my side of the bed. I found a hanger and hung the dress on the back of the closet door. I tossed the long skirt over the top of the hanger. Ted was flipping through papers in his briefcase.

"So, when I see something, I take care of it," he said.

"Yeah, we've got a lot of things to take care of Ted, but we have a To-Do List. And according to the To Do List, I should buy my own wedding dress."

I retrieved the To Do List and pointed to dress next to my name.

"Look at this, Ted."

He stopped rummaging through his briefcase. He held up a piece of paper. He had his own To-Do List!

"Your dress is done. Tomorrow I have to buy my tuxedo and shoes. I'm on a roll!"

On Saturday, I took the train to Herald Square and roamed from store to store in search of a wedding dress. I found and bought a long, white, sack dress in eyelet fabric with a white matching shawl. It had two ruffles, one just off-the-shoulder and another at the hemline.

With my dress done, I needed something for my hair. I had no veil, only a shawl. I needed something that would compliment my dress and not crush my flip. I decided to mimic the look of one of my favorite singers, Billie Holiday. I decided to go with flowers. She always wore white gardenias in her hair. I bought two silk white roses for my hair.

I brought home my wedding dress and flowers and hid them both in the back of my closet. I ran my finger along the side of my To Do List and drew a line through the words Wedding Dress with my blue Bic ballpoint pen.

"Guess what I did today?"

Ted had come home from the bread store on Broadway. I smelled the freshness of bread. He was holding a bread bag. I could see the slices through the plastic.

"I hired musicians!" he said.

"You did? Who?"

"Yeah, for the wedding. They're students from the Manhattan School of Music, just across the street. They were playing violins next to the bread store, beautiful music. So, I asked them if they play weddings. It was so cute. They said they never had, but we could be the first. They're cheap, fifty dollars each for two hours."

He pulled a piece of scrap paper from his pocket.

"So, the music is done."

I found the To-Do List on the kitchen table. I ran my finger along the side. I located the word Musicians. I drew a line through it with my blue Bic ballpoint pen.

"We got to go to see my friend Harry next week. He's a professor at LaGuardia College and he's a minister. He said he will marry us. We just need to meet with him first, on Saturday."

I found the To-Do List on the kitchen table. I ran my finger along the side. I located Minister. I drew a line through it with a number two pencil.

Ted pulled a scrap of paper from his jeans pocket.

"I spoke to Mr. Girard. I told him we will have thirty-two guests and we want seafood crepes as the main course."

"We're only inviting thirty people. Why did you tell him thirty-two?"

"Oh, I forgot to tell you. Joe, my Teachers College friend, and his wife asked me if their best friends could also come. I think they are Mexican, so I said Ok."

"You know we only have twelve hundred dollars to spend, and that's supposed to cover the wine too! If we keep adding random..."

"What was I supposed to say, 'No, you can't bring your friends'?"

Two days before the wedding, Ted left the apartment mid-morning saying he had some last-minute things to take care of. I saw him looking at his scrap paper to do list. He came home in the early afternoon. I was washing dishes in the kitchen sink. He stood near the sink. I dried my hands on a dish towel.

"I wasn't going to tell you, but we forgot to buy wedding rings!"

"Oh, my goodness! We have no rings?" I cupped my face in my towel. "Why wasn't that on the list?"

I grabbed the To Do List from the kitchen table and ran my finger along the sides.

"Calm down...calm down."

Ted took the To Do List clipboard from my hands.

"We just forgot. It's all taken care of. That's where I went this morning. Look."

He pulled a small white netted jewelry bag with a yellow drawstring from his pocket and poured two gold bands into the palm of his left hand.

"These are our rings. I saw this place near the daycare center. They're not expensive, but they're fine. Looks like gold for just thirty-five dollars each!"

I took my ring and slipped it on my left ring finger and held up my hand in front of my face.

"Mrs. Baskins. That has a nice ring to it, doesn't it?"

At the beginning of May, I figured it was time to tell Laura that I was leaving the country and would not be returning for the next school year. When I approached her open door, I could see that she and Eddie were sitting at a corner table with their heads leaning into quiet conversation. I assumed they were having a briefing session since she had just recently returned from medical leave.

Their being together gave me an opportunity to tell them both that I was leaving. I knocked on the door. They both bolted to attention, turned, and stared at me and back at each other like I had caught them in some misdeed. I smiled at the two of them, not caring what they were talking about. *I'm on my way out!*

"Hello, excuse me. Hope I am not interrupting anything."

I entered the room.

"No, no, come on in," Laura said. "I was going to speak to you. I heard you are leaving to go to India. Well, good luck over there."

Damn...you stole my thunder! I wanted to watch your face when I told you I was quitting...I am really pissed at Malik and Betty!

"Yes," I said, with a sigh. "Thank you."

"When will you be leaving for India?" Eddie asked.

He was feigning interest in my future. He was trying to show Laura his leadership skills by asking a question. He couldn't stop tapping the palm of his left hand with a black Bic ballpoint pen.

I answered his question with the fewest words possible.

"After July 4 sometime. Still working on the exact date."

I was careful to use 'I' and not 'we.' They didn't need to know that I was getting married and going to India with my husband.

"Oh, we got plenty of time, then. I'll see you before you leave." Laura gave me a toothy grin. Laura's grin gave Eddie permission to break into a grin also.

I never saw Laura again. She went out on another medical leave that lasted the remainder of the year.

I wonder what her parting words to me would have been.

27
ONCE UPON A TIME

Today is my wedding day, Saturday, June eleven. A blue line had been drawn through all the items on the To Do List except: Nails, Dress and Terrace – 6:45 p.m. My friend Betty is coming over at 4:30.

By four p.m., I had showered, rubbed my body down with Avon lotion, squeezed into a pair of new pantyhose and slipped into an underwire black bra. I was wearing my oversized pink cotton bathrobe when Betty arrived. She was wearing a flowered beach sundress and sandals. I was glad to see a black vinyl bag hanging from her arm. Her wedding attire must be in that bag.

My Flesh Pink nail polish, four cotton balls and a plastic bottle of nail polish remover were waiting on a small white plate on the coffee table.

Betty said, "Getting your fingernails filed and painted is one of the things brides-to-be always do on their wedding day. This is your wedding day...so sit...relax! Let's have a cup of tea."

I liked having my tea made and brought to me. I was glad she also liked her tea with milk and sugar.

"Let's do your nails now. What's this?"

She picked up the bottle of Flesh Pink, shook it vigorously and watched the color settle down.

"You don't want this pale color…you want something bold."

She reached into that black vinyl bag. Her fancy wedding attire was not in that black vinyl bag. She found a Red Red and a Hot Pink. She painted my nails Hot Pink.

I found myself listening to her, relying on her. I wasn't looking at the clock, she was.

"Time for your dress."

I slipped on my white off-the-shoulder wedding dress with eyelet, ruffles, and no waistline. I sat on the bed while she fastened onto my feet a pair of white, low-heeled prom shoes that I bought from TJ Maxx on Broadway.

"Is this your makeup?" she asked. She opened the box of face powder, ran a finger across a red rouge compact, and decapped tubes of lipstick arranged on top of my three-drawer dresser. She checked the color of the two eyeliner pencils.

"I'll use mine," she said. From her black vinyl bag, she pulled out three small bags with zippers. She brought a brown wooden kitchen chair into the bedroom.

"Sit," she said.

I could feel her warm hands on my face. She was sponging, patting, and dabbing. I could hear her raking through the three bags on the dresser. She stood back, then she moved back in. She brushed my cheeks, penciled my eyelids, and painted my lips. She moved back again and stared at my face.

"Look in the mirror and see what you think," she said.

I followed her directive.

"Oh, it looks really nice…I like it. You should think about becoming a makeup artist." I didn't tell her that I could see spots where I would be adding an extra layer of coverage.

"It's 5:15. We need to leave in thirty minutes." Betty was putting her makeup back into the three little zip bags.

"Ok," I said. "Just gotta do my hair."

I removed bobby pins that were keeping my hair flipped under. The flip stayed in place when I pushed both sides of my hair behind my ears. I clipped the two white silk roses in my hair on the left side. *I like the look.* After a final makeup check, a purse check, and a bathroom visit, I walked out into the living room."

"Oh my God, just look at you!"

Betty cupped her cheeks in her hands.

"You look beautiful…has Ted seen you in this dress?"

She was picking at something in my hair.

"No…that's bad luck, I think."

She was now fussing with my off-the-shoulder ruffle and the silk petals on my roses.

"Well, when he sees you, he's gonna be knocked off his feet… beautiful! Let's see, I've got your shawl and your purse…and my bag. Ok, let's go, girl, you gotta man waiting for you at the altar! Hold your dress up out of that dirt!"

Betty stepped off the elevator and peered through the door's small glass window into the main dining room. I could hear violin music, and lively chatter. I stood behind Betty raising up my dress out of the dirt.

"It's not seven o'clock yet," Betty said looking at her watch. "I'm going in…you just wait. Here, take your shawl." She placed my triangular white eyelet shawl around my shoulders.

I heard a voice from the dining room…it's Kate. *She is my emcee. I almost forgot.*

"Everybody, outside…ready to start."

I peeked through the small window into the dining room.

Wow, I see Larry and Bob and Sandra. And wow, it looks so nice, white tablecloths. There's Ray and that must be Betty's Pakistani boyfriend…

Kate bursts through the door. I stepped back just in time. With both hands, I raised my dress up out of the dirt.

"Oh...oh my...you look beautiful!" She bends and hugs my bare shoulders. *Don't mess up my makeup!* I couldn't hug her back since my hands were raising my white ruffled hem out of the dirt. She's smiling and looking down upon me in her leopard-patterned, long wrap-around dress. Her bobbed hair is bouncy and her cleavage deep.*She looks like a lioness in heat!*

"Everybody's ready...you look beautiful! Ted's a lucky guy."

She exists through the dining room door. Voices quiet. Classical violinists start making music.

Kate is back. My sister Kay is behind her carrying flowers wrapped in white paper. She removes the paper. She holds a small bouquet of white daisies surrounded by wide, triangular fern leaves.

"Alright," Kate said. "Kay, since you are the Maid of Honor, you go and stand to the right of the minister."

She holds open the dining room door while Kay, in her long, green high-collared dress and her bouquet of white daisies walk out to take her place to the right of the minister. That done, Kate starts making sharp cutting signs in the air with her right hand.

The classical violin music stops. I hear violins playing *Here Comes the Bride.* I look at Kate. She returns my gaze with teary eyes and praying hands. I let the ruffled hem of my eyelet wedding dress drop to the floor and wrap my shawl just below my shoulders. She hands me my wedding bouquet of yellow, purple, and pink wildflowers infused with white baby's breath.

Kate holds open the dining room door. I walk tall through the door around tables with white tablecloths, white rolled napkins and tall wine glasses. I walk past camping friends, work buddies, university friends, and family members. I walk out to the terrace surrounded by panoramic views of the Manhattan skyline—the Twin Towers, the George Washington Bridge, the Empire State Building. I take my place next to Ted. And as the sun sets, and before we said, "I do!" he said, "You look gorgeous. Where did you get that dress?"

I am first in line for the buffet. I request two seafood crepes, two asparagus sticks, and one small potato. Before I put the first bite of crepe in my mouth, a waiter pours me a glass of white wine. I am being pulled away by Kate.

"It's time for your dance," she says to me and to everybody else within shouting distance.

"Gather round everybody. It's time to dance. Come on, you two…this is your song."

She is guiding Ted and me into the clearing made by the guests.

"May I present to you Dr. and Mrs. Baskins!"

Everyone applauds or whistles or shouts, "Yeah, yeah!"

"'You Are So Beautiful" begins to play from a jukebox in the corner. Seth is the tape master.

While slow dancing with Ted, I put a big smile on my face and moved my face close to his ear.

"Is 'You Are So Beautiful' our song?"

"It is now," he said, grinning and kissing me on the cheek. He twirls me away from him and pulls me back in. He whispers in my ear. "Kate has to be in control...it's really *her* song."

I throw my head back and flash a big smile towards where Kate should be. I spotted her directing the rollout of our two-tier white wedding cake.

A waiter puts a glass of white wine in my hands. I take a few sips and put it down on a table to give Joe and Vonnie a hug. I am still pissed at them for having the audacity to increase our wedding tab by sixty dollars. And only one of their best friends is Mexican!

A waiter puts another glass of wine in my hand. I put that glass on a table to take a Baskins' family picture. I put another glass down to take a picture with Ted and his co-workers from the Children's Psychiatric Center.

A waiter puts another glass of wine in my hand. I beckon Kate to take a picture of Ted and me with my family, Frank, Kay, and Joyce. I put my glass of white wine on the table.

The two student violinists are the first to leave. Each accepts an envelope from Ted containing a fifty-dollar bill. The good-byes and hugs from our guests begin slowly, but escalate quickly after I look at my watch and realize our reservations end at ten p.m. The waiters are clearing dishes and removing buffet trays from the center aisle. Ted and I take our place at the exit door and smile, hug and shake hands. I am pleased to see Ted accepting, with thanks, any and all gift envelopes. He slips each into the pocket of his black tuxedo jacket. When the last guest has left and Ted and I are gathering shawls, bouquets, and leftover wedding cake, I ask one of the waiters to bring me a glass of wine with club soda.

"This is my first one tonight!"

We are invited to join the owner, Mr. Girard, at one of the cleared tables near the kitchen. He spreads out the various tabs for the evening. He points to the cost for the venue, the catering for thirty-four people, plus the nine bottles of wine. His total amounts to seventeen hundred dollars.

"Seventeen hundred dollars!" I exclaim. "...so much...I thought...twelve...!"

My abbreviated English is to help Mr. Girard's understanding of my complaint.

Mr. Girard used abbreviated English to help me understand the reason for the extra costs. He taps on the papers spread out on the table.

"You say thirty people for food. Thirty-four people eat food. And wine...so much bottles...guests love wine. You much vin, aussi!"

Yes, I did leave a lot of glasses on the tables.

I hold up my glass of wine with club soda to the owner and say, "Un moment."

I turn and speak quietly to Ted.

"You know, he's right. We added those two people from D.C.

What were their names? Anyway, why would people invite their friends when we have to pay by the head? Some people are so selfish."

Ted is jabbing his pointer finger in the air.

"You know, I bet the two violinists ate dinner too. That accounts for the thirty-four people. That explains it."

"Yeah...and the wine…it was flowing like water. I know I wasted a few glasses. Anyway, we got to pay the bill. What money are we gonna use?"

"I don't have that much money in my account. Do you have it?" Ted asks.

"Yeah, but this is gonna empty my account. Let's hope those envelopes in your pocket will put a smile on our faces."

We walked out the door to the elevator. I held up my dress out of the dirt. We drove to our apartment on 122nd Street in Ted's 1974 blue Toyota.

28
EYES WIDE OPEN

During the month before our departure on Sunday, July 10, the school sent us information to help facilitate our entry into India. We were told to read the book *Freedom at Midnight* to get some idea about India and the history of the region.

We also got information about clothing. I was told to bring clothing that covered my arms and legs. There was no information about what clothing Ted should bring.

We were told not to bring electronics like record players or toasters.

A week after my wedding, I got a call from my friend, Betty.

"You're what?" I was screaming into the phone.

"Yes, yes...I'm getting married! Malik asked me last night." Betty sounded so happy. I wanted her to hear my happiness.

"Wow," I said, raising my voice tone to a screech and giggling into the phone.

"This is sooo exciting! I am really happy for you. When is the wedding?"

"We're not having a wedding. Malik just wants to go to a justice of the peace. That's fine with me. We'll have the blood tests and hopefully get the license this week. So, we already made an appointment to get married next Wednesday."

I tried to remain giddy. "Wow! This is exciting and quick! Do you have everything you need? What are you wearing?"

"Well, it's not like that. It's gonna be very small, just Malik and me and two witnesses. I was wondering if you will be one of the witnesses…or my witness? Malik's friend will be a witness, also."

"Of course I will. Just let me know the time and I'll be there."

I went to City Hall at eleven on Wednesday and stood with Betty and Malik and his friend. I left the three of them at eleven-thirty standing together on the steps of City Hall.

On Friday morning at eleven, my phone rang.

"Hello."

"Marge…he's gone."

"Betty? What's the matter? Who's gone?"

I could hear sniffles. I could feel distress.

"Malik," she said, barely audible. "He didn't...come home…he just left."

Betty was crying and sniffling and mumbling words through tissues.

"I'm so angry at myself. He never wanted to be with me. He didn't want to be seen with me, a Black woman. He never took me out..."

Sniffling, crying, mumbling.

I needed to verbalize what she was thinking and already knew about Malik. "Betty, you think he married you because he wanted a green card?"

"I know that's what he wanted—but I thought he would stay at the apartment one night! He told me in the car—after we got married—that he was moving…to Colorado. Then he dropped me off at my apartment. I don't know where he is…"

"So, Betty, you should turn him in. I don't know where--immigration department, I think."

"No," she said, decidedly. "I want nothing else to do with him. He's not a part of my life anymore. He never was."

Sounded like she had accepted her fate and decided to move on.

29

HELP WANTED

After we were married, Ted continued to go to his day job at The Children's Psychiatric Center and to his night job at LaGuardia College.

On the weekends we dined with Kate and Seth. They were smiling and hanging on to each other and giving us credit for their decision to move in together. We even went to a reception hosted by Elana, one of Ted's cousins. None of Ted's other family, aside from his two siblings and his sister-in-law, had shown any interest in coming to our wedding or in communicating to us their good wishes. The exception was Elana. Ted was pleased. I was pleased for him.

Our main focus now was to rid ourselves of all our possessions. We sold my green, year old Datsun the last weekend in May. Ted was in charge of selling it for a good price. He advertised in the Morningside paper. A round, White woman with short brown hair showed up with her tall, lanky high school son. Both emerged from an old black Ford. The car needed a wash. *Good move. She's playing the "I'm poor" move.*

Ted's counter move was to tout the upgrades to the car.

He pointed to scuff-free floor mats, new windshield wipers and new cassette tape system. She opened the hood, uncapped pipes, and pulled out rods. Ted kicked tires and flashed the turn signal lights. She pointed to a dent in the front fender.

"We'll need three hundred off for that."

I didn't like this woman. She was probably a mechanic. But I felt compelled to defend that dent.

I stepped up to the car, leaving my lanky companion picking at his face. "This little dent," I said, bending and pointing in the direction of the dent, "was not caused by an accident. It was caused by ice on the Fifty-Ninth Street Bridge. My car slid into the rear of a dump truck. The dump truck driver never knew my car had hit him. He just drove away because it was such a minor bump!"

I stood next to Ted on the curb of 122nd Street with a check for sixteen hundred dollars. Together we watched the spindly boy drive away in my green Datsun with the small front dent. His mother, in her dirt splattered black Ford, followed close behind.

Ted said, "We have to get serious about clearing out this apartment. I'm still working, so you have to get things ready."

I organized an "everything must go sale." I made flyers with a thick black marker on pieces of typing paper: "Apartment Sale—Everything must go!"

I wrote prices on little pieces of masking tape and stuck the tape on every sale item. I priced and taped random pieces of silverware, lidless pots and pans, side tables and two standing lamps without shades. The plaster hands Ted made in high school art class with one finger pointing upward, sideways, and downward were priced at a dollar each. I priced and taped a broom and a dustbin, two tennis rackets, lifeless tennis balls, a record player and empty cassette tapes.

I also priced sleeveless blouses, shorts, and sling back heels.

I did my job. Everything saleable in our apartment was sticker priced and the For Sale signs announcing the date were written with a large red marker. Everything not for sale like our bed, the brown couch, the dresser, and the kitchen table with three chairs had a sign that said, "Not For Sale." These items were already bought by our friend who wanted to sublet our apartment for the two years we would be away.

The voluptuous clay bust sitting next to the dining room window was not for sale. I didn't want anybody to think we were dealing in porn.

Saturday, July 2, was the date of our sale. Anything not sold by five p.m. would either go in the dumpster or be left on the curb. At seven a.m. Saturday morning, Ted went out to post and hand out flyers. I stayed back to handle the customers.

At 7:15 a.m., I answered a knock on the door. I was pushed aside by our neighbors, old, young, Black, and White. Then came random people I had not seen before. They were grabbing at silverware, rug pieces, lamps, and pads of paper. They grabbed ash trays, ice trays, flower baskets, and clay hands with pointing fingers, tennis rackets and couch pillows.

I need smaller bills! I need coins! I need help! *Where is Ted?*

How much time does it take to hang a few flyers! I am pissed!

"No, that's not for sale…that's been sold."

"I can't break that...ok, pay later."

"I want the bed."

"Please look at the sign…Not For Sale."

"Where's the hotpot? You said you had one…where is it...?"

An hour after that knock on the door, I am standing alone in the middle of the scavenged living room, dazed, frazzled, and perturbed. I am holding a size eight Bass shoe box brimming with bills. Ted bursts through the front door.

"How's the sale going?"

He checks himself. He looks around the room.

"Where is everything? Is everything sold?"

He holds his head and exclaims with wide eyes, "How did that happen? The stuff is already sold?" He laughs and throws up his arms and turns around in circles. "Don't you think it's funny? I'm out there running around putting up flyers…and handing them out to people and...you have already sold everything! Isn't that funny?"

I was not laughing.

"Ted, you think it's funny that I was here by myself with all these crazed people grabbing stuff...with no help! Where were you? You should have been here to help! I had no change and…"

Ted interrupted me.

"Ok, Ok…" He gathered me and the shoebox in his arms and spoke softly to me.

"I'm sorry I was not here to help. I can imagine what you went through. You were stuck at home with hordes of strangers coming in and picking over old spoons and forks and plates and saucers and poor you…you just had to collect the money…" He started laughing at his own sad tale.

I pushed him away.

"It is not funny, Ted."

"Ok…how about this...for all your trouble, you get to count… and keep all the money you collected."

There was prankishness in his face. But I took the shoebox to the bedroom and sat on the edge of the bed covered with a brown blanket. I emptied the bills and coins onto the brown blanket. I heard Ted yell from the living room, "You gotta admit, the whole thing is pretty funny."

I was still not laughing.

The last possession that had to go was Ted's blue well-used 1974 Toyota. For the past four years, it had hauled couches, chairs, tables, tents, and rugs. It had bedded down campers and traversed the logging roads of his almost fifty acres upstate. No buyers responded to his ad in the Morningside newspaper describing the car as a "workhorse in need of love and care." He took it to a used car lot and accepted the offer.

30

THE DEPARTURE GATE

On Sunday, July 10, we were ready to leave. Our travel documents were checked and rechecked. Our bags were packed, two large green ones and a black carry-on for me. I sold my green matching carry-on at the apartment sale for two dollars and bought a larger, black one with extra stuffing space. Ted had two large black duffel bags and the backpack from his motorcycle days.

In one of my two large green bags, I packed all my clothes for summer, winter, spring, and fall. I packed pants, long dresses and skirts and long-sleeved blouses. I packed two coats, two sweaters, a sock hat, and wool gloves. I packed my eyelet wedding dress and Ted's long, rayon wedding dress.

My other green bag had lingerie like underwear, off-black pantyhose, and pajamas. But mostly I packed hair and face products. I had never met a Black person who had been to India, so I packed all the things I used on my hair and my face in New York. I also packed all the things I thought I might need, like perm creams, shampoo and conditioners, wide tooth combs and stiff brushes. I packed dark brown shades of makeup and pink lip gloss.

The American School allowed us to plan our route to India. Our only guidelines were "fly economy and provide your arrival date." Pan American was the airline of choice to India. Since it made stops in various countries enroute to India, we decided to honeymoon along the way. We planned to spend a night in Vienna and Rome, three nights in Israel, and two nights in Kabul. Upon our arrival in New Delhi, a school facilitator would meet us at Delhi's Palam Airport and help us through the immigration process.

Everything I needed for each of these stops was in my carry-on. I had enough underwear for seven days. I packed two long-sleeved shirts, one striped, and one plain. Inside a pair of folded jeans, I tucked my burgundy spiral notebook.

For the trip, I pinned my hair up tight to the back. Ted's hair was cut short, especially around his ears. I dressed in travel clothes, loose khaki pants, short-sleeved beige shirt and brown jacket hanging over the handle of my black extra-large carry-on.

Ted spoke to his parents. He didn't tell me what they said. I spoke to my mother. She said, "Y'all be kaful ova dere."

At one p.m., Ted stood in the doorway of our apartment in his brown striped shirt and jeans surrounded by my two green bags and his two big black duffel bags. I did a final walkthrough. I walked into the kitchen and the bedroom. I walked through the living room where the bronze lady stood alone in the corner in the light of the living room window.

Ted yelled, "Let's go!"

Ted insisted on a five-hour airport arrival time before our flight. I let him have his way. We arrived, checked our bags, went through security, and walked around the shopping areas looking at tie-dyed shirts, and fingering a camera at the Everything Under Five Dollars store.

I had a taste for Chinese food. I wanted shrimp egg foo young. Two years in India...it would be a long time before I had Chinese food again. I wanted to sit in a coffee shop and have a cup of tea. Ted said we had to keep moving.

I took a few deep breaths. I felt unencumbered. We had divested ourselves of all our worldly goods, except what we could carry in four suitcases and two carry-ons.

Here I am being hurried along by my month-old husband who keeps looking at his watch.

"We should be picking up the pace," he said. "Kate and Seth said they are going to meet us at the gate."

I looked at my watch.

"Don't you think it's too early? We've got almost two hours before boarding."

He didn't respond.

We passed a donut stand.

"Let's get a donut," I said, almost pleading.

Ted checked his watch.

"You have to take it with you."

We bought two, a chocolate glazed for me and a buttermilk glazed for him. I tucked mine in my purse for later.

There were so many people milling around the gate. They were mostly Indian people. We stood back just watching. I had never seen so many Indian people in one place before. Most of them were speaking their language...very loudly. Most of the men were dressed in white, long-sleeved shirts and matching baggy pants. Struggling with the little kids who insisted on running around in the seated areas seemed to fall to the women in their brightly colored saris.

I was looking at the Indian families. Ted was looking at his watch. He was scanning the crowd like he was looking for someone. I was gazing around, too. I spotted a White woman standing in the midst of saris and white turbans. She was straining her neck looking around like she was looking for someone, too.

I know that woman...that's Rose! Ted's mother! What is she doing here? She is standing arm-in-arm with a front heavy man. He has a receding hairline. She is wearing a white cropped jacket. The man is wearing a black suit jacket with a white shirt. The two of them are standing arm-in-arm like they are guests at someone's wedding. Rose seems to be propping up the man holding on to her arm. She's wearing a tight smile on her face. The man's face is wearing sadness. He looks like a penguin.

I nudged Ted.

"Ted, your mother is here!"

"Where?" he said, craning his neck in the direction of my nodding head. She spotted my Black face. I turn my head away to avoid her eyes. My eyes are accustomed to looking straight ahead and avoiding disappointed eyes.

"There," I said. "At the gate. Why is your mother here, Ted?"

"Ok," Ted said, letting out a deep sigh of guilt. "I told my mother what time we were leaving…but I didn't think she would show up...and especially with Dad. She forced him to come, I'm sure."

"Well, I've never met your dad…and I don't intend to meet him now."

Ted left my side with a hesitant smile on his face. He headed in the direction of his parents. An announcement broke through conversations, "Pan Am Flight 1707 to New Delhi, India is now ready for boarding."

I watch Rose release the arm of the man at her side long enough to give Ted a quick cheek to cheek. The man reached out a quick hand, like he is trying to keep Ted at bay. Rose looks in my direction. I acknowledge her look this time with a nod of my head. I turn and hurry to the other side of the waiting area.

I spotted Kate and Seth. "What are you guys doing here?" I ask as I approach them. My big green purse is hanging on my left shoulder and my black carry-on bag is hanging on my right shoulder.

"We are going to miss you…we want to say goodbye," Kate said, pouting as she wraps her long arms and slender body around my shoulders, my green purse, and my black carry-on. My face gets buried on the right side of her neck. I smell lemon, probably from her morning tea. She releases me into the arms of Seth. My face is buried in his chest. *Is that Brut I smell? I prefer Aramis. I have to buy some Aramis for Ted.*

Ted joins me on the Kate and Seth side of the gate. He gets the same goodbye hugs from Kate and Seth, but with some welling up in the eyes from Kate. Seth pulls out a Kodak and someone takes a picture of the four of us smiling into the camera. I take one last glance at Rose still standing with the man in their same propped up position.

"Pan Am flight 1707 to New Delhi now boarding."

"Ted, let's go," I said.

I head to the line for boarding. Indian people are moving through the line. I hear Ted ask, "Seth, can you take a picture of me and Marge? Hey, Mother, come take a picture with us…Marge."

I am in the line to board. I am holding my ticket to India with coupons for stopovers in Vienna, Rome, Tel Aviv, and Kabul. There are so many men in white turbans and women and grandmothers wrapped in white and red and sparkling colors pushing me along.

Ted wants a picture with his parents, now. I am not abandoning my place. I am moving forward. A young woman in tan and a red cap reaches for my boarding pass. I look to the end of the line. Ted is there. He waves. I smile and wave back.

The young woman in the tan and red cap examines my boarding pass.

"So, your final destination is New Delhi, India," she said. "Welcome aboard. Enjoy your flight."

"Thank you." I smile, take a deep breath, and follow the wave of her hand.

ABOUT THE AUTHOR

Margaret Edwards attended Southern Illinois University (SIU), Columbia University, and Harvard University. She received a Ph.D. from The American University in Washington, DC, and spent thirty years working abroad in International Education. She is the mother of two children. She lives in Florida with her husband.

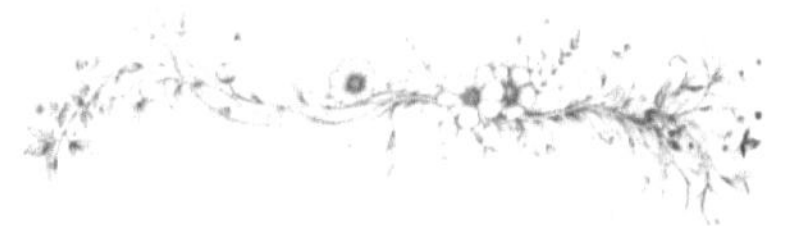

www.ingramcontent.com/pod-product-compliance
Lightning Source LLC
Chambersburg PA
CBHW020857060726
47591CB00004B/984

* 9 7 8 1 9 5 1 1 8 8 8 7 0 *